WO~~RLD TR~~AVEL
D~~ICTION~~ARY

The Dictionary for the Travel Industry

WITHDRAWN

ISBN: 1-902221-77-X

Highbury Columbus Travel Publishing
Jordan House
47 Brunswick Place
London N1 6EB
Tel: +44 (0)20 7608 6666
Fax: +44 (0)20 7608 6965
Email: booksales@columbus-group.co.uk
web: www.columbustravelguides.com

Editor
Brian Quinn

Consultant Editor
Graeme Payne

Design and Production
Space Design & Production Services Ltd, London N1

Publisher
Pete Korniczky

Printed by
Stephens & George Ltd, Merthyr Tydfil

The Editor would like to thank all the organisations and individuals who provided specialiat help in the preparation of this edition, with particular thanks to James Anderson, Ned Middleton, Guru Sachdev of the GITO in London, Fred Belcher of the MCS, Pat Collinge of Sunsail, Giles Murray, Jim Maynard, Kate Roberts, Keith Betton of ABTA, Steve Austen, Steven Jackson, Jim Maynard, Neil Davidson, Emma Baillie of Sixt Rent-a-Car, Annemarie Kruse, Madeleine Marsh, Helen Argent, David Burles, Richard Peacocke of Marcus Hearn, Nick Symons, Rob Collister, Patrick Fitzgerald, Karen Henderson, Patrick Thorne of Snow 24, Sarah Ebbutt, Kev Howett, Roy Osborne, Penny Locke, Peter Walton of IAGTO, Brendan Fox of Thomas Cook Timetables, Charlotte Evans, Christine Newton, Twanna Duncan, Dave Henderson, Dominic Williams, Robina Brown of APTG and Stuart Ingram of the BMC. Apologies to anyone omitted from this list in error.

The Editor welcomes any comments or suggestions as to how the title can be further improved for future editions. He can be contacted at wtd@brianquinn.demon.co.uk

Contents

Introduction

Welcome to the third edition of the Columbus *World Travel Dictionary* – the specialist dictionary for the travel trade in the 21st century.

In general, the successful format of the previous two editions has been followed. The alphabetical listing has been fully revised and updated, and over 700 new terms added. The emphasis, as ever, has been on words or phrases which are of central importance to those working in the industry, or studying travel- and tourism-related courses. This edition has also set out to further expand the coverage of terms in related areas, which are widely used in guide books, brochures and web-sites but often without their meanings being clearly explained. These areas include sports and activity holidays (such as golf, climbing, yachting, skiing and diving), geography, history, religion, cartography and insurance.

The following points are worth bearing in mind when using this dictionary:

- Many of the terms have many more possible definitions than those offered here. In such cases, the dictionary has generally limited itself to usages specific to, or common in, the travel industry.

- Words or phrases of foreign origin (other than proper nouns) that may not be accepted as English are shown in italics.

- In the interests of clarity, words or phrases used in the definitions which are themselves defined elsewhere have not been cross-referenced. At the end of some definitions, however, reference has been made to complementary or related entries. These are indicated by >.

- Terms that are proper nouns, or are generally regarded as such, have been capitalised: otherwise, lower-case has been used. This sometimes gives rise to more than one definition for the same term.

- Countries and capital cities have only been defined where an ambiguity needs to be clarified, such as where there are two or more with similar names.

- The description (UK), (US) or (Australia) indicates that the definition that follows is specific to that country, although it may also be correctly understood elsewhere.

- Some commonly used abbreviations and alternative spellings of terms are provided: others may exist, particularly where the term has been translated from another language or transliterated from another alphabet.

- For consistency, all acronyms that are defined have been written in capitals with no punctuation, although where they appear in the definitions they may be in lower case if this is an acceptable usage. Where these are abbreviations of phrases like 'gross registered tonnage', rather than abbreviations of organisations like 'ABTA', they can generally be written in lower case or in capitals, with or without full stops.

- Imperial units of measurement (miles, inches and the like) have generally been written in full: metric units (km, cm and the like) have generally been abbreviated.

- Many aspects of English writing, such as the use of capital letters, inverted commas, hyphens and apostrophes, are open to individual interpretation. The usages in this book represent the Editor's preferences and not necessarily those of any other organisation. In many cases, there is no 'correct' usage.

- Throughout, British, rather than American, spelling has been used, except where American terms are being defined or American usages quoted. See Appendix 6 for more on these points.

The list of worldwide attractions featured as an appendix in the second edition has proved so popular that it has since formed the basis of a separate book, the Columbus *Guide to Tourist Attractions and Events of the World*. This section has therefore been removed. The other appendices, revised and updated, remain. These cover phonetic alphabets (new to this edition); an expanded list of travel trade associations (now with web and email addresses); a country-by-country reference chart (in this edition combined with the list of nationalities and languages that previously formed a separate appendix); a US-UK/UK-US interpretation guide; the Greek and Russian alphabets; and a list of the states, provinces and territories of the USA, Canada and Australia.

Many individuals and organisations have provided specialist assistance in the preparation of this title, and these are all thanked by name on the credits page. Two particular debts of gratitude are owed: firstly to Graeme Payne, whose considerable knowledge and experience of the travel trade was so invaluable during the updating; and secondly to Richard English, who edited the first two editions of the Columbus *World Travel Dictionary* and on whose excellent work this third edition has been based.

Any suggestions as to how the title can be further improved for future editions will be gratefully received. Please contact the Editor at the email address shown on the credits page.

A
B
C
D
E
F
G
H
I
J
K
L
M
N
O
P
Q
R
S
T
U
V
W
X
Y
Z

Aa

A clamp   A device fitted to air hose, manifold or regulator which may be attached to a diving cylinder pillar valve.

A flag   A small blue and white pennant used in the seafaring 'international code of signalling' which represents the letter A. When flown independently above any craft, this flag also denotes diving is in progress – translated as 'stand well clear, I have divers down'. Also called flag alpha.

à la carte   1. A restaurant menu that lists a wide range of choices, individually priced. 2. A term often used by tour operators to denote a higher class of package holiday, possibly one that can be varied to meet a customer's individual tastes. > *tailor-made*.

A sizes   One of the ranges in the international system of metric paper sizes, used virtually everywhere in the world except in North America. A sizes are used mainly for stationery, books and magazines. The most commonly used size is A4 (297mm x 210mm).

AA   Automobile Association. *See Appendix 5a.*

AAC   Association of ATOL Companies. *See Appendix 5a.*

AAS   Alternative air source.

Abacus   A GDS operated by a consortium of Far Eastern airlines.

abaft   The stern half of a ship.

ABC   1. *See Advance Booking Charter.* 2. An informal term for the Caribbean islands of Aruba, Bonaire and Curaçao.

abeam   On a line at right-angles to the length of a ship or aircraft.

ABLJ   *See adjustable buoyancy life-jacket.*

aboard   On or in a ship, aircraft, train or bus.

Aboriginal   (or **Aborigine**) Of or relating to the original inhabitants of Australia before the arrival of European settlers.

aboriginal   The original inhabitant of a place.

ABP   Able bodied passenger. Usually selected to sit near the emergency exits on an aircraft.

ABPCO   Association of British Professional Conference Organisers. *See Appendix 5a.*

abroad   A foreign country. From wherever a person happens to live, other countries are abroad.

abseiling   The act of making a controlled descent of a cliff or other steep ground by sliding down a rope. Also known as rappelling.

absolute pressure   The total pressure exerted at any depth (including atmospheric pressure).

ABTA   Association of British Travel Agents. *See Appendix 5a.*

A

ABTA Travel Agents Certificate An examination-based qualification developed by ABTA and TTC Training, operated in conjunction with City & Guilds.

ABTA Association of British Travel Agents. *See Appendix 5a.*

ABTAC *See ABTA Travel Agents Certificate.*

ABTOF Association of British Tour Operators to France. *See Appendix 5a.*

ABTOP The tour operating equivalent of ABTAC.

ABTOT Association of Bonded Travel Organisers Trust Ltd. *See Appendix 5a.*

abyss An exceptionally deep chasm.

AC 1. An abbreviation for air conditioning, in a car, train, hotel room, coach or other enclosed space.
2. *See alternating current.*

ACAV Associació Catalana d'Agencies de Viatges. *See Appendix 5c.*

accident An unexpected event causing physical injury. Most insurance policies can offer cover against the various consequences of an accident while travelling (including curtailment, disablement, medical expenses and repatriation). The conditions under which such a claim can be made will be set out in the small print and will vary from policy to policy. > *travel insurance.*

ACCKA Association of Czech Travel Agencies. *See Appendix 5c.*

acclimatisation The process of gradually adjusting the body to a different environment, such as a lower level of oxygen at higher altitudes. By limiting the amount of ascent each day and resting frequently, the body can adapt to live normally at altitudes up to around 5,000m. > *altitude sickness.*

acclimatise To become accustomed to new or changed conditions.

acclivity An upward slope.

accommodation 1. A hotel or other similar facility.
2. Specifically, the provision made in such a facility for its guests' sleeping arrangements.
3. Sleeping space and facilities available for passengers in a form of transport such as a ferry or a train. This can range from a reclining seat to a private cabin.
4. The term used by the WTO to quantify the amount of sleeping space available in a country, defined as 'the total capacity in rooms of establishments offering accommodation available in the entire country'.

accommodation grading and listing organisations The bodies that operate classification schemes for hotels and other accommodation. These include:
• *Government-run bodies.* Some governments operate an official registration scheme. The department responsible will allocate an official classification, and may impose certain conditions on the establishment's operation. When government classifications exist, registration is normally obligatory.
• *Transport-related organisations.* These include the AA and the RAC in the UK and the Michelin Guides in France. Other organisations such as airlines and railways may also produce lists of recommended establishments. Inclusion criteria will vary from guide to guide.
• *Consumer organisations.* Perhaps the best known in the UK is the series of *Which?* guides that give details of a wide range of properties.
• *Commercial organisations.* Several publishers specialise in hotel guides. The most-used by the UK travel trade are DG&G travel information's *Hotel Gazetteers* and *Hotel and Travel Index.* Such guides use a grading system that incorporates other 'official' grades in place.

• *Holiday companies.* Most tour operators try to give their customers an indication of the quality of the accommodation they are considering and indeed, it is a requirement of the ABTA Code that the 'official' classification (if one exists) is shown. However, many operators will also provide their own description and rating. > *accommodation grading systems.*

accommodation grading systems Any method by which different hotels or other properties are compared by examining factors such as facilities, room sizes, number of staff and location and, as a result, allocating each property one of several grades: these are either named or given a rating by symbol, such as stars or crowns. There are many different accommodation grading systems in use in the world: by far the most important are those which relate to hotels. Some systems are international, some national, some regional. Some cover a wide range of properties, some only those certain types. Some have been developed by publishers, some by national tourist offices and some by hotel chains. While each is useful enough in its way, comparisons between properties listed in different sources may be impossible to draw: even if both use the same grade names (such as one to five stars), each might be based on different criteria. > *accommodation grading and listing organisations.*

accommodations (US) Accommodation.

accredited agent A passenger sales agent that has met the necessary conditions specified by the appropriate organisation (such as IATA).

ACE Association for Conferences and Events. *See Appendix 5a.*

Acela Express The high-speed train service running between Boston and Washington via New York in the USA.

acre An imperial measurement for an area

of land equal to 4,840 square yards (approximately 0.405 hectare).

acronym A name, such as ABTA and UK, which is made up of the initial letters of other words.

ACTA Association of Canadian Travel Agents. *See Appendix 5c.*

activity holiday Any holiday that involves some type of structured or organised activity. There are many holidays offered by tour operators to meet the special needs of enthusiasts for the various different types of activity.

actual flying time The time an air journey takes, disregarding local time differences. This expression is gradually replacing the earlier 'EFT' (elapsed flying time), which has the same meaning.

ACV *See hovercraft.*

AD 1. Agent's discount. On air tickets, the letters will appear with a secondary code to indicate the amount of discount allowed. For example, AD75 = 75% discount. 2. *Anno Domini* (the year of our Lord), describing the dates of the Christian Era. It is written before the date in question.

ad hoc Anything that is arranged for a specific (usually exclusive) purpose. Typically, ad hoc arrangements will be made at relatively short notice to suit the needs of an organisation or individual.

ad hoc charter A one-off arrangement by which a vehicle, usually an aircraft, is hired in order to meet special demand or cover an unforeseen circumstance.

ADA room (US) A room complying with the requirements of the Americans with Disabilities Act.

add-on An expression, more common in North America, that means anything that can be bought by a customer that is an extra to the basic cost of the holiday or

A

other arrangement. Shore excursions for cruise passengers are an example. In the UK the term optional extra is more commonly used.

add-on fare   An amount added to the fare to a gateway in order to construct a through fare to a final destination. For example, a London to New York fare would require an add-on for a passenger wishing to continue their journey on another flight to Norfolk, Virginia.

adjoining rooms   Rooms in a hotel or similar establishment which are next to each other.

adjustable buoyancy life jacket   An inflatable collar, worn by divers, that can be partially inflated and then deflated to suit underwater buoyancy requirements. When fully inflated at the surface it also act as a lifejacket.

administration   The management of a bankrupt company under a court order, often with the intention of finding a purchaser for it. Such a company is said to be in administration.

administrative county   Any of the various and successive sub-divisions of England, Wales or Scotland created as a result of administrative reforms since the 1880s. In some cases these adopted the names, and sometimes the frontiers of, the far more ancient geographical counties which still exist for some non-administrative purposes. > *geographical county*.

administrative office   The principal office of an accredited agent.

Adriondack   The rail service between New York in the USA and Montréal in Canada.

adult   A person who will normally have to pay the full charge for a travel facility. Normally this will be anyone over 12 years of age, although this varies from service to service. > *child*.

advance booking charter   An obsolete type of charter flight previously available to customers booking in advance.

advance purchase rate   A lower price charged to someone who is prepared to pay in advance for a product or service, such as a hotel room, where post-payment is more common.

AEA   Association of European Airlines. *See Appendix 5d.*

AEDAVE   Associación Empresarial de Agencias de Viajes Españolas. *See Appendix 5c.*

AEO   Association of Exhibition Organisers. *See Appendix 5a.*

aerodrome   An obsolete term for airport, still occasionally used to describe a small airport.

aero-engine   (UK) An aircraft engine.

aerofoil   Any one of the curved surfaces on an aircraft designed to give lift.

aeroplane   (or **airplane**) A heavier-than-air flying machine.

aerostat   An airship or balloon, especially one that is tethered.

aerotrain   A train supported on its track by a cushion of air.

affinity card   A card that identifies members of an affinity group.

affinity group   A group of people linked by a common interest or purpose. Some suppliers and brokers offer special rates for affinity groups.

Africa   One of the world's continents. As with most continents, opinions differ as to its exact composition and area. > *continent*.

aft Towards the stern of a vessel. When a person or object moves toward the stern of a vessel they will be going aft.

AFTA Australian Federation of Travel Agents. *See Appendix 5c.*

after On a ship, nearer to the stern or aft.

agency list The list maintained by a trade body of their members.

agent A person or organisation that acts for another. Technically, an agent should be paid for the facilitation of the transaction regardless of its outcome. In practice, the term is often used to describe those, such as travel agents, who are paid by the supplier on the basis of sales made. Consultancy fees are beginning to erode this practice. > *travel agent.*

agent's coupon The coupon of a ticket or voucher that is retained by the issuing agent.

agonic line An imaginary line joining the north and south magnetic poles, along which a magnetic compass will point without deflection.

agriculture One of the three types of profession (manufacturing and services being the others) into which economic activity is generally divided for statistical purposes.

agri-tourism Holidays spent working on a farm.

aground The situation of a ship having run into the bottom of an area of water.

Agulhas Current A very strong north-south current off the south-west coast of Africa.

AH&LA American Hotel & Lodging Association. *See Appendix 5b.*

ahead When used as a nautical term

means to move forward, as in 'full steam ahead'.

AIDS *See HIV.*

aiguille A sharp peak of rock, especially in the Alps.

aileron The hinged part of the wing of an aircraft used to control lateral balance.

air brake 1. A brake operated by compressed air, commonly used on larger vehicles.
2. A movable flap or other surface used to reduce an aircraft's speed.

air bridge (UK) The removable walkway set against an aircraft for transferring passengers to and from the departure gate.

air corridor A route to which aircraft are restricted, especially when flying over a foreign country.

air hostess (UK) A female aircraft cabin attendant.

air mile A nautical mile when used as a measure of distance flown.

Air Miles A passenger loyalty programme operated in conjunction with British Airways and its associated companies. The term is sometimes more loosely used to describe such loyalty programmes generally.

air pocket A region of low pressure that can cause an aircraft to lose height suddenly.

air rage An act of violence on an aircraft, directed either at cabin crew or other passengers.

air sickness A feeling of nausea when flying, usually caused by a combination of nervousness and turbulence.

air taxi A small aircraft that can be

A

chartered for one-off journeys. Most air taxis are relatively small (generally carrying less than 20 passengers) and the journeys they undertake relatively short (generally less than 250 miles).

air terminal   1. (UK) The location in a town or city from which passengers travel to and from the airport.
2. One of the passenger buildings at an airport.

air testing   The analysis of an air sample to ascertain whether it conforms to the appropriate air purity standards.

air traffic control   The system or organisation responsible for the safe routing of aircraft while in flight.

Air Travel Organiser's Licence (ATOL)   A certifying document which any company in the UK must have obtained before it can operate any form of package-style travel arrangement by air.

air-boat   A vessel propelled by an enclosed fan or propeller, used for travelling over shallow water and marshland.

Airbus   Originally an aircraft designed to carry large numbers over relatively short routes. Now used to describe many types made by the Airbus Industrie consortium.

aircraft   Any machine that flies. Nowadays the term almost always refers to an aeroplane or helicopter, rather than to lighter-than-air vehicles such as balloons and dirigibles.

airfield   An area, possibly grass-covered, where aircraft can take off and land.

airfoil   (US) Aerofoil.

airframe   The body of an aircraft.

airline   A carrier providing regular public air transport.

airline accounting code   The unique

three-digit code which is allocated to and used by each airline. This appears before the ticket number on tickets and other travel documents. The accounting code is distinct from the more widely used *airline code.*

airline code   The unique code – usually of two letters, sometimes of a number and a letter, and (rarely) of three letters – which is allocated to and used by each airline, and which appears as a prefix to the flight number. Occasionally two airlines will have been allocated the same code but these will be in different geographical locations. Often one of these operators will be a passenger airline while the other is a cargo carrier. This is known as a controlled duplication. In recent years, as the number of new airlines in the market has exhausted the supply of two-letter prefixes available, some codes have become partly numerical. Some airlines have a three-letter identification but these are rarely used as they may be confusing when used next to the city and airport codes described above. Such codes are only seen on the departure indicators at some Spanish airports.

airliner   A large passenger aircraft.

air-miss   When two or more aircraft get closer to one another than safety regulations permit.

airplane   (US) Aircraft.

airport   The complex of buildings, runways, car parks and administrative areas that make up the overall facility for the handling of civil aircraft.

airport code   The unique three-letter code which is allocated to and used by each airport in the world. This is often the first three letters of the city's name, such as ALG for Algiers, but it is not always the case: Toronto, for example, even though it is in a major city, has a code of YYZ. It is important to remember that where a city has more than one airport, each airport will have its own code, and these, rather than the city's code, will be the ones used on ticketing. Thus London, England (LON) has Heathrow (LHR), Gatwick (LGW), Stansted (STN), Luton (LTN) and London City (LCY).

Apart from airports, other travel destinations such as major railway and bus stations have also been allocated three-letter codes, although these will very rarely bear any resemblance to the city or the name of the station. Thus Birmingham Colmore Row Bus Station in the UK has a code of ZBC, and Berlin's Friedrichstrasse Rail Station of QWE.

airport surcharge   An additional charge which may apply for hiring a vehicle at certain airport locations.

airport transfer   The transport provided for passengers between their arrival or departure airport and their accommodation or other specified points.

airscrew   An old-fashioned term for an aeroplane's propeller.

airship   A powered aircraft that is lighter than air. The first ever passenger air service was operated by the German airline DELAG, before the First World War, using Zeppelin airships.

airside   The area of an airport reached after passing through immigration and other security controls.

airspace   The part of the sky available for aircraft to fly in, especially that part subject to the jurisdiction of a particular country.

airspeed   An aircraft's speed relative to the surrounding air.

airstrip   An area of land suitable for aircraft take off and landing which has few of the facilities normally provided at airports.

AITO   Association of Independent Tour Operators. *See Appendix 5a.*

AKA   Also known as.

Al Andalus   A luxury six-day rail cruise in Spain which starts and finishes in Seville and visits Antequera, Granada and Ronda.

Alaska Standard Time   One of the time zones used in North America, nine hours behind UTC.

Aleutian/Hawaiian Standard Time   One of the time zones used in the Aleutian Islands and Hawaii, ten hours behind UTC.

Algarve   Portugal's southern coast and the country's main resort area. The main towns include Lagos, Albufeira, Faro and Tavira.

alien   A person from a foreign country.

all hands   The entire crew of a ship.

all-aboard time   The time (generally 30 minutes before sailing) by which all passengers should be on board ship at a port of call.

alleyway   A passageway or corridor on board a ship.

all-inclusive   A package holiday, resort or hotel which includes accommodation, meals and certain drinks, entertainment and sporting facilities. These will generally be pre-paid. > *inclusive resort.*

allocation   Space or accommodation reserved in advance by a principal for an intermediary, such as a tour operator, for onward sale to a customer. Space held on allocation will not be sold directly by the principal without reference to the allocation holder. Sometimes known as an allotment.

allotment   *See allocation.*

aloft   At or near the top of the mast.

alongside   Beside a pier, dock or other landing area, or another vessel.

alp A high mountain, generally snow-capped.

alpenglow The rosy light at sunrise and sunset seen on high mountains.

alphabetical The ordering of information by the first and, if necessary, subsequent letters of the alphabet. Confusions can be caused with entries that begin with numbers or with abbreviations such as 'St', with names such as 'McDonald' or 'MacDonald', and with acronyms.

alpine Of or relating to high mountains, particularly the Alps.

alpine skiing The main form of modern downhill skiing as practised by most people visiting ski resorts, invented in the early 20th century.

Alps The main mountain range in Europe, extending from southern France to western Austria, and from northern Italy to southern Germany.

alternating current (AC) An electrical supply that varies in voltage from zero to a peak, then to zero, then to a trough, then back to zero many times a second. Such a complete cycle is known as a Hertz. Most countries have an AC supply at either 50 Hertz (such as the UK) or 60 Hertz (such as the USA). Travellers need to ensure their appliances work on the different frequencies. > *direct current.*

altimeter An instrument that shows a pilot the height of an aircraft.

altitude The height of an object or place, normally measured from sea level. Altitude will directly affect its air pressure and will have implications for any activities undertaken.

altitude sickness (or **mountain sickness, AMS**). A variety of physical problems caused by the lack of oxygen in the air at altitude. It can occur anywhere above 2,500m if proper acclimatisation procedure is not followed and may manifest itself up to 36 hours after travel to height. Symptoms include headache, nausea, vomiting, poor appetite, insomnia a racing heart and extreme fatigue. If untreated, it may develop into its more rare but life-threatening forms, HACE and HAPE. The only cure is rest and descent. > *acclimatisation.*

AM Ante meridiem – used in 12-hour clocks and timetables for the period between midnight and midday. Most transport schedules in the United States are listed using am and pm. Note that IATA regulations require that am and pm be written without full stops.

Amadeus A GDS operated by a consortium of European airlines.

AMAV Asociacion Mexicana de Agencias de Viajes. *See Appendix 5c.*

ambient Local, immediately surrounding. The term is often used in relation to pressure and temperature.

amenity 1. A pleasant or useful feature, often mentioned in sales literature to stimulate interest.
2. (US) Kitchen facilities in a property.

amenity kit A pack provided by some airlines, generally to premium passengers, containing such items as slipperettes, eyeshades and washing kit.

America 1. The Americas. *See the Americas, continent.*
2. A commonly used unofficial term for the USA.

American plan A hotel rate that includes accommodation and all meals. Also known as full board.

American Of or relating to the Americas. Without qualification, the term is generally taken to relate to North America and often specifically to the United States of America.

Americas The land mass comprising North, Central and South America. > *continent.*

amidships (US amidship) The longitudinal centre part of a boat or ship.

amphibian A mode of transport that can operate on land or water.

amusement park *See theme park.*

anchor The heavy fluked metal weight used to moor a ship to the sea bed.

anchor ball A black ball hoisted above the bow of a ship to show that it is at anchor.

anchorage A place where a ship may be anchored.

ancient monument (UK) An old building or similar, often preserved under government control.

ancillary services In travel, extra services provided such as visas, foreign exchange and insurance.

Andean Of or relating to the Andes mountains of South America.

Andes The main mountain range in South America, extending along the entire western coast.

anemometer A wind speed gauge.

anemometer An instrument for recording the speed or direction of the wind.

Anglo 1. Used as a prefix to denote anything of English or British origin.
2. (US) A person of British or Northern European origin.

Anglophile A person who is well disposed towards England or the English.

Anglophobe A person who dislikes or distrusts England or the English.

Anglo-Saxon 1. Of English descent.
2. (US) The modern English language, especially when referring to a plain form of it.
3. Of or relating to the language, people and culture of England between the unification of the 9th century and the Norman Conquest of 1066.

annexe A separate or added building giving extra accommodation in a hotel or similar.

annular eclipse *See eclipse.*

Antarctic Of or relating to the continent of Antarctica.

Antarctic Circle The parallel of latitude at 66° 30' S, which marks the southernmost point at which the sun can be seen during the southern hemisphere's winter solstice. Any point south of this will experience at least one period of 24 hours without a sunrise and a similar period without a sunset.

Antarctic Circumpolar Current The ocean current that runs around Antarctica.

Antarctic Travellers' Code A set of regulations, enforced by the expedition cruise companies operating in this area, designed to prevent pollution and to preserve the continent's eco-systems.

Antarctica One of the world's continents, a vast, ice-bound landmass surrounded by the Southern Ocean and containing the South Pole. > *continent.*

anticyclone A system of winds rotating outwards from an area of high pressure, usually producing fine weather.

Antilles 1. *See Greater Antilles, Lesser Antilles.*
2. *See French Antilles, Netherlands Antilles.*

antimacassar Paper or cloth placed on

A

A

the headrests of aircraft or other seats.

antipasto The Italian equivalent of hors d'oeuvre.

antipodes The opposite point on the earth to where one is. From the UK, the antipodes is Australasia.

anti-trust (US) A collective term for the state and federal legislation in the USA designed to protect consumers from anti-competitive behaviour by companies.

ANTOR Association of National Tourist Office Representatives. *See Appendix 5a.*

ANVR Algemeen Nederlands Verbond van Reisondernemingen. *See Appendix 5c.*

AOA Airport Operators Association. *See Appendix 5a.*

aparthotel A hotel in which the accommodation is provided as self-catering apartments or suites with additional communal facilities.

apartment A room or collection of rooms. When used as holiday accommodation it will normally be rented out on a self-catering basis.

APAVT Associação Portuguesa das Agências de Viagens e Turismo. *See Appendix 5c.*

APEX Advance Purchase Excursion Fare. A type of advance booking fare.

appetiser A small amount of food or drink, taken before a main meal, to stimulate the appetite.

appointment The situation of a travel agent being authorised by a supplier to sell its products or services in exchange for a commission or a consultancy fee. *> travel agent.*

approved location A location for the sale of passenger tickets, including head offices, branch offices and satellite printers, that appears on the appropriate agency list.

après ski The social activities taking place after a day's skiing.

apron The hard surfaced area of an airfield used for loading and unloading aircraft. Also known as a ramp.

APTG Association of Professional Tourist Guides. *See Appendix 5a.*

aqualung Portable breathing apparatus for use underwater. *> scuba.*

aquapark A water-orientated amusement park.

aquarium A place where fish and other marine species are kept in captivity for scientific study or the enjoyment of visitors.

aqueduct A bridge, similar to a viaduct, but designed to carry water.

Arab 1. A member of the Semitic peoples originally inhabiting the area around what is now Saudi Arabia. 2. Of or relating to Saudia Arabia, the Arabian peninsula, or the Arabs.

Arabian Gulf *See Persian Gulf.*

Arabian peninsula The geographical region comprising Bahrain, Oman, Qatar, Saudi Arabia, United Arab Emirates and Yemen.

Arabian Sea The area of the Indian Ocean between the Indian sub-continent and the Arabian peninsula.

Arabic civilisation Of or relating to the culture of Arabia and the Arab peoples. Arabic influence extended from the Pyrenees to the Indian sub-continent as a result of the spread of Islam in the centuries following Mohammed's death in AD632.

Arabic numerals The system of numbers from 0 to 9 and then combining from 10 onwards. These are now almost universally used. > *Roman numerals*.

arc Part of the circumference of a circle or other curve. Since the Earth is spherical, a 'straight line' journey between any two points is actually an arc.

archipelago A group of many islands.

Arctic Circle The parallel of latitude at 66° 30' N, which marks the northernmost point at which the sun can be seen during the northern hemisphere's winter solstice. Any point north of this will experience at least one period of 24 hours without a sunrise and a similar period without a sunset.

Arctic Ocean *See oceans*.

arête A sharp mountain ridge.

arrival tax Taxation raised on passengers arriving at a port or airport. Arrival taxes do not only apply to international arrivals but may on occasions be raised on domestic arrivals as well.

arrondissement An administrative division of a French city or *departement*.

Art Deco A style of architecture that flourished in the 1930s, characterised by geometric shapes and symmetrical patterns. Supreme examples include the Chrysler Building in New York and the Art Deco District in Miami Beach.

ARTA Association of Retail Travel Agents. *See Appendix 5b*.

artificial respiration A means of resuscitation by re-oxygenating the blood of an unconscious person.

Aryan A member of the peoples speaking any one of the languages of the Indo-European family.

ASAP As soon as possible.

ASATA Association of South African Travel Agents. *See Appendix 5c*.

Ascension Day A festival in the Christian religious calendar, celebrated 39 days after Easter.

ascent The process of rising towards the water's surface from any depth.

ASEAN The Association of South East Asian Nations. A regional organisation comprising: Brunei, Laos, Malaysia, Myanmar, the Philippines, Singapore, Thailand and Vietnam.

Ash Wednesday A festival in the Christian religious calendar, celebrated 46 days before Easter. It marks the start of Lent.

ashore Towards or on the shore or land.

Asia One of the world's continents. As with most continents, opinions differ as to its exact composition and area. > *continent*.

Asian Of or relating to the continent of Asia.

ASIRT The Association for Safe International Road Travel. *See Appendix 5b*.

ASR Bundesverband mittelstndischer Reiseunternehmen. *See Appendix 5c*.

ASTA American Society of Travel Agents. *See Appendix 5b*.

astern A nautical term meaning the rear of a vessel. When a ship goes astern it will go backwards.

ASVA Association of Scottish Visitor Attractions. *See Appendix 5a*.

asylum, political Protection given by a state to political refugees from another country.

A

ATA Air Transport Association. *See Appendix 5b.*

ATB *See automated ticket and boarding pass.*

ATC *See air traffic control.*

Athens Convention An international agreement that limits the liability of shipping companies in respect of loss or damage to passengers and their luggage.

Athens of... A term used to market a town or city by virtue of its cultural heritage (such as the 'Athens of the North' or the 'Athens of America').

ATII Association of Travel Insurance Intermediaries. *See Appendix 5a.*

Atlantic Ocean *See oceans.*

Atlantic Standard Time One of the time zones used in North America, four hours behind UTC.

atlas A book composed entirely or principally of maps.

Atlas Mountains The main mountain range in North Africa, extending from the Atlantic coast of Morocco to Tunisia.

ATM (US) Automated Teller Machine: an automatic cash dispensing machine. (UK cashpoint).

ATOC Association of Train Operating Companies. *See Appendix 5a.*

ATOL *See Air Travel Organiser's Licence.*

atoll A ring shaped island formed by a coral reef.

atrium A central open area in a hotel or other building. There will often be access to natural light, either through an opening or a transparent roof.

attraction In tourism terms, something that a tourist wants to see or visit. Attractions can be natural (such as Table Mountain in Cape Town) or man-made, such as Disneyland. For more information, consult the Columbus *Guide to Attractions & Events of the World.*

auberge A French inn.

AUC Air Transport Users Council. *See Appendix 5a.*

auditor's coupon The coupon of a ticket or voucher that is used for accounting purposes. Usually it will be submitted to the principal with the sales return.

Aurora Australis The southern hemisphere's equivalent to the Aurora Borealis that can be seen regularly below 70° south. Also known as the southern lights.

Aurora Borealis Spectacular luminous phenomena caused by electrical solar discharges and visible every dark night in the higher latitudes above 70° north but less frequently the nearer an observer is to the Equator. London can expect a maximum of seven sightings a year. Also known as the northern lights.

Australasia One of the world's continents. As with most continents, opinions differ as to its exact composition and area. *> continent.*

auto 1. An abbreviation for automatic transmission (on a car). Standard in the USA; an extra in most other countries. 2. (US) An abbreviation for automobile.

autobahn The German word for motorway.

autogiro An aircraft with rotating wings, somewhat similar to a helicopter, but where the rotors are turned by their motion through the air and not by an engine. Autogiros were the first successful type of rotating-wing aircraft.

automated ticket and boarding pass A document containing details of a passenger's flight booking and seat allocation.

autopilot A device that maintains the course and, in the case of an aircraft, the attitude of a vehicle without the pilot's intervention.

autopista The Spanish word for motorway.

autoroute The French word for motorway.

autostrada The Italian word for motorway.

auxiliary A sailing boat with an additional source of power, such as an engine.

avalanche A rapid, dangerous and often unpredictable fall of snow and ice down a mountain.

avalanche corridor *See couloir.*

avalanche transceiver A radio transmitter, used by skiers travelling off-piste, which sends a signal that can help rescuers locate users in the event of their being buried in an avalanche.

AVE The Spanish high-speed rail service, operating between Madrid and Seville via Cordoba.

aviation The skill or practice of operating aircraft.

avionics The electronic systems used in navigating and flying aircraft.

awning A cover, usually of canvas, set up to provide temporary protection against sun or rain. Often used over an open deck of a ship.

AWTE Association of Women Travel Executives. *See Appendix 5a.*

axis The imaginary straight line around which something rotates. In the case of the earth, this imaginary line joins the poles.

Azores A group of nine islands in the Atlantic, west of, and politically part of, Portugal.

Aztec The dominant civilisation in Mexico before the Spanish conquest in the 16th century.

A

Bb

B sizes   One of the ranges in the international system of metric paper sizes, used virtually everywhere in the world except in North America. B sizes are used mainly for posters.

B&B   *See Bed and Breakfast.*

BAA   British Airports Authority. *See Appendix 5a.*

Babylonic   Of or relating to the ancient Babylonian civilisation (c.1500BC until 538BC).

BACD   British Association of Conference Destinations. *See Appendix 5a.*

back-to-back   1. The principle on which a charter flight series works. The flight taking a group out to a destination will return with those travellers who have finished their holiday, and so on.
2. The combination of two restricted return tickets to create a fare that undercuts the cost of a full-priced journey.

backcountry   (US) An area away from settled districts.

backdate   The often illegal practice of issuing a ticket or voucher later than the date shown in the issuing stamp box. This is usually done to circumvent the regulations covering advance purchase restrictions.

backhaul   A fare construction rule that states that it is not possible to apply normal fare rules to journeys that double back on themselves. This rule prevents the undercutting of fares to a more distant point than that where the journey ends.

backing   Change of wind direction in an anti-clockwise manner.

back-pack   1. A ruck-sack.
2. A harness attached to a diving cylinder, comprising shoulder and waist straps, that allows the diver to wear the cylinder.

backwash   1. The wave of waters created by a vessel's passage.
2. A similar wave of air caused by the passage of an aircraft.

badlands   Extensive, uncultivatable tracts of land, usually arid and bare of vegetation.

Baedecker   One of the first travel guides published. The term is still sometimes used as a generic term for a guide book.

Baffin Bay   The area of the North Atlantic Ocean between northern Greenland and northern Canada.

baggage   The luggage and personal effects that a traveller might reasonably carry on a journey.

baggage allowance   The amount of luggage which a passenger may take with them without additional charge. This is most commonly encountered in air travel, where the usual baggage allowance is 20kg (44 pounds) in economy class and 30kg (66 pounds) in first class. Most other forms of public transport have a limit of some kind, although this is generally very high and few travellers will exceed it.

baggage check   (US) A receipt for baggage. > *baggage tag (1)*.

baggage claim area   The part of an airport where arriving passengers collect their baggage.

baggage tag   1. The labels, usually adhesive, that are issued at check-in to identify checked baggage. One part will be given to the traveller as a receipt.
2. The label noting the passenger's name and destination address which should be attached to each item of luggage before starting a journey.

BAHA   British Activity Holiday Association Ltd. *See Appendix 5a*.

Bahama Islands   The group of islands comprising the Commonwealth of the Bahamas and the Turks and Caicos Islands.

BAHREP   British Association of Hotel Representatives. *See Appendix 5a*.

bail bond   The security paid to an authority to enable someone to be released from custody pending trial. Some insurance companies offer bail bond cover.

bailiwick   The district or area of jurisdiction of a bailee or bailiff. The administrative areas of Guernsey and Jersey in the Channel Islands are balliwicks.

baksheesh   A term of Middle Eastern origin meaning a tip or gratuity.

balconette   A small balcony, rarely more than a few inches deep, generally outside French windows.

balcony   A platform or terrace on the outside of a building with access from the room.

Balearic Islands   A group of three islands situated in the western Mediterranean, politically part of Spain.

Balkans   The geographical region of the Balkan Peninsula (bordered by the Adriatic Sea to the west, the Aegean and Black Seas to the east and the Mediterranean to the south). The countries in this region are generally known as the Balkan States and comprise Albania, Bosnia-Herzegovina, Bulgaria, Croatia, Greece, the former Yugoslav Republic of Macedonia, Romania, Slovenia, Serbia & Montenegro (formerly the Federal Republic of Yugoslavia) and the European part of Turkey.

ball lightning   A very rare natural phenomenon where a glowing mass of energised air moves around until it strikes an earthed object, whereupon it discharges and disappears.

ballast   1. Heavy weights put in the hold of a vessel to give stability. They are often used when a voyage is being made without cargo or passengers.
2. The stone chippings on which railway lines are laid.

balloon   A lighter-than-air vehicle that cannot be steered. Now often used for sightseeing trips in such places as game parks where their quietness and slow speed avoid disturbance to wildlife.

BALPA   British Airline Pilots Association. *See Appendix 5a*.

Baltic Sea   The area of sea between Scandinavia and the coasts of north-eastern Germany, Poland and the Baltic States.

Baltic States   Any country with a coastline on the Baltic Sea. However, the term normally refers to Lithuania, Latvia and Estonia.

bamboo curtain   The political and cultural divide that exists between communist China and the rest of the world. > *Iron Curtain.*

banana republic   A derogatory term for a state, often in a deprived area, dependent on one type of trade (such as banana growing).

bangstick   A long rod containing an explosive-charged head (normally a shotgun cartridge) which detonates on contact. It is used by divers to repel sharks.

bank holiday   (UK) A day when the banks are officially closed and which is generally designated a public holiday.

bank settlement plan   The previous name for billing and settlement plan.

banqueting rooms   Rooms set aside in a hotel or similar for private and public functions.

bar   1. A place that serves alcoholic drinks and, on occasions, simple food. This can be within a hotel, ship or similar, or a place in its own right.
2. (UK) As definition 1, but the term does not usually include pubs.
3. (UK) Any one of the various public rooms in a pub.
4. A barrier of sand or sediment, usually caused by tidal action, near to shore or in the mouth of a river.
5. An abbreviation for barometric, used as a unit of pressure.
6. To forbid someone from entering a particular place, now or in the future.

BAR UK Ltd   Board of Airline Representatives in the UK. *See Appendix 5a.*

Barbary   An old name given to the western part of North Africa, now preserved in the name of the monkeys living on the Rock of Gibraltar known as Barbary Apes.

Barbary Coast   The coast of North Africa from Morocco to Egypt, named after the infamous Barbary Corsairs who once preyed on ships in the Mediterranean.

bareboat charter   A form of charter whereby the vessel is provided without supplies or crew.

barge   A cargo vessel, usually towed, that plies rivers and canals. The expression is often used (technically incorrectly) to describe the narrow boats common on British inland waterways.

barograph   A barometer that records its readings.

barometer   An instrument for measuring air pressure. .

baroque   A highly ornate and extravagant style, popular in the 17th and 18th centuries. Commonly used to describe architecture of that period.

barotrauma   Internal physical damage to human body caused by expanding or contracting air. Divers are most at risk from such damage, which can include burst ears, air embolism, emphysema and spontaneous pneumothorax.

barque   A type of sailing ship, usually with four masts.

barrage   A structure built across a tidal river or estuary to control the flow of water. In some countries the word is synonymous with dam.

basement   A storey in a building that is below ground level.

basin   A geographical term meaning a portion of land that is lower than the surrounding area. The term may also be applied to an area drained by a river.

bassinet   A little-used term that describes a cot provided for a baby on an aircraft.

BATA British Air Transport Association. *See Appendix 5a.*

bathometer An instrument used to measure the depth of water.

bathometric Of or relating to the depth of water.

bathroom 1. (UK) A room containing a bath and other washing facilities.
2. (US) A lavatory.

batten down To secure the hatches of a ship against bad weather. The term derives from the original practice of using wooden battens to secure the tarpaulin covers over a ship's holds.

bay A part of an ocean or sea that is partly or mainly surrounded by land.

Bay Area The urban area surrounding San Francisco Bay. Includes San Francisco in the west, Oakland in the east and San Jose and Silicon Valley in the south.

Bay of Bengal The area of the Indian Ocean between the Indian sub-continent and Indochina.

Bay of Biscay The area of the Atlantic Ocean between the northern coast of Spain and the western coast of France.

bayou A name given to a marshy creek or tributary in the southern USA.

bazaar An oriental market.

BC Before Christ, describing the dates before the Christian Era. It is written after the date in question.

BCH Bonded Coach Holiday Group. *See Appendix 5a.*

beach The area of rocks, sand or shingle making up the shore of a lake, sea or river.

beach buggy A small, wide-wheeled motor vehicle used mainly for recreation, for travelling on sand or similar.

beam The width of a vessel at its widest point.

beamy A ship that is broad in the beam.

beanery (US) A slang expression for a cheap restaurant.

bearing The direction of a journey, usually expressed as an angle relative to magnetic north.

beating the lung A diving term that means breathing at a rate faster than an aqualung is able to deliver air.

Beaufort scale The scale used to measure wind speed. In the USA an extension of the scale, up to scale 17, is sometimes used. The levels are:

0	Calm	Less than 1 knot
1	Light air	1 - 3 knots
2	Light breeze	4 - 6 knots
3	Gentle breeze	7 - 10 knots
4	Moderate breeze	11 - 16 knots
5	Fresh breeze	17 - 21 knots
6	Strong breeze	22 - 27 knots
7	Near gale	28 - 33 knots
8	Gale	34 - 40 knots
9	Strong gale	41 - 47 knots
10	Storm	48 - 55 knots
11	Violent storm	56 - 63 knots
12	Hurricane	Over 64 knots

becalm To deprive a ship of wind.

bed and breakfast 1. A guest house providing simple accommodation and breakfast.
2. A hotel rate or arrangement which includes accommodation and breakfast.

Bedouin A nomadic Arab people, usually living in the desert.

beerhouse (UK) A public house licensed to sell only beer and wine, not spirits.

bell boy (US) A page or porter in a hotel.

B

bell captain (US) The head porter of a hotel.

bell hop *See bell boy.*

bells A method of recording the passage of time on board a ship, with one bell measuring each progressive half-hour to a total of eight. The series starts at half past the hours of 4, 8 and 12. Each 4-hour period makes up a watch.

below Anything beneath the main deck of a ship.

beltway (US) A ring road.

bend A knot used for joining two pieces of rope.

bends, the The common term for decompression sickness, so named because the patient is often found bent over with pain.

benefit An insurance term describing the amount that will be paid to the insured in the event of a successful claim for a specific incident. The term is often used to describe any such payment from an insurance company, but more properly refers to payments which are made on a fixed scale, usually reflecting some degree of inconvenience (such as £30 per 12-hour period for a delayed departure), rather than those which are made to cover a quantifiable loss or expenditure covered under the policy. > *travel insurance.*

Benguela Current A cold-water current running northwards up the coast of West Africa and then westwards into the south Atlantic ocean. Its significance is the up-welling of nutrient-bearing water it brings from the seabed that supports vast numbers of fish in the area.

berg A South African term for mountain.

berg wind A hot dry wind blowing from the interior of Africa to coastal districts.

Bering Sea The area of the North Atlantic Ocean between eastern Siberia and Alaska.

Bering Strait The narrow channel where the Bering Sea meets the Arctic Ocean, between eastern Siberia and Alaska.

Berlin The capital of the Federal Republic of Germany. During the period when the country was divided, Bonn was the capital of West Germany. The eastern part of Berlin (East Berlin) was the capital of East Germany, divided from West Berlin by the infamous Berlin Wall. > *Germany.*

Berliner 1. A resident of Berlin.
2. A type of yeast bun with a jam filling.

berm A narrow path or earthwork beside a slope, road or canal.

Bermuda Agreement An air travel agreement developed in the 1940s that restricted air travel between Britain and the USA to the services of the national carriers. The agreement was substantially modified in the 1970s and few such restrictions now exist.

Bermuda plan A hotel rate that includes accommodation and full breakfast.

Bermuda Triangle A triangular area of the Atlantic Ocean stretching between Bermuda in the north-east, Puerto Rico in the south-east and south Florida in the south-west, in which there is supposed to have been a disproportionately high number of unexplained disappearances of ships and aircraft. The area first gained its reputation following the mysterious loss of several US warplanes in the 1940s.

berth 1. A bed on a ship or train. Berths can usually be folded against the wall when not in use and can be situated one above another. Obviously an upper berth can be inconvenient to passengers who are not fully able.
2. The name given to an area where a ship ties up when in port.

BH&HPA British Holiday & Home Parks Association Ltd. *See Appendix 5a.*

BHA British Hospitality Association. *See Appendix 5a.*

BIBA British Insurance Brokers' Association. *See Appendix 5a.*

Bibby cabin A cabin that has a narrow corridor leading to a porthole, thus getting some natural light and fresh air. It had the advantage of being away from the ship's side and was thus cooler when the plates are heated by the sun. The term is now rarely used.

Bible Belt The parts of the United States where Fundamentalist Christianity exerts a dominating influence on local politics and culture. The term was first used in the 1920s to describe rural communities and small towns in the South. Parts of the South-west and the Midwest are now often included in the term.

Big Foot A large ape-like creature reputedly living in the mountains of North America.

big foot A short fun-ski, shaped like a giant foot.

bight 1. A curve or recess in a coastline or river.
2. A loop in a rope.

bike A two-wheeled vehicle driven by pedal power. > *cycle.*

bilateral agreement An agreement between two parties (for example, countries). Often used in connection with airlines' agreements with each other.

bilge The lowest part of the hull of a ship.

bilharzia A disease of the tropics caused by a parasitic flatworm.

bilingual 1. A person who can speak two languages fluently.

2. Something that is written in, or spoken in, two languages.

bill of fare *See menu.*

billabong (Australia) A branch of a river forming a backwater.

billing and settlement plan (BSP) An IATA payment system whereby agents hold one type of ticket, rather than separate documents for each airline. Payment for all tickets sold is made through a bank in the agent's own country and BSP arranges for the airlines to be paid. Agents do not therefore have to make individual payments to airlines participating in the scheme.

bin The enclosed luggage container situated above the seats of an aircraft.

binding 1. A special clip that fixes the ski or snowboard to the ski boot or snowboard boot. They are normally designed to release the user in a fall to minimise the risk of injury and can be set according to the ability of the skier.
2. Any of the methods by which the pages of a magazine, book or similar are held together.

binnacle A receptacle for a ship's compass.

bioinvasion The phenomenon whereby indigenous species of plants and animals are being invaded by other types carried in by travellers. Many fragile ecosystems, such as the Florida Everglades, are under threat from bioinvasion. The effects of this phenomenon are known as biopollution.

biopollution *See bioinvasion.*

biosphere That part of the earth in which life exists.

biplane An aeroplane with two pairs of wings. Biplanes can usually operate at lower speeds than monoplanes and are thus still used in regions where STOL capabilities are important.

B

bisque   Fish soup.

bistro   A small, often informal, restaurant.

BITOA   British Incoming Tour Operators Association. *See Appendix 5a.*

bitumen   (Australia) A tarred road.

bivi   *See bivouac.*

bivouac   (or **bivi**) An overnight stop in the middle of a climbing or mountaineering route without the benefit of a tent.

black box   *See flight recorder.*

black diamond run   *See black run.*

black ice   Thin, hard, transparent and shiny ice, dangerous to climbers and motorists alike.

black run   The grading given by most ski areas to the most difficult, and usually the steepest, of ski runs. In North America the toughest runs are called black diamond runs.

Black Sea   The sea between the Mediterranean, Ukraine, the Caucasus and Turkey.

black tie   (UK) The name given to the mode of formal evening dress for men that involves the wearing of a dinner jacket and bow tie.

black-water rafting   An extreme sport that involves rafting down underground streams in the dark.

blimp   A non-rigid airship.

blizzard   A violent snowstorm with high winds.

bloc   A combination of parties, governments or other groupings sharing a common purpose or ideology.

Blue Badge Guide   (UK) The highest category of professionally qualified tourist guide.

blue channel   *See customs clearance.*

Blue Flag beach   A beach that meets the strict environmental requirements set by FEEE. These cover water quality, environmental education and information, environmental management, and safety and services. Each beach is inspected annually, and any blue flags are awarded only for one year.

Blue Peter   A blue flag with a white square, raised on a ship when leaving port.

blue run   The very easiest ski run category in Austria and German-speaking Switzerland. In France and Italy it is the second easiest category after a green run. In North America this is defined as green circle trail.

blue square trail   (US) A ski run of moderate difficulty in North American resorts. > *red run.*

Blue Train   The luxury rail service in South Africa which operates regularly between Pretoria and Cape Town, and less frequently on other routes, including the Garden Route (to Port Elizabeth), the Valley of the Olifants (to Neispruit and Hoedspruit) and the service to the Victoria Falls in Zimbabwe.

blue water   The open sea.

bluff   A steep cliff or headland.

BMC   British Mountaineering Council. *See Appendix 5a.*

board   1. To get onto or into a vehicle. 2. Food and lodging.

boarding card   *See boarding pass.*

boarding house   (UK) An old-fashioned term for a private home whose owner rents out rooms and may provide meals. The term 'guest house' is now more commonly used.

boarding pass   A document given to a passenger in exchange for a ticket coupon. This proves their entitlement to board an aircraft or other vehicle subject to immigration and security clearance, and (where applicable) indicates their class of service and seat allocation.

boardroom seating plan   A common configuration at meetings, conferences or seminars whereby the delegates are seated around one main table.

boardwalk   1. A wooden walkway across a sandy or marshy area.
2. (US) A seaside promenade.

boat   A small water-borne vessel. The distinction between a large boat and a small ship is vague but any vessel that is large enough to have more than one lifeboat is probably a ship.

boat deck   The deck of a ship on which the lifeboats are located.

boat drill   See *lifeboat drill.*

boat stations   The designated meeting points for passengers prior to the lowering of the lifeboats.

boat train   A train transporting passengers to or from a ship.

boatel   (Also **botel.**)
1. A waterside hotel with facilities for mooring boats.
2. A floating vessel converted to a hotel.

boatswain   Pronounced, and sometimes spelt, bosun. The ship's officer in charge of equipment and crew.

bodega   A shop selling wine and food, especially in Spanish speaking countries.

bog   An area of wet, spongy ground.

bogie   A wheel set on a locomotive or other railway vehicle.

Bohemian   1. Of or relating to Bohemia, a former kingdom in central Europe, roughly corresponding to the area of Slovakia and the Czech Republic.
2. A socially unconventional person.

boiler   The tank fitted to a steam engine in which the water is boiled into steam.

bollard   A stout post, either on shore or on board ship, used for fixing mooring lines.

bond   A guarantee of repayment in the case of financial failure of the bondholder. Most travel principals require a bond to protect themselves against loss through the financial failure of a travel agent. Many insurance companies will arrange a bond in consideration of an appropriate premium.

book   To make a reservation of some kind.

booking form   Originally an essential document, completed and signed by customers to show in writing the arrangements requested. These days many bookings are made on the telephone or electronically and booking forms are not usually needed by principals. However, it is good practice for agents to hold a written and signed copy of a customer's request, since, in the event of a later dispute, this may avoid arguments about what was agreed or requested at the time.

booking reference   A name, number, letter or a combination of any or all of these that identifies a specific booking. Ideally a booking reference should enable immediate access to the reservation in question without any need for cross-referring.

boom   A spar that supports the base of the sail.

booster   1. A further vaccination after the initial one that prolongs the period of immunity.

2. A type of seat for small children, usually strapped onto a chair for use at meal-times.

Bora   A strong, cold, dry north-easterly wind blowing in the Adriatic region.

Borneo   An island in the Malay Archipelago divided between Brunei, Indonesia (the provinces of Central, East, South and West Kalimantan) and Malaysia (the states of Sabah and Sarawak).

borough   (UK) A large town.

Borough   One of the administrative divisions of London (32) or New York (5), and some other cities.

botel   *See boatel.*

bottom time   The duration between commencing a dive (i.e. leaving the surface) and beginning the final ascent.

bouldering   A climbing activity that takes place on large boulders. Ropes and other climbing gear are not generally used.

Bourbon   1. Of or relating to the kings of France between 1589 and 1793 (and, less commonly, also between 1815 and 1848), and to those periods of French history generally (particularly the former). 2. Of or relating to the kings of Spain between 1700 and 1808 and 1831 to 1931, and to those periods of Spanish history generally (particularly the former).

bow   The front of a ship. Usually used as the plural, bows.

bow thruster   A screw mounted at the front of a ship, facing sideways, that assists docking. Many car ferries use bow thrusters.

bow wave   The wave set up by the bows of a moving ship or other vessel.

bowsprit   A spar projecting from the bows of a boat or ship.

BPA   British Ports Association. *See Appendix 5a.*

BR   *See British Rail.*

BRA   British Resorts Association. *See Appendix 5a.*

brae   A Scottish term for a steep bank or hillside.

Brahman   (or **Brahmin**) A member of the highest Hindu caste.

branch office location   An accredited agent's place of business, other than its head office, listed on the appropriate agency list as a branch office location.

break-even point   The number of sales required on a given service to cover the direct costs of its operation. Profit will not be made until sales in excess of the break even are made.

breakaway   A short holiday.

breakwater   A barrier built out into the sea to mitigate the force of waves and currents.

bridge   1. A structure built to carry a road or railway across an obstruction. 2. The control point of a ship.

bridleway   A route or track intended for the use of horse-riders.

brig   A two-masted, square-rigged ship.

British   Of or relating to the British Isles, its inhabitants and culture.

British Crown Dependency   *See British Overseas Possessions.*

British English   The form of English spoken in the UK, rather than in, say, the USA.

British Isles   The geographical region comprising the United Kingdom, the

Republic of Ireland, the Isle of Man and the Channel Islands. > *Great Britain, UK.*

British Overseas Possessions The various former British colonial possessions which now enjoy varying degrees of autonomy. Since the 2002 British Overseas Territories Act, the nomenclature of these has been simplified. There are now three British Crown Dependencies (Guernsey, Jersey and the Isle of Man) and 14 British Overseas Territories. For more information, please consult the Columbus *World Travel Guide.*

British Overseas Territory *See British Overseas Possessions.*

British Rail The former name for the rail network of the United Kingdom prior to its break-up into a track authority and several private train operating companies.

British Summer Time The daylight saving time used in the UK. > *daylight saving time.*

British Virgin Islands *See Virgin Islands.*

Britisher A term, used by races other than the British, to refer to a British subject or someone of British descent.

Briton 1. A member of the peoples that inhabited the southern part of Britain before the Roman conquest. 2. A native or inhabitant of Great Britain.

broad gauge A railway track gauge of more than the standard four feet eight and a half inches.

brochure The catalogue issued by tour operators and others that gives details of the products on offer.

BSP *See billing and settlement plan.*

BSP Committee A committee composed of representatives of IATA members, established in accordance with the Provisions for the Conduct of IATA Traffic Conferences and having general responsibilities with respect to Standard Bank Plans.

BSP Coordinator A person appointed by the plan management as required, to act in accordance with its rules on behalf of airlines and IATA members.

BSP Panel A panel composed of IATA members who operate services, or issue traffic documents through agents, in the country or area of a Billing and Settlement Plan. The panel also includes non-IATA airlines which participate in Billing and Settlement Plans.

BSP Steering Panel The IATA panel which, in accordance with the instructions and directions of the BSP committee, is charged with the implementation and certain supervisory aspects of BSP.

BST *See British Summer Time.*

BTA British Tourist Authority. *See Appendix 5a.*

bubble car (US) *See observation car.*

Bucharest The capital of Romania. Not to be confused with Budapest, the capital of Hungary.

buck (US) A colloquial term for a US dollar.

bucket shop A now redundant term for a travel agency which specialised in selling discounted air tickets. In the past, many fares created by these outlets were contrary to IATA rules, and the bucket shops themselves were often perceived as being untrustworthy. Such operations have ceased to exist now that almost all travel agents are able to offer reduced priced tickets.

bucket-and-spade A term used to describe a traditional type of family holiday, typically at a beach resort and

B

with young children, taken in a relatively low-price destinations.

buckshee   (UK) A slang expression meaning free of charge.

Budapest   The capital of Hungary. Not to be confused with Bucharest, the capital of Romania.

Buddhism   The philosophy or belief observed by the followers of Guatama Buddha, who lived in India during the 5th century BC. > *religion*.

buddy   In sub-aqua terms, a fellow diving companion.

buffet   1. An eating establishment, often on a railway station, where customers serve themselves from a counter. 2. The food service system where customers help themselves from a counter or table.

buffet car   The carriage on a train which is wholly or partly devoted to providing snacks and beverages for passengers.

buffeting   An irregular oscillation of an aircraft, caused by air turbulence.

bulkhead   A vertical partition or wall in a ship or aircraft.

bulkhead seats   Seats in an aircraft or other form of transport that either face or back on to a bulkhead. The former may have more leg room, but less storage space; the latter may not recline. Families with babies are usually seated immediately behind a bulkhead.

bullet train   A general term for the high-speed passenger trains in Japan running on Shinkansen lines.

bulwarks   The sides of a ship above the top deck.

bumboat   A small boat plying between ships and the shore with provisions.

bump   1. The act of denying carriage to a passenger with a confirmed booking. This happens when the service is overbooked and the customer is requested to travel on a later flight, usually in exchange for compensation. 2. (US) A mogul.

bunk   A sleeping berth, especially one projecting from a wall or partition, often in pairs.

bunkering   The taking on of fuel by a ship.

bunkers   The space on ship where the fuel is stored.

buoy   A floating marker that indicates a channel or hazard.

buoyancy compensator   An inflatable jacket worn by divers which can be partially inflated or deflated to suit underwater buoyancy requirements.

bure   A South Pacific term used to describe a thatched-roof bungalow, especially in Fiji.

burst lung   A condition brought about by the diver holding his breath during ascent, thus causing the air in the lungs to expand dangerously.

bus   1. A large passenger-carrying road vehicle. In the UK a distinction is made between buses, which operate short-distance scheduled services, and coaches, which operate longer-distance and chartered services. This distinction is not applied in many other parts of the world. 2. The act of transporting passengers by bus.

busboy   (US) A person on a cruise ship or in a restaurant in North America who clears the table during a meal.

business centre   A room for business travellers, usually including telecommunications equipment, secretarial assistance and other office facilities.

business class An airline class of service in which passengers are offered extra comforts compared to economy class, but not to the luxurious standards of first class.

business house An obsolete term for business travel agent or implant.

business travel agent *See travel agent.*

business traveller A traveller who makes a journey for the purpose of trade or commerce, rather than for leisure or other personal reasons.

button lift *See drag lift.*

BVRLA British Vehicle Rental & Leasing Association. *See Appendix 5a.*

BW British Waterways. *See Appendix 5a.*

B

bwana A polite form of address used in many African countries. From the Swahili for 'sir'.

bypass A route, usually a road, that avoids a town centre or other congested area.

byway A minor road.

Byzantine Of or relating to the Eastern Roman Empire (AD325 to 1453), and in particular to the highly decorated style of art and architecture which flourished there.

Cc

c. (or **circa**) Approximately.

C card The diver certification card issued by each authority responsible for awarding qualifications in scuba diving.

C sizes One of the ranges in the international system of metric paper sizes, used virtually everywhere in the world except in North America. C sizes are used mainly for envelopes. The number corresponds to the A-sized sheet it is designed to hold. Thus a C5 envelope is designed to hold an A5 sheet.

CAA Civil Aviation Authority. *See Appendix 5a.*

cab An alternative name for a taxi. > *minicab.*

cabaña A US and South American term for a beach hut.

cabin 1. A small hut or shelter.
2. A room for sleeping on a ship.
3. The interior of an aircraft.

cabin bag A small bag suitable for carriage in the passenger cabin of an aircraft.

cabin baggage *See hand baggage.*

cabin class An obsolete expression denoting a class on a ship that is between first and tourist.

cabin crew Those members of an airline's staff who are responsible for the comfort and safety of the passengers on board the aircraft.

cabin cruiser A large motor boat with living accommodation.

cable A nautical measure of length equal to 100 fathoms (600 feet).

cable car 1. A large cabin attached to a cable along which it travels. They are able to travel up steep gradients, and are thus much used in ski resorts.
2. (US) A tram.

cable railway A railway along which a train is drawn by means of an endless cable. Examples can be found in Llandudno (Wales), Hong Kong and San Francisco.

Cabo da Roca The westernmost point of mainland Europe, west of Lisbon, in Portugal.

cabotage 1. The navigation and movement of ships in coastal waters.
2. Air travel between territories of the same sovereign state. This may be between points within the same country (such as London to Manchester) or between a country and its dependencies (such as London to Gibraltar). The air fares for cabotage journeys are not governed by the normal international fare agreements.
3. The act of reserving such air travel to the exclusive control of the state concerned.

caddy A person who carries golf clubs on a golf course and otherwise assists a golfer.

café 1. (UK) A small, relatively informal,

eating establishment, usually not serving alcohol.
2. (US) A bar or night-club.

cafeteria 1. The full name for café, to which it is usually abbreviated.
2. A self-service restaurant.

caique A small rowing boat used on the Bosphorus.

cairn A mound of stones built as a monument or landmark.

Cajun Country Area of southern Louisiana settled by a group of people of French origin, expelled from Nova Scotia in the 18th century by the British.

Caledonian Of or relating to Scotland.

calendar 1. The system by which the start, finish, duration and sub-divisions of years are fixed. The most widely used is the western (Gregorian) calendar However, there are several other systems, of which the Chinese, Jewish and Muslim are the most important.
2. A table of dates for a year, usually showing festivals and events important to a particular occupation or interest group.

California Current A wide, cold and sluggish current that runs north to south off the west coast of the USA.

California Zephyr The rail service between Chicago and San Francisco in the USA.

calm See Beaufort scale.

Camino de Compostela The medieval pilgrim routes from south-western France to the tomb of St James in Santiago de Compostela. The monuments and churches erected along the way, and the route as a whole, have now become tourist attractions. Also known as the Way of St James.

campground See campsite.

camping holiday A holiday where holidaymakers stay in temporary accommodation such as tents or caravans.

camping site See campsite.

campsite An area where campers can pitch their tents or where static tents can be rented. In the USA most sites will accept motorhomes and caravans, but in the UK this is not always the case.

Canadian 1. Of or relating to Canada.
2. The rail service between Toronto and Vancouver in Canada.

Canadian Technology Triangle An area south-west of Toronto, Canada, famous for its concentration of high-tech industries.

canal An artificial waterway. Most canals were originally built for goods traffic, but many are now used by leisure travellers.

Canary Current An extension of the North Atlantic Drift flowing south along the north-west African coast and moderating temperatures in the coastal region.

Canary Islands A group of seven islands in the Atlantic off the north-west coast of Africa and politically part of Spain.

cancel To release, withdraw or revoke a reservation.

cancellation and curtailment insurance See travel insurance, curtail.

cancellation charge A fee charged to a customer who cancels a booking. In general, the more notice is given of the cancellation, the more money will be refunded. Since it is always difficult to collect such charges, it is important for agents to collect in advance an amount sufficient to cover any likely charges. The scales of cancellation charges can be complex, and it is important that travel staff do not refund any part of a pre-payment without having proper authority from the principal involved.

canoe   A small, narrow boat usually propelled by paddling.

cantina   A Spanish term, especially common in Mexico, for a bar or wine-shop.

Canuck   A Canadian, especially a French Canadian.

canx.   A commonly used abbreviation for 'cancelled'.

canyon   A deep valley or ravine with steep sides.

canyoning   *See gorge walking.*

cap   As applied to commission, to place a ceiling or limit on the maximum amount that can be earned.

capacity   The maximum number of people, or amount of goods, that a vehicle, hotel, room or similar can physically, or legally, accommodate.

cape   A point of land projecting into a body of water, usually a sea or ocean.

Cape Agulhas   The southernmost point of the African continent, in South Africa.

Cape Cod   A long, sandy peninsula in Massachusetts, USA.

Cape Comorin   The southernmost point of India, south of Nagercoil.

Cape Doctor   A strong south-easterly wind experienced in South Africa.

Cape Farewell   The southernmost point of Greenland.

Cape Horn   The southernmost point of the South American continent, in Chile.

Cape of Good Hope   A headland in South Africa, south of Cape Town.

Cape Sable   The southernmost point mainland Florida, USA.

Capetian   Of or relating to the kings of France between AD987 and 1328, and to that period of French history generally.

capital   The city or town of a country, province or state which is the administrative centre and which has officially been designated as such. The capital may be the largest city, but this by no means always the case: only three of the world's ten most populous cities are capitals; only four of the world's ten most populous countries have their largest city as the capital; and out of Europe's 19 urban agglomerations with a population of over 2 million, only seven are capitals. In some cases (such as the USA, Canada and Australia), the capital was deliberately not established in the largest city in order to counterbalance its influence, and the same policy was adopted by many US States (such as New York, California and Florida). In recent times, some countries (such as Nigeria, Côte d'Ivoire and Brazil) have established new capital cities away from the major centres, and others may do so in the future. A few countries (such as South Africa, Bolivia and Sri Lanka) have administrative, legislative or judicial pre-eminence split between more than one capital. > *Appendix 1.*

Capital Region USA   A US regional marketing organisation covering the states surrounding Washington DC. > *US regional marketing organisations..*

Capsian   Of or relating to the Palaeolithic culture of North Africa and Southern Europe.

capsize   Of a boat, to overturn or upset.

capstan   A thick revolving spindle used for winding a rope or hawser, commonly found on marine vessels to haul in mooring ropes.

capsule hotel   Accommodation, commonly used in Japan, that provides sleeping compartments in drawer-like capsules, just large enough for one person.

captain   The person in charge of a waterborne vessel or aircraft.

car   1. (UK) A private motor vehicle having three or more wheels.
2. A railway carriage.
3. Any passenger compartment in a vehicle such as a lift.

car ferry   A vessel, usually a ship, designed to carry vehicles as well as passengers.

car hire   *See vehicle rental.*

car rental   *See vehicle rental.*

carafe   An open-topped glass jug used for serving water or wine in a restaurant.

caravan   Originally a trailer vehicle providing accommodation, but now also applied to many types of semi-permanent accommodation on special sites.

caravan park   *See caravan site.*

caravan site   An area where caravans may be parked. Sites may be semi-permanent, where the caravans may be parked for months or years, or short-stay.

caravanette   A motor-caravan.

cardboarding   A method of falsifying the audit coupons of a manually issued ticket. It is, of course, fraud and thus a criminal offence.

Cardinal   The rail service between Chicago and Washington DC in the USA.

cargo   Goods, other than a passenger's personal effects, carried on board a ship or aircraft.

carhop   (US) A colloquial expression for a waiter at a drive-in restaurant.

Caribbean   A general term used to describe the islands of the Caribbean Sea and, in many cases, the parts of the countries of Central and South America which have a Caribbean coastline. For convenience, the term may also include the Bahamas and the Turks and Caicos Islands.

Caribbean Sea   The area of the Atlantic Ocean between South America, Central America and the Antilles.

carnet   1. A term of French origin that describes an official document that allows the temporary importation of goods without payment of duty.
2. On some transport networks (including the London Underground and the Paris Métro) a book of tickets sold at a discount.

Carnival of Colour   *See Holi.*

Caroline Islands   An archipelago in the western Pacific Ocean. The islands comprise the Federated States of Micronesia and Palau.

Carolingian   Of or relating to the kings of France between AD751 and AD987 and the Holy Roman Emperors between AD800 and AD911, and those periods of those countries' history generally.

carousel   1. A rotating delivery system for the collection of luggage, especially at an airport.
2. (US) A merry-go-round at a funfair or similar.

carriage   1. (UK) A passenger vehicle on a railway.
2. Transportation between two points by a company existing for that purpose.

carriageway   That part of a road intended for vehicles.

carrier   A generic term for any transport operator.

carrier identification plate   A small

C

embossed plate that is fitted into a ticket validating machine and which endorses the name of the carrier onto the ticket or other document. Also known as a plate.

carsickness   Nausea caused by travelling in a car or other road vehicle.

cartel   An association or group of manufacturers or suppliers that seeks to control prices and other aspects of its members' trading. It is common practice for cartels to fix prices at a high level. Although cartels are now illegal in many countries, it is often difficult to detect and prevent their activities.

cartogram   A map with statistical information in diagrammatic form.

cartography   The art and practice of map-making.

carving skis   A current design of skis, shorter than the skiier and wider at the tip and tail than was previously popular, which helps the skis to turn more easily. They are sometimes called shaped skis or hourglass skis: particularly wide models are sometimes known as fat boys.

casbah   *See kasbah.*

cascade   A small waterfall.

cash basis   A method of payment for goods or services where no credit facilities are offered and settlement must be made in full before the goods or services are provided. The term 'cash' can in certain cases include a banker's draft or a cheque.

casino   A building used for gambling, especially roulette, sometimes attached to a hotel.

casita   A bungalow, especially in Mexico.

Caspian Sea   The inland sea in west central Asia, bordered by Russia, Kazakstan, Turkmenistan, Iran and Azerbaijan.

caste system   The system practised in the Hindu culture whereby different personal levels of purity or pollution are said to be inherited. In a strict caste system, members of different levels will have no contact with each other.

CAT   Clear air turbulence. The disturbance caused to an aircraft when flying through inclement weather or air pockets.

cat's paw   A very slight breeze that just ripples the surface of water.

catacomb   An underground cemetery, generally Roman.

catamaran   A boat with twin parallel hulls.

cataract   A large waterfall or cascade, often with a relatively slight drop.

catchment area   The area from which an attraction or resort derives most of its customers.

Caucasian   Of or relating to the white or light-skinned division of humankind.

Caucasus   The range of mountains between the Black Sea and the Caspian Sea.

causeway   A raised road or tract across low or wet ground or shallow water.

cave   A large hollow in the side of a hill or cliff or underground.

cave tubing   *See black-water rafting.*

caveat emptor   A Latin expression meaning 'let the buyer beware', used to point out that the buyer is responsible for their satisfaction with a purchase.

cavern   A cave, usually large.

cay   A small island (sometimes spelled key, as in the Florida Keys).

CBT   *See Certificate in Business Travel.*

CDW *See vehicle rental insurance.*

ceiling 1. The maximum height at which an aircraft can fly under a given set of conditions.
2. The inside planking of a ship's hull.

Celebes Also known as Sulawesi, an island in the Malay Archipelago and politically part of Indonesia.

Celsius *See centigrade.*

Celtic Of or relating to the pre-Roman inhabitants of Britain and Gaul and their descendants.

centi- A prefix commonly found in the metric system, meaning one-hundredth part of. Thus a centilitre is one hundredth of a litre.

centigrade The temperature scale in which water freezes at 0° and boils at 100°. A quick way approximately to convert Centigrade to Fahrenheit is to double the Centigrade figure and add 30. Thus 25°C x 2 = 50 + 30 = 80°F. Also known as Celsius.

centimetre A unit of measurement in the metric system, equal to approximately 0.4 of an inch.

Central America The geographical region comprising Belize, Costa Rica, El Salvador, Guatemala, Honduras, Nicaragua and Panama.

Central Standard Time 1. One of the time zones used in North America, six hours behind UTC.
2. One of the time zones used in Australia, nine and a half hours ahead of UTC.

Certificate in Business Travel (CBT) The qualification run by the Guild of Business Travel Agents and validated by City and Guilds. It is an examination-based qualification at several levels designed for those working, or intending to work, in business travel.

Ceylon An island off the south-east coast of India, now Sri Lanka.

chain 1. An obsolete imperial measurement of distance equal to 66 feet (one eightieth of a mile). The railways of Britain were surveyed using chains and certain measurements may still be referred to in these units.
2. A group of shops, restaurants, hotels or other retail businesses owned by the same person or organisation.

chair lift A lift with one to eight seats, common in ski resorts but sometimes used at other visitor attractions. Chairs are carried on a constantly moving cable up a slope. The oldest and slowest lifts typically seat one or two people, and are known as single and double chairs. The most modern and fastest lifts detach from a faster moving cable at the bottom of the lift, moving on a slower cable and thus allowing the chair to move slowly to pick up users. The same process takes place in reverse for dismounting. These modern chairs typically seat four (quad chairs), six (six-pac) or eight people in a row.

chalet A small, wooden house or bungalow, usually with an overhanging roof. Traditional in Switzerland and Austria and often used as accommodation for winter sports enthusiasts.

chambermaid A housemaid in a hotel.

champagne powder Very light powder snow, typically falling in western North America. The name has been trademarked by Steamboat resort.

channel A length of water, wider than a strait, joining two larger areas of water.

Channel Islands A group of islands off the north-west coast of France comprising Alderney, Guernsey, Herm, Jersey, Sark and Jethou. They are British Crown Dependencies and not part of the United Kingdom, although close ties are maintained.

C

Channel Tunnel The under-sea tunnel that provides a direct rail link between England and France, carrying Eurostar (passenger) and Eurotunnel (vehicle and freight) services.

Channel, the (UK) The English Channel.

Chanukah (or **Hanukah**) A festival in the Jewish religious calendar, lasting for eight days, generally in December.

charabanc An old-fashioned term for a motor coach.

charge card Similar to a credit card, although the extended payment facility is not automatically offered.

chart An alternative name for map, usually applied to the very accurate navigational maps used on aircraft and ships.

charter The act of a person or organisation paying for the exclusive use of part of or the whole of a vehicle. The term is usually applied to aircraft but can apply to any form of transport. An ad hoc charter is a one-off arrangement; a series charter is several journeys between the same points; a time charter is when the vehicle is chartered for a period of time.

chasm A deep, wide fissure or opening in the earth or rock, either on land or under water.

chauffeur The paid driver of a motor car.

chauffeur-drive A vehicle rented with a driver.

check (US) A cheque.

check digit A number, following a document number, that bears a mathematical relationship to that number. It is used to verify the accuracy of the number and thus identify any transcription errors. Also known as check sum.

check sum *See check digit.*

checked baggage Baggage that is registered to a traveller's destination and is conveyed in a special container or in the aircraft's hold.

check-in 1. The process of registering at a hotel or other accommodation.
2. The process of completing formalities before boarding a flight or other transportation.
3. The location or time at which a vehicle rental ends, and the formalities associated with this. Also known as drop-off.

check-in time The time by which a person must have checked in. In the case of accommodation, this may also refer to the earliest time at which the guest may take possession of the room.

check-out 1. The process of removing luggage and finalising the bill when a guest vacates a hotel or other accommodation.
2. The location or time at which a vehicle rental begins, and the formalities associated with it. Also known as pick-up.

check-out time The time by which a person must have checked out. In the case of accommodation, this is rarely later than noon. Late check-out, which may incur an additional charge, should ideally be agreed with the establishment in advance.

check-point A place where traffic is stopped for inspection and clearance.

chef A cook in a restaurant or similar establishment.

cheque (UK) A written order to a bank, usually on a pre-printed sheet, to pay a specified sum of money to a specified person or organisation. The increasing use of credit and debit cards has led to a decline in their use. Furthermore, cheques are generally not acceptable outside their country of issue.
> *travellers' cheques.*

cheque card (UK) A card that guarantees payment of a cheque up to a stated amount.

chevron seating plan *See herringbone seating plan.*

Chicago Convention The international agreement that defined the freedoms of the air in 1944. > *freedoms of the air.*

child In travel, a young person who will not have to pay the full fare, but who may be entitled to a reduced one. The age at which a child ceases to be an infant, and the age at which a child becomes an adult, will vary from service to service, but for most airlines these cut-offs are 2 and 12 years respectively. Some organisations, such as amusement parks, will define a child by height, not age. > *adult, infant.*

chill factor The perceived lowering of temperature caused by wind. The chill factor is often more important in determining comfort than is the actual temperature.

chimney A wide crack, generally with three sides, that can accommodate a climber (or most of one).

China, People's Republic of The official name for mainland China. Not to be confused with the Republic of China (ROC), the term used by Taiwan to describe itself.

chine A deep narrow ravine, especially in the Isle of Wight or Dorset.

Chinook 1. A warm dry wind that blows east of the Rocky Mountains.
2. A warm wet southerly wind that blows west of the Rocky Mountains.
3. A make of helicopter.

chit A note, memorandum or similar document.

chocks Blocks placed either side of an aircraft's nose-wheel. Exact departure and arrival times are usually determined by the time at which the chocks are taken off or put on.

cholera An infectious intestinal disease transmitted by water and endemic in countries with poor standards of sanitation. Current WHO policy advises that immunisation is not effective in stopping the spread of the disease. > *health precautions.*

chondola The name for a modern ski lift that can carry either chairs or cabins.

chopper A colloquial term for a helicopter.

Christian 1. A person believing in or following Christianity.
2. A general term for countries or areas where Christianity is the dominant religion, particularly with reference to the aspects of its culture which Christianity has influenced. > *religion.*

christian name A person's first or given name. This term is not generally used in countries where Christianity is not the main religion and the expression 'given name' may be better understood.

Christianity The religion based on and following the teachings of Jesus Christ and his disciples. > *religion.*

Christmas A festival in the Christian religious calendar, generally celebrated on 25 December, but on 6 January by the Orthodox church.

chronological The ordering of information by date, usually with the most recent appearing last. Confusions can be caused when dates written in the date-first system are sorted using the month-first, and vice-versa. > *date order.*

chronometer An instrument that measures time, particularly at sea. Accurate navigation across meridians of longitude was not possible until the invention of the chronometer by the

C

C

Englishman, John Harrison.

Chunnel   A colloquial term for the Channel Tunnel. *See Channel Tunnel.*

chute   1. A narrow, short, steep ski run, off-piste in Europe.
2. An inflatable slide used as a means of emergency exit from an aircraft.
3. A very steep gully.

CIMTIG   Chartered Institute of Marketing Travel Industry Group. *See Appendix 5a.*

Cinque Ports   The ports of Sandwich, Dover, Hythe, Romney and Hastings on the south-east coast of England. From the 11th century they were granted privileges in exchange for defensive obligations. The term is retained today for ceremonial and touristic purposes.

CIP   *See commercially important person.*

circle trip   A return journey which is continuous back to its starting point and via two or more intermediate points, each of which carries a different fare.

circuitous   A journey that is indirect and usually a long way around. Such routes are often discouraged or prohibited by many carriers.

circumnavigate   To sail around, especially around the world.

circumpolar   Around or near to one of the earth's poles.

cirque   A deep, bowl-shaped hollow at the head of a valley or on a mountain.

cirrus   A form of white, wispy cloud found at high altitude. Often known as 'mare's tails'.

CIS   *See Commonwealth of Independent States.*

citizen   A native or naturalized inhabitant of a country.

city   1. (UK) A large town which has formally been designated as a city by Royal Charter.
2. In most of the world, a large town.

city terminal   A point in a town or city where airline or boat passengers may check in for flights or sailings rather than at the airport or docks. Passengers may be taken into a city terminal at the end of their journeys.

City, the   1. The administrative area of the City of London.
2. The financial institutions which exist in and around the City of London.

claim   To submit a request for compensation or reimbursement.

claimant   A person making a claim.

clan   A group of people with a common ancestor, especially in Scotland.

class   In travel, the segregation of passengers according to the fare paid. Once simply first, second and third, the demands of marketing have resulted in many special names for the different classes. Some are unique to one carrier, and all may be subject to change.

classroom seating plan   A common configuration at meetings, conferences or seminars whereby the delegates are seated at rows of tables arranged one behind the other.

clay pan   (Australia) A hollow in the soil that retains water after rain.

clearance   1. The specific permission granted to an aircraft or other mode of transport to allow it to begin or continue with its journey.
2. The act of being allowed through customs.
3. The act of moving funds from one bank account to another, and the time taken to do this.
4. An amount of clear space needed for

the safe passage of two objects, such as a lorry and a bridge, or two ships.

clearing house   The bank or other organisation appointed under BSP to perform various functions, including: receipt of sales transmissions; extraction and processing of data; rendering of billings to agents; receipt of payments from agents.

clearstory   (US) *See clerestory.*

cleat   1. A projecting piece on a spar or gangway to give secure footing.
2. A clip to which a rope may be secured.

clerestory   (or **clearstory**) (US) A raised-roof section of a building or railway carriage that contains windows and ventilators. Rarely seen these days on transport.

CLIA   Cruise Lines International Association. *See Appendix 5b.*

cliff   A steep rock face.

climate   The general condition of an area in terms of its temperature, rainfall, humidity and other meteorological factors, arrived at by compiling weather statistics over a period of time (generally at least 30 years) and averaging the results. Unlike weather, variations in climate are relatively regular and predictable.

climate zones   The climatic types, in approximately ascending order of average temperatures over a 24-hour period are:
• *Polar.* Extreme cold with vicious winds. Rainfall or snowfall is low, but as there is little evaporation, polar regions are snow-covered for much of the year.
• *Mountain.* Each rise in altitude of 15,000 feet (4,500 m) has the same effect as a change in latitude towards a pole of around 15°. At the tops of the tallest mountains, the climate is often as cold as at the poles, even in equatorial latitudes.
• *Tundra.* The area of cold, coniferous

forests that extends across the northern parts of Siberia, Europe and North America, with long, cold winters and brief, warm, summers. There is relatively little rainfall. Tundra only occurs in the northern hemisphere since there are no large land masses at the equivalent southern latitudes.
• *Temperate.* Temperature and rainfall are reasonably evenly distributed throughout the year and there are no extremes of either. Temperate regions are characterised by very changeable day-to-day weather. The UK is in a temperate region.
• *Mediterranean.* Hot, dry summers and warm wet winters characterise the climate of west-facing coastal regions between the temperate and desert latitudes. Mediterranean climates can be found in every continent except Antarctica and all are popular with holidaymakers.
• *Savannah.* Areas such as the prairies of North America, the pampas of Argentina and the veldt of southern Africa are all screened from the moisture-laden sea air. There is only enough rainfall to support grass and similar plants.
• *Hot desert.* Desert areas have high daytime temperatures and little rainfall. With irrigation, desert areas can be made fertile.
• *Subtropical.* High temperatures throughout the year but with marked seasonal variations in rainfall.
• *Tropical.* High day and night temperatures and high rainfall give rise to luxuriant growth of many types of vegetation. Where unchecked this results in a typical rain forest.

climbing clinic   (US) A climbing school.

climbing grades   A way of describing the relative difficulty of different kinds of climbing trips. While each operator tends to rank the various climbs featured in their programmes in some way, there is no common system, even within one country, such as exists with skiing. This makes direct comparisons difficult. Most companies will grade climbs into one of between three and six levels, with the higher number or letter generally being the hardest. In addition, some will have two grading systems: one referring to the technical difficulty of the climb and the amount of equipment needed; the other referring to level of fitness required by the climber. The second is at least as important in deciding whether a particular trip is suitable for a particular person. These issues also apply to trekking, hill walking, scrambling, ice climbing and mountaineering, each of which will have its own grades. A grade-three walk, for example, is thus a very different proposition from a grade three climb.

climbing school An institution where rock climbing is taught at all grades. Often called a climbing clinic in the USA.

clime An alternative and old-fashioned name for a region or climate.

clip The act of removing a small piece from a ticket (usually one for rail travel) to show that it has been used.

clip-joint A slang expression for a night club or similar establishment that swindles its guests by overcharging.

clipper A large, fast sailing vessel.

cloakroom 1. A room where outer garments and baggage can be left.
2. A lavatory.

closed dates Days for which reservations can no longer be taken because there is no availability.

closed-U-shape seating plan A common configuration at meetings, conferences or seminars whereby the delegates are seated around the outside of tables arranged together in a hollow rectangle.

cloud The visible masses of condensed water vapour floating in the atmosphere.

club car (US) A railway carriage equipped with a lounge and other amenities.

coach 1. (UK) A motor vehicle carrying a large number of passengers and used mainly for longer distance journeys and tours.
2. (US) Economy class.
3. A railway carriage.

coach class (US) Economy class.

coaming Small raised partitions at the doorways and around the hatches on a ship that prevent the access of water.

coast The border of the land near the sea.

coaster A ship that travels along the coast from port to port.

coastguard A person or organisation keeping watch on the coasts and on local shipping to maintain safety and prevent smuggling.

coastline The line of the seashore, especially as regards its shape and characteristics.

cockpit 1. The part of an aircraft where the flight controls are located.
2. The control position of a yacht or motor launch.

code-share An arrangement whereby two or more airlines are allocated seats on the flight and sell them independently under their own airline prefix, although the actual aircraft will be operated by another airline.

co-development The situation where a plot of land, a building or other feature is jointly constructed or modified by two or more commercial partners (such as a hotel and a sports club) engaged in complementary business activities.

co-extensive Having the same extent, frontiers or limits.

coffee shop A small informal restaurant in a hotel or similar.

cog railway A form of railway used on steep gradients where the normal friction between wheels and track would give insufficient grip. An extra toothed wheel engages with a toothed rack on the track.

col The lowest passage between two mountain tops.

collection charge See *delivery charge*.

collision damage waiver See *vehicle rental insurance*.

colonial Of or relating to a colony or colonies. The term is also used pejoratively to describe a patronising attitude towards other cultures.

colony A group of settlers in a country, subject to a mother country.

colours The national flag or emblem flown by a ship.

commercially important person (CIP) Similar to VIP but where the traveller's importance derives from commercial or business activities rather than status. > *VIP.*

commis A junior waiter or chef.

commission The amount paid by a principal to its agents for selling their products or services, usually calculated as a percentage of the sum paid by the client.

commissionable Any product or service the sale of which will result in a commission being paid to the seller.

common carrier A carrier that undertakes to transport any person or goods in a specified category or categories.

common-rated The name given to two or more destinations to which the fare is the same.

commonwealth A nation, viewed from the point of view of all its members having a stake or interest in it. The term was originally coined to help express a political philosophy, but has survived in the name of some international institutions, and also as part of the formal title of some countries.

Commonwealth, The A free association of independent states (currently 54) most of which were at one time under British administration.

Commonwealth Games A major international athletics event, which takes place every four years in a different Commonwealth city on each occasion. Accommodation and transport arrangements may need to be made months, and sometimes years, in advance.

Commonwealth of Independent States (CIS) The short-lived political entity in the 1990s which was created after the demise of the USSR and lasted until the establishment of its constituent republics as independent states. It included all the republics of the USSR except Estonia, Latvia and Lithuania.

communicating cabins The shipboard equivalent of connecting rooms.

communism The political and economic philosophy derived from Marxism, the main principles of which include the common ownership of property, the central control of economic and political activity and the subordination of the individual to the common good. In various forms, communism formed the guiding philosophy of many countries in the 20th century although has survived in only a few (notably China, Korea DPR and Cuba).

commuter Anyone who travels regularly on a route, usually to and from work.

commuter aircraft An aircraft, usually with fewer than 30 seats, that operates on relatively short routes.

C

comp. *See complimentary ticket.*

companionway A staircase on a ship, technically to a cabin, but often used loosely to refer to any stairway on board.

compartment 1. A small separate section in a railway carriage. On railways in Britain, these days compartments tend to be restricted to use by holders of first-class (or equivalent) tickets. 2. A watertight division in a ship.

compass An instrument used to determine direction. Magnetic compasses point to the magnetic north, other types of compass, such as a giro compass, can give a true north reading.

compatriot A fellow countryman.

compensate To make restitution for loss or damage.

compensation An amount of money or other reimbursement made as restitution.

complement (or **full complement**) The number of persons required to fill or crew a ship or other conveyance.

complimentary ticket A free ticket given as thanks for a service provided or to be provided, or possibly as compensation.

complimentary upgrade The situation whereby a passenger or customer is upgraded to a higher class of accommodation, facility or service without additional payment.

comprehensive Complete or all-inclusive. Often used to describe insurance cover.

compressor A pump used to compress air to the high pressure necessary to charge diving cylinders.

computerised reservation system (CRS) The former name for *global distribution system.*

concierge A term of French origin that refers to a person in a hotel who provides information and arranges the transfer of the guests and their luggage to their rooms.

concourse An open area in a large building, station or airport, where people can wait for a short while before moving on.

conditions of carriage The special terms and conditions under which principals will carry passengers and their baggage. The purchase of a ticket is deemed to indicate acceptance of these terms and conditions, even if the passenger is not familiar with them. Many conditions of carriage exclude the rights that people have under the law.

condominium 1. (US) A block of flats or apartments, often rented out on a long term or timeshare basis. Often abbreviated to 'condo'. 2. A region administered by two or more powers.

conducted tour A tour led by a guide on a predetermined and fixed itinerary.

confederation A union or alliance of states.

conference The generic name for any sort of medium to large gathering for discussion, especially one held annually.

conference rooms Rooms set aside for business and similar meetings.

confidential tariff The rates offered by principals, such as hotels and excursion companies, for the use of agents and premium customers when arranging travel.

configuration The way in which the seats and other parts of an aircraft's interior are laid out.

confirmation A written, emailed or printed document that verifies the existence and details of a booking. Many travel bookings are now no longer confirmed in writing, although under CAA regulations, package holidays still must be.

confluence   A place where two rivers meet and join.

Congo, Republic of   A country in central West Africa. Not to be confused with the Democratic Republic of Congo.

Congo, Democratic Republic of   A country in central West Africa formerly known as Zaire. Not to be confused with the Republic of Congo.

conjunction tickets   The issuing of multiple flight tickets to cover a complex itinerary. A journey of four or more sectors cannot be fitted onto one ticket and in such instances, two or more tickets will be issued 'in conjunction' to cover the entire itinerary.

connecting rooms   Two or more rooms in a hotel that have a private connecting door, so that occupants can move from one room to another without using the external corridor.

connecting service   A flight or other service that links with another to provide a transfer, whereby a passenger completes a journey to a final destination travelling on two or more scheduled services with a change at the intermediate point/s.

consequential loss   An insurance term meaning a loss arising from an original loss, for example loss of business incurred by a traveller as a result of a delayed flight. Partly because it is so difficult to evaluate, consequential loss is often excluded from cover in travel policies.

conservation area   A region protected against damage or undesirable change. Many tourist destinations such as safari parks are also conservation areas.

consol. fare   See consolidation (2).

consolidation   1. The action whereby a charter flight or tour operator combines two or more departures, thus maximising the passenger load.
2. The general term for the practice of selling discounted air tickets. Various regulations prohibit the public sale of air fares at a discount, but airlines often wish to maximise their profits by selling off surplus seats. They circumvent the various rules by selling their surplus seats, at heavily discounted rates, to a 'consolidator'. The consolidator then sells the seats on to agents or travellers at a price that includes his profit, but which is far lower than the official fare. These fares are colloquially known as 'consolidation' or 'consol.' fares.

consolidator   A person or organisation dealing in discounted airfares, especially those made available by scheduled carriers. > consolidation (2).

consortium   An association of companies.

constellation   A group of stars whose outline or appearance in the sky is considered to represent the outline of a figure or mythical being.

consul   A government official, stationed in a foreign country, who represents the interests of the nationals of the represented country when they are in that foreign country. Consuls can render assistance to travellers who find themselves in difficulty, but generally only to the extent of ensuring they are treated in the same way as nationals of the country in question.

consulate   The office where the consul works.

consultancy fee   A mark-up that a travel agent adds to the price when no commission is paid by the supplier.

contents gauge   A gauge which indicates the pressure of air inside a diving cylinder.

C

C

contents, table of A list, in order of appearance, of the items appearing in a book or manual.

contiguous Neighbouring, touching or in contact with. The 48 states of the USA (excluding Alaska and Hawaii, but generally also including Washington DC) are sometimes described as the contiguous states; Alaska and Hawaii as the non-contiguous ones.

continent The Earth's landmass is divided into eight (some say five, six or seven) continents. These are:
• Africa
• Europe
• North America
• South America
• Asia
• Australasia
• Oceania
• Antarctica
Australasia and Oceania are often bracketed together, as are (less commonly) North and South America. For obvious reasons, Antarctica is often ignored altogether. Sometimes, still other divisions are used, reflecting the needs and usages of the particular sector or industry being addressed.
Despite being what might be termed the largest objects in the world, there is – with the exception of Antarctica – no universally accepted agreement as to the exact composition or area of any of the continents. One organisation will employ its own definitions which are, if consistently applied, as valid as those used by another. Turkey and Russia, for example, can reasonably be seen as being in either Europe or Asia, or both, and a similar problem exists with Panama, Egypt, Greenland and Papua New Guinea. The whole of Central America (sometimes including Mexico) is often regarded as a separate entity, as is the Caribbean: the widespread use of the term Latin America only adds to the confusion. Terms such as 'the Caribbean', 'the Middle East' and 'the Mediterranean' are often more widely used – and useful – in the travel industry

than are the names of the continents (sometimes more than one) in which these regions are to be found. Some places, such as French Guiana, Hawaii and the Canary Islands, are politically fully part of one country but geographically somewhere else altogether. Organisations such as IATA and the WTO will often use names such as 'Europe' or 'Asia' in a specific sense which might conflict with the generally understood area of that name. So too do many other high-profile organisations with no connection with the travel industry, such as international sporting bodies. For more information, see the Columbus *World Travel Atlas*. (This book divides the world into six continents – Europe; Africa; Asia; Australasia & Oceania; Latin America & the Caribbean; and the USA & Canada.)

continental breakfast A light breakfast, generally of rolls, coffee and fruit juice.

continental plan A hotel rate that includes accommodation and continental breakfast.

contour lines Lines drawn on a map to connect points of equal height.

contour map A map that shows heights and depths by means of contour lines.

contraband Items that are prohibited or illegal for export or import.

contrail An abbreviation of condensation trail. The visible trail of condensation left by a high-flying aircraft.

contremarque A term of French origin meaning a simple document issued to identify passengers, usually those travelling by rail, on a group ticket. This avoids the necessity for issuing separate tickets to each passenger.

contribution An insurance term for the principle that any liability is shared between all insurers involved.

control tower   The building at an airport from which aircraft movements are controlled.

controlled duplication   *See airline code.*

conurbation   An extended urban area, often when several towns and their suburbs merge.

convenience   A public lavatory.

convention   1. A widely held agreement about standards of behaviour and dress in specific circumstances.
2. A formal meeting or conference.
3. A formal agreement about standards and practices (such as the Warsaw Convention, relating to air travel).

Convention and Visitors' Bureau (CVB)   (US) A tourist office, generally regional or local.

convertible   1. A car with a roof that can be folded down.
2. An aircraft whose layout can be changed rapidly from cargo to passenger configuration and vice-versa.
3. A currency for which a market exists, and which can thus easily be exchanged.

cooling-off period   The period of time during which the purchaser of a service, such as an insurance policy, may cancel the agreement and obtain a full refund. This will vary depending on the type of service, the policy of the individual company and the rules of any regulatory authority.

co-pilot   The second pilot of an aircraft.

coracle   A small boat made of wickerwork and covered with watertight material. Used on Welsh and Irish lakes and rivers.

coral   The shells of various marine animals. When laid down over time, these form reefs, islands and atolls.

Coral Coast   The northern coast of Tunisia, the main town on which Bizerte.

Coral Sea   The area of the Pacific Ocean between the Great Barrier Reef and Melanesia.

cordillera   A chain of mountains, especially one (such as the Andes) that forms the axis of a large land mass.

cordon bleu   Cookery of the highest possible standard of preparation and presentation.

corduroy road   A road made of tree trunks and laid across an unsound area such as a swamp.

Corinthian   1. Of or relating to ancient Corinth in southern Greece.
2. An amateur in sport; and the attitude of doing something for its own sake, rather than for profit, associated with this.

corkage   The sum a restaurateur may charge customers who wish to bring their own drinks into their establishment.

corked   The result of the contents of the bottle reacting with the cork and spoiling the wine.

corkscrew   The movement of a ship or boat when it is both pitching and rolling as it meets oncoming waves.

corniche   A road cut into the face of a cliff.

Corniche   Three roads in the French Riviera running parallel to the coast between Nice and Menton and cutting through spectacular cliffs.

Coromandel Coast   The coast of south-east India. The main ports include Nellore, Chennai (Madras), Pondicherry, Cuddalore and Nagappattinam.

corona   A ring of light that appears closely around the moon or sun under certain meteorological conditions. > *halo.*

C

corporate rate Specially discounted rates offered to major purchasers of travel products. These rates are usually offered by hotels and car rental operators, although other principals are now adopting the idea.

corridor (UK) The passage in a railway carriage from which compartments can be accessed. > *korridorzuge*.

cosmopolitan Of, or knowing, many parts of the world.

Cossack One of the people of southern Imperial Russia, originally famous for their military skill.

Costa Blanca 'White coast': the resort area on the eastern coast of Spain from Denia to Torrevieja. The main town is Alicante: other resorts include Calpe and Benidorm.

Costa Brava 'Wild coast': the coast of the province of Gerona, north of Barcelona, with many popular tourist resorts. The coast south of Blanes is strictly speaking the Costa del Maresme.

Costa Calida 'Warm coast': the coast in the provinces of Andalucia and Murcia in Spain between Cabo de Gata and Cartagena.

Costa de Almería The eastern part of the Costa del Sol in southern Spain. The main town is Almería.

Costa de la Luz 'Coast of light': the Atlantic coast of southern Spain, principal towns are Huelva and Cádiz. More popular with the Spanish than with foreign tourists, the main resorts are Sanlúcar de Barrameda, Rota and Chipiona.

Costa de Lisboa The resort coast around Lisbon in Portugal, also known as the Costa do Sol or the Costa do Estoril. The main resorts are Cascais and Estoril.

Costa de Prata 'Silver coast': the Portuguese coast stretching from Oporto in the north to the Costa de Lisboa in the south. The main resorts include Figuera da Foz and Nazaré.

Costa del Azahar 'Orange-blossom coast': the Spanish resort area on the Mediterranean coast between the Costa Dorada in the north and the Costa Blanca in the south. The main town is Castellón de la Plana.

Costa del Maresme *See Costa Brava.*

Costa del Sol 'Coast of the sun': the resort region of southern Spain, stretching along the Mediterranean coast from Tarifa in the west to Cabo de Gata in the east, with the main concentration of resorts between Marbella and Motril. The main town is Málaga: resorts include Marbella, Fuengirola, Torremolinos, Nerja, Almuñécar, Salobreña and Almería.

Costa do Estoril *See Costa de Lisboa.*

Costa do Sol *See Costa de Lisboa.*

Costa Dorada 'Golden coast': the coastal resort area in Catalonia south of the Costa Brava. The main centres are Barcelona and Tarragona.

Costa Dourada 'Golden coast': Portuguese coastal region between Lisbon and the Algarve. The main towns are Sines and Vila Nova de Milfontes. Also known as the Costa de Ouro.

Costa Verde 'Green coast': the resort coast in Portugal north of Oporto. Also the Spanish coast of the Asturias region, principal town Gijón.

cot A small bed, usually only suitable for a child.

Côte d'Argent 'Silver coast': the coastal area in south-west France running from Arachon to the Spanish border. The main resorts include Vieux-Boucau-les-Bains, Mimizan, Bayonne and Biarritz.

Côte d'Azur 'Azure coast': the coast of south-east France, also known as the French Riviera. The main towns include St Tropez, St Raphaël, Cannes, Antibes, Nice and Monte Carlo. > *Riviera.*

Côte d'Emeraude 'Emerald coast': the coastal region in Brittany in north-east France between St Malo and Cap Fréhel, including Dinard.

Côte d'Opale 'Opal coast': the coast of north-east France in the Nord-Pas-de-Calais region, centred on Boulogner.

Côte des Calenques 'Coast of rocky inlets': the section of coast between Hyères and Marseilles in southern France.

Côte des Landes 'Coast of moors': the section of coast in south-west France, running from the Gironde estuary to Cap Ferret.

Côte Vermeille 'Ruby-red coast': the coast of south-western France between the Etang de Leucate and the Spanish frontier.

co-tidal line A line on a map connecting points at which tidal levels (such as high or low tide) appear simultaneously.

couchette A type of sleeping accommodation offered on European trains, which provides six fold-down berths to each standard class compartment. Only basic bedding is supplied and there is no segregation of the sexes. Couchettes are not used on UK rail services.

couloir A steep gully on mountainside that can be used as a transit route, which are sometimes prone to avalanching. Also known as an avalanche corridor.

count (**countess** when feminine) A noble of high rank. Where the term survives, it is mainly honorific.

counterfoil Part of a receipt, ticket or other document retained by the issuer.

country 1. The territory of a nation with its own independent government, and recognised as such by other countries and international bodies. In practice, the definition of what is and what is not a country is not clear-cut. There are several areas of confusion:
• *Overseas territories that are politically part of another country.* These include Hawaii, the Canary Islands and French Guiana. These are administratively part of another country from which they are geographically separated. This may result in their being treated as if they were separate countries in some cases, particularly where they are seen as wholly separate travel destinations.
• *Overseas dependencies, with some degree of self-government.* There are over 30 of these. Most are islands or groups of islands, and most were previously directly administered by another country. These include Gibraltar, Wallis and Futuna, Guam, Greenland and the Cook Islands. For the same reasons as the overseas territories above (although with more justification) these are also often regarded as separate countries.
• *Countries within a federal union.* Before 1991, the republics of the USSR were examples of this, but nowadays, the United Kingdom provides the best instance. England, Scotland, Wales and Northern Ireland are in many ways separate countries and are generally marketed as separate destinations, and yet all are politically united.
• *Countries which are attempting to gain, or are in the process of gaining, independence.* By their nature, such places are in a state of some turmoil and are thus of less importance for the travel industry. These include Palestine NAR, East Timor and Western Sahara. Throughout the world there are many other separatist movements at work which may, in the future, result in the formation of new countries.
• *Countries which are de facto independent but are not recognised by a*

C

C

sizeable number of other states. These places will generally have a bitter dispute with neighbouring countries which may claim some or all of the territory. The significance here is that travel to the countries with which the dispute exists may be impossible if the traveller has an entry visa for the disputed country or shows any other strong connection with it. These include Israel, the Turkish Republic of Northern Cyprus and Taiwan. > *Appendix 1.*
2. The term 'country' is often used as part of a region created for travel marketing purposes, such as 'Shakespeare Country' and 'Mississippi River Country'.

county   1. Any of the territorial divisions of a country (or in the USA, a state), forming the main unit of local administration.
2. The territory of a count or countess. Where the term survives it is mainly honorific.

coupé   A car with a sloping roofline and usually with two doors and limited seating in the rear. The term coupe (pronounced coup) is generally used in the USA. Note that different manufacturers and rental companies may use these and other descriptive terms to mean slightly different vehicles.

coupe   *See coupé.*

coupon   1. A page of a multi-part ticket. Such tickets will have at least four types of coupon:
• *Exchange coupons* which are presented in exchange for the service;
• *Passenger coupons* which are the passenger's record and details of conditions of carriage;
• *Agency coupons* which are for the agent's records;
• *Audit coupons* which are used for accounting purposes.
2. A marketing term that refers to that part of an advertisement which is designed to be returned to the advertiser as a request for further information.
3. A discount voucher offering a price

reduction on a specified item or service.

courier   1. *See tour guide.*
2. A person who delivers messages or portable items.

courier flight   A journey undertaken by a messenger carrying documents, samples and the like.

course   The direction in which a vehicle is heading.

courtyard   An area, enclosed by walls or buildings, often with access to a street.

cove   An inlet from a sea or other body of water, smaller than a bay.

cover charge   An extra charge levied in some restaurants and night-clubs.

coxswain   1. The person who steers a boat. Usually pronounced cox'n.
2. (UK) The senior petty officer on a small ship.

CPT   Confederation of Passenger Transport UK. *See Appendix 5a.*

CRAC   Continental Rail Agents Consortium. *See Appendix 5a.*

crachin   A light rain that falls in the coastal regions and mountains of Vietnam.

craft   A general term for any boat or plane.

crag   A steep or rugged rock.

crampons   Metal devices with spikes fitted to boots to give a grip on hard packed snow and ice. For personal safety it is better to receive training in the use of crampons before embarking for areas where their use may be required.

crater   The mouth of a volcano.

creative ticketing   A term describing the means by which an agent seeks to obtain a lower fare by taking advantage of what are sometimes perceived as ambiguous or unenforceable fare regulations. If detected by carriers or their agents, this can result in denied travel and the imposition of financial or other penalties.

credit card   A small plastic card that identifies a customer and allows the purchase of goods or services. Payment for the goods or services is made to the credit card company, which generally allow the debt to be discharged over a period of time if required. Interest is charged for this facility.

creek   A small bay or harbour.

Creole   1. A descendent of European settlers in the West Indies or Central or South America.
2. A white descendent of French settlers in the southern United States.
3. A person of mixed European and African descent.
4. A former pidgin that has developed into a formalised language.

Crescent   The rail service between New Orleans and New York in the USA.

crest   The very top of a ridge or arête.

crevasse   A deep crack, especially in a glacier.

crew   Those who work on board a ship, aircraft or similar vehicle.

crewed charter   A form of charter whereby the vessel is provided complete with supplies or crew.

cross trees   A pair of horizontal timbers at the top of a lower mast of a ship, supporting the topmast.

cross-border ticketing   The practice of issuing a ticket to start from a country other than that of the passenger's home or real origin. This is done to take advantage of a more favourable fare structure or exchange rate and is obviously discouraged by carriers.

cross-country skiing   A method of skiing on generally flat land, as opposed to Alpine or downhill skiing. Cross-country skis are long, thin and light, connected to a lightweight shoe at the toe only, unlike downhill ski equipment which involves heavier, rigid boots connected at toe and heel to the ski.

crossroad   (US) A road that joins or crosses a main road.

crossroads   An intersection of two roads.

croupier   A person who operates the gaming table at a casino.

crow's nest   A small lookout position, near the top of the mast of a ship.

Crown Colony   The former name for what is now a British Crown Dependency. *See British Overseas Territories.*

CRS   *See Computerised Reservation System.*

cruise   A voyage taken for pleasure, rather than purely for the purpose of transport.

Crusader states   Any of the four territories in the Middle East (the Kingdom of Jerusalem, the Principalities of Antioch and Tripoli and the County of Edessa) established by the Christians in the aftermath of the First Crusade (1098-1100), some of which survived in some form until 1291. Many castles and churches in the area date from this period.

CTA   China Tourism Association. *See Appendix 5c.*

CTC   Coach Tourism Council. *See Appendix 5a.*

CTO   Caribbean Tourism Organisation. *See Appendix 5a.*

CTT   Council for Travel & Tourism. *See Appendix 5a.*

C

cultural attraction   An attraction that capitalises on its importance as a centre for cultural pursuits.

culture   1. The distinctive characteristics, achievement, attitude or way of life of a group or nation.
2. A general term for artistic, intellectual, musical or literary activities.

cumulus   A type of cloud, generally dense and with sharp outlines, looking rather as if it were made of cotton wool.

cupola   A rounded dome forming all or part of the roof of a building.

curfew   A restriction on the public movement of people, typically during the hours of darkness. Curfews are usually imposed during periods of conflict or civil unrest.

currency   Money in circulation in a specific country or countries in which it is officially recognised as a means of exchange for goods and services. In general, each country has its own currency which is used only within its borders (although it can often be exchanged elsewhere). Sometimes, however, a common currency may be used within a geographical or political area, even if each constituent country produces its own design of notes and coins: the Eastern Caribbean dollar, the CFA franc and, most recently, the euro are examples of this. In some cases, currencies of one country may be very widely accepted in others in addition to their own: some countries do not have their own currencies at all, but instead use a foreign hard currency as the preferred means of exchange. Such places are often dependant territories or former possessions. The US dollar and, to a lesser extent, the pound sterling are examples. The US dollar could fairly be described as a global currency, being widely accepted throughout the world, often in preference to local money.

currency exchange   The act of converting one currency into another, such as through a bank or a bureau de change.

currency restrictions   Controls put in place by governments to restrict the flow of money into and out of their countries.

current   1. A flow of water.
2. The measure of flow of electricity usually rated in amperes (generally abbreviated to amps). UK appliances are usually protected by a fuse in the plug rated at 3, 5 or 13 amps. Travellers should be aware that, if they adjust an appliance to run on a lower voltage, the fuse may need to be upgraded. This is because a halving of the voltage will lead to a doubling of the current drawn.

curtail   To cut short. Most insurance policies can offer cover in the event that a holiday or other trip abroad needs to be curtailed. The conditions under which such a claim can be made will be set out in the small print and will vary from policy to policy. > *travel insurance.*

customer profile   Information stored by business travel agents and similar organisations about their clients, such as class of travel, passport details and credit card details. Such information will generally be protected by legal restrictions as to its future use, particularly with regard to its sale or rental to a third party.

customs   1. The manners, morals and behavioural patterns of a country or society.
2. The government agency that seeks to control the movement of goods into and out of a country, particularly those which are prohibited or subject to customs duty.

customs clearance   The act of passing through customs control when entering a country. This is normally facilitated by a series of channels, usually colour-coded: red generally indicates the traveller has goods to declare; green usually indicates that the traveller has no goods to declare; blue is used for people travelling within the EU (but not the Canary Islands, the Channel Islands or Gibraltar) who have no goods to declare. Whichever channel is used, travellers may be stopped by a customs officer and searched. If goods that are prohibited, restricted or in excess of the appropriate customs allowances are discovered, travellers risk heavy fines and possibly a prison sentence. Customs regulations vary from country to country and should be established in advance.

customs duty   A tax levied on goods being imported.

cut-off date   The last date by which an arrangement must be confirmed or completed.

cutter   A small boat, other than a lifeboat, carried by a ship.

cutting   An excavated channel through high ground for a railway or road.

CVB   *See Convention and Visitors' Bureau.*

cycle   Technically any wheeled vehicle, but usually used to refer to lightweight vehicles such as bicycles.

cycle route   A track or path reserved for the use of those on pedal cycles.

cyclone   1. A circular storm revolving around a relatively calm centre.
2. An area of winds rotating inwards towards an area of low pressure, usually causing bad weather.

cylinder   *See diving cylinder.*

Cyprus   1. A large island in the eastern Mediterranean, the southern part of which is the Republic of Cyprus, and the northern part the Turkish Republic of Northern Cyprus, an entity not recognised by most governments.
2. The Republic of Cyprus.

Cyrillic   The alphabet used by the Slavonic people of the Orthodox Church, especially in Russia and Bulgaria. > *Appendix 8.*

C

Dd

Dakar   The capital of Senegal. Not to be confused with Dhaka, the capital of Bangladesh.

Dalmatia   The Adriatic coast of most of former Yugoslavia, stretching from Zadar, Croatia in the north to Montenegro in the south, generally barren but with some excellent harbours. Principal towns are Zadar, Split and Dubrovnik.

dam   An artificial barrier built across a river or other watercourse to hold back water and create a reservoir.

DAN   Divers Alert Network. A US-based, non-profit organisation which provides emergency medical advice and assistance for scuba divers all over the world.

Danelaw   The parts of northern and eastern England administered by the Danes in the 9th, 10th and early 11th centuries.

dangerous activity   Any one of a range of hazardous sports and pastimes, such as winter sports, scuba diving and mountaineering, participation in which may invalidate an insurance policy unless specifically included in it. The conditions under which such a claim can be made will be set out in the small print and will vary from policy to policy. > *travel insurance.*

Dark Ages   The period of European history from the collapse of the Roman Empire in the 5th century AD to the emergence of nation states and the revival of trade in the 10th century.

data   Information of any kind. These days the term is commonly used in connection with information stored on a computer.

date order   The convention for expressing dates as numbers. Most countries in the world, with the important exception of the USA, use the date-first system, whereby 9th August 1998 is written 9/8/98. In some computer systems and on some forms, leading zeros must be used (09/08/98); in others, the year must be written in full (09/08/1998). In the USA, however, the convention is month-first: 9th August 1998 would thus be written 8/9/98 (or 08/09/98, or 08/09/1998). In the USA, the month is generally expressed first even when written or spoken in full (August 9th rather than 9th August). IATA regulations require that all travel documents be written using the date-first system, but other communications between companies in the USA and the rest of the world can be fraught with confusion as a result of this difference of usage. If space permits, dates in such communications should ideally have the month written out, or abbreviated (Aug.).

davit   A special crane built into a ship for loading and unloading goods and for lowering lifeboats.

day care   (US) *See Ski Kindergarten.*

day delegate rate   A rate offered by a hotel or similar venue to organisers of conferences and training events. The rate usually includes room hire, refreshments and lunch, as well as basic meeting facilities and equipment.

day out   (UK) A short trip or excursion completed in a single day.

day rate   A rate offered by a hotel or similar to a guest wishing to stay for a short time and not overnight.

day return   A fare, often discounted, that is valid for travel out and back during the same day. Day return fares are usually cheaper than the single and therefore may not be used for a one-way journey. In cases where the non-usage of the return is detected (for example on a cross-Channel car ferry), the principal may retrospectively charge the full fare.

day trip   *See day out.*

daylight saving time (DST)   A practice observed in many countries, generally outside the tropics, whereby clocks are advanced by one hour in the local spring and put back by one hour in the local autumn. Countries which observe DST do not always do so across the whole of their territories (USA, Brazil, and Australia are examples). Nor will all countries that observe DST necessarily make their changes on the same day; moreover, the dates of change will differ from year to year to reflect national circumstances. Countries may have names, such as British Summer Time, to describe this change of time. > *time zones.*

daylight time   (US) Time adjusted for daylight saving. > *daylight saving time.*

DC   1. *See direct current.*
2. District of Columbia, the Federal District of the USA, co-extensive with the national capital, Washington.

DCA   *See deposit collection advice.*

DCS   *See decompression sickness.*

de luxe   The term usually applied to the very best accommodation or facility. It has no official meaning unless it is related to other terms within the classification to which it belongs.

dead calm   No measurable wind.

dead reckoning   A method of calculating a vessel's position from existing data when fresh observations are not possible.

D

deadheading   (US) The circumstance of a vehicle or crew operating without passengers or payload. When aircrew travel on flights as passengers in order to position for another flight, they are said to be deadheading.

deadlight   1. A cover for a ship's porthole fixed to prevent the entry of light or sunlight. Deadlights may also be fitted to the portholes of the lowest decks in stormy weather conditions.
2. (US) A skylight that cannot be opened.

debark   To land from a ship.

debit card   A card, similar in size and shape to a credit card, but which takes money directly from its holder's bank account.

deck   A horizontal division of a ship. The upper decks are often given names such as sun deck, boat deck and lido deck. Lower decks tend to be numbered or lettered. There is, however, no standard system.

deck plan   A diagram showing the layout of cabins and public rooms on a ship.

deckhand   A person employed to do jobs on the deck of a ship.

decompression   1. The sudden loss of cabin pressure in an aircraft.
2. The reduction in pressure experienced by divers when ascending, during which dissolved gases such as nitrogen escape from the body tissues.

decompression sickness   A physical condition caused by a sudden or too rapid reduction in pressure, thus allowing

D

dissolved nitrogen to form bubbles within the body tissues.

decompression tables A published list of stages at various depths of water at which a diver must pause and wait in order to allow for decompression to occur safely within the body.

Deep South The south-eastern states of the USA. Often considered as an area embodying traditional southern culture and values. > *South, the.*

deep vein thrombosis (DVT) A potentially fatal condition, which can affect those undergoing a prolonged period of inactivity, such as on a long flight, in which blood clots form in deep veins. Certain groups. including the overweight, those with heart problems and pregnant women, have an increased risk of DVT, but it can affect anyone. During a long flight, the risks can be reduced by taking regular exercise and drinking plenty of water. The condition has also been dubbed 'economy class syndrome', as it is argued that passengers in cramped conditions are less easily able to move during the flight and are thus more at risk. Some airlines have recently increased the seat pitch on certain long-distance services in response to this. > *health precautions, seat pitch.*

deep-sea Used to describe activities, such as diving or fishing. in the deeper parts of a sea or other body of water.

degree A measurement of angle denoted by the symbol °. There are 360 degrees in a circle. All bearings and positional measurements on a sphere (such as the earth) or a circle are expressed in degrees measured from a base line or point. Each degree is subdivided into 60 minutes (symbol '), and each minute into 60 seconds (symbol").

delivery charge The charge for delivering a vehicle to, or collecting a vehicle from, an address requested by the renter.

delta An area of land, usually roughly triangular, at the mouth of a river. This will have been formed from the sediment deposited from the river and its flatness will allow the river to create a large number of small channels.

delta wing An aircraft wing of triangular shape.

demand valve A regulator that supplies air as demanded by the diver.

demi-pension A hotel rate which includes room, breakfast and one other meal. Also known as half-board or modified American plan.

democracy A system of government whereby power is vested in elected representatives, and any state so governed.

demographics The factors concerning the characteristics of a population. Demographics can include aspects such as age, income, family size and employment.

demurrage An amount payable to the operator of a cargo vessel because of failure to load or unload a cargo by an agreed time.

dengue A tropical viral disease, transmitted by mosquitoes.

denied-boarding compensation The compensation to which passengers are generally entitled when they have a confirmed reservation for a flight but for which the airline cannot provide a seat, usually due to overbooking. The amount of compensation will vary according to a number of factors, including the carrier, the type of service and the length of the delay.

denizen An inhabitant or occupant of a place.

denomination The range of values of coins or banknotes in a particular currency.

departure The act of going away from a place, and specifically the time or place at which this journey begins.

departure delay insurance *See travel insurance.*

departure tax Taxation raised on passengers leaving a port or airport. The tax can be collected either at the time of ticketing or at the time of departure. Departure taxes do not only apply to international departures and may on occasions be raised on domestic departures as well.

dependency A country or province that is controlled by another.

deplane (US) To get off an aircraft.

deportation The lawful forced removal of a foreign national from a country. At the point of attempted entry this is often because of the lack of correct documentation; at other times often because of violation of local laws or of the conditions of their visa.

deportee A person who is being deported.

deposit A partial payment made to hold space or show goodwill.

deposit collection advice A document issued by travel agents to confirm collection of a customer's deposit. Agents will be billed at agreed periods for the total value of deposits collected. DCAs are becoming less common as electronic payment systems take over.

deposit reservation A reservation for which a hotel has received pre-payment for at least one night and is committed to holding the room, regardless of the guest's actual arrival time. This policy varies from hotel to hotel.

depot 1. (UK) A storage place. 2. (US) An alternative name for a terminal or station.

depression A low pressure air circulation in temperate latitudes. The condition is usually associated with wet weather.

depressurisation *See decompression.*

depth gauge An instrument used by divers which measures changes in pressure and calibrates these in terms of depth.

D

derail When a railway locomotive or its train leaves the tracks, usually as a result of an accident.

deregulation The term given to the gradual removal of government controls over an industry, such as air travel.

desert A dry and barren area, often sandy, and characterised by its lack of water and vegetation. > *climate zones.*

desolate Of a place, abandoned, uninhabited or neglected.

destination The end point of a journey.

detour 1. A deviation, voluntary or otherwise, from a planned route. 2. A voluntary deviation from the most direct route.

detrain (US) To alight from a train.

developing country A poor or underdeveloped country that is seeking to become more advanced.

devolution The act of certain legislative, administrative or judicial powers being relinquished by a central government and handed over to a regional authority to exercise. This has recently happened to some degree in the UK, particularly in relation to Scotland and Wales.

Dhaka The capital of Bangladesh. Not to be confused with Dakar, the capital of Senegal.

dhow A lateen-rigged ship used on the Arabian Sea.

D

dialect A form of speech peculiar to a particular region or group.

diarchy A region governed by two independent authorities.

diarise The act of recording an item in a diary or other scheduling system.

dictator A ruler who is not restricted by laws, a constitution, free elections or an effective opposition, and who governs in an arbitrary or tyrannical fashion.

dictatorship A state ruled by a dictator, or the government of such a state.

diesel engine An internal combustion engine in which the heat of compression of the air in the cylinders ignites the fuel.

diesel-electric A vehicle propelled by electricity generated by a diesel powered generator, carried on the same vehicle.

diesel-hauled A railway train that is pulled by a diesel-powered locomotive.

diligence A legal term referring to the attention and care required in a given situation.

diner 1. (US) An informal roadside restaurant.
2. (US) A restaurant car on a train.

dinghy A small boat, often carried by a ship.

dining car (UK) A restaurant car on a train.

dinner jacket (UK) Formal evening wear for men comprising a jacket (usually black) and trousers, worn with a shirt and bow tie. The expression 'dinner jacket' does not refer simply to the jacket but generally to the whole ensemble. Both the jacket individually, and the outfit collectively, are also known as a tuxedo.

diphtheria An acute contagious bacterial disease, endemic worldwide, causing severe inflammation of the throat. Children are particularly at risk. > *health precautions.*

direct current An electrical supply whose direction does not alter. Battery-operated appliances run on DC, whereas most mains appliances run on AC. Travellers must take care in countries where DC supplies still exist as AC equipment may be damaged if it is used. > *alternating current.*

direct sell *See disintermediation.*

direct service A flight or other journey that does not require a passenger to change services. A direct service is not necessarily non-stop.

directional fare A fare that only applies in one direction of travel.

dirigible A steerable, lighter-than-air, aircraft. Also known as an airship.

disclaimer A clause, or series of clauses, in or appended to a contract or other form of agreement, which limits the right of one or other party (usually the purchaser) from making certain claims, for example for compensation.

discount A reduction given from the published fare, price or tariff.

Discover New England A US regional marketing organisation covering some of the states of New England. > *US regional marketing organisations.*

disembark To get off an aircraft, ship, train or other method of transport.

disintermediation The act of selling a product or service directly to the ultimate consumer, without recourse to a middle man. In travel, the middle man is generally the travel agent. The practice has long existed, with some tour operators specialising in direct selling. In recent times it has become more popular due to

D

the information and purchasing possibilities of the internet.

displaced person A person who has been forced to leave his or her home country because of persecution, disease, famine, war or other serious problem.

displacement effect A tourism term given to the phenomenon where workers move from primary jobs (such as agriculture) to tourism-related jobs, such as hotel work.

distribution channel A means by which a product or service is made available to customers. Tour operators, for example, can choose either to use travel agents as their distribution channel, or maybe to sell via the internet.

distributory A branch of a stream that does not return to the main channel once having left it.

district 1. A territory or region marked off for special administrative purposes. 2. A part of a town or city.

ditch 1. A long, narrow gully that provides drainage. 2. To bring an aircraft down in the sea.

diuretic A substance that increases the amount of water passed in urine. Coffee, tea and alcohol are examples. Diuretics should be avoided as far as possible on long flights due to the low relative humidity of aircraft cabins. > *humidity, jet lag.*

Divers Alert Network *See DAN.*

diving cylinder A metal container designed to hold air at high pressures underwater. Sometimes called bottle or tank.

Diwali A festival in the Hindu religious calendar, celebrated at the time of the new moon in late October or early November.

docent (US) A guide, usually voluntary, in a museum, art gallery or similar.

dock An area designed for the safe mooring of ships and the handling of their passengers and cargoes.

doldrums A region of unpredictable weather near the Equator. In the days of sail the doldrums were feared because of the possibility of long periods of completely calm weather.

Dolphin Coast The stretch of coast in South Africa from Durban in the south to the Tugela river in the north.

domain An area owned by, ruled by or under the influence of a person, government or organisation.

dome car (US) *See observation car.*

Domesday Book A record of the land and property in England made on the orders of William the Conqueror after the Norman Conquest and completed in 1086. Many places stress their antiquity by claiming to have been mentioned in it.

domestic Within one's own country. Domestic tourism is tourism within the country where a person lives; domestic flights are those within the airline's own country.

domestic inbound tourism A term defined by the WTO as comprising 'any person residing in a country, who travels to a place within this same country. The unit of measure used to quantify this concept is the number of nights by resident.' Note that the term 'tourism' refers to travellers generally, rather than those travelling purely for pleasure. > *tourism.*

domestic tourism *See tourism.*

domicile A person's own home or dwelling place.

D

Dominica, Commonwealth of   One of the Lesser Antilles in the Caribbean. Not to be confused with the Dominican Republic.

Dominican Republic   A country occupying the eastern part of the island of Hispaniola in the Caribbean. Not to be confused with the Commonwealth of Dominica.

dominion   *See domain.*

doorman   An employee of a hotel, restaurant, club or other similar, and usually high-class, establishment, who will be responsible for such services as greeting guests, hailing taxis, providing directions and assisting with luggage.

dory   A small flat-bottomed fishing boat with high sides.

douane   The French word for a customs post.

double   An abbreviation for a double room.

double chair   *See ski lift.*

double room   A room with one double (large) bed. The term is sometimes used casually to describe any room that can accommodate two people, even if it has two small beds, but this is not strictly correct. > *twin.*

double-booking   When two or more reservations are made for the same seat, accommodation or service. When done in an attempt to maximise load factors, it is usually known as over-booking. *See over-booking.*

double-decker   A bus with an upper and lower deck.

double-double   A room with two double (large) beds.

double-headed   A train hauled by two locomotives.

downgrade   To move to a lower grade of accommodation or service.

downriver   At or towards the mouth of a river.

downtown   (US) The lower or more central part of a town or city, particularly where this forms a distinct area.

down-under   (UK) A colloquial term for Australia or New Zealand.

downwind   In the direction in which the wind is blowing.

drag   The air resistance a vehicle, such as an aircraft, is subjected to when in motion.

drag lift   The commonest type of ski lift which pulls a skier or snowboarder uphill by means of an attachment to a moving cable. Common types include button lifts (also known as Poma lifts after the main manufacturer), or as surface tow lifts in North America. Another type is the T-bar named after its shape which, unlike the single-person button lift, can drag two skiers per T-bar side by side.

draught   The depth of water a ship draws. In effect, the minimum depth that is required for it to float clear of the bottom.

dress code   The standard of dress which is expected, required, or prohibited at an event or in an establishment.

DRF   Danmarks Rejsebureau Forening. *See Appendix 5c.*

drift   Deviation from the set course, due to the effect of side-winds or currents.

drift diving   A dive where divers allow the current to move them along.

drive-in   (Also **drive-through**) (Mainly US) Of a place, such as a bank, into which customers may drive and transact business without leaving their vehicles.

drive-on   A ferry or similar, onto which

vehicles are loaded by their own drivers, rather than by a crane or other method.

drive-through   *See drive-in.*

drophead   (UK) A car with a collapsible fabric roof.

drop-off   *See check-in (3).*

drop-off charge   The name given to the charge levied by a car rental company in connection with a one-way rental.

droshky   A Russian small four-wheel open horse-drawn carriage.

DRV   Deutscher Reisebüro- und Reiseveranstalter Verband e.V. *See Appendix 5c.*

dry dock   A structure large enough to contain a ship and from which the water can be emptied. Dry docks allow work to be undertaken on those parts of the hull of a vessel that would normally be submerged.

dry lease   The rental of a vehicle, such as an aircraft, without supplies or crew. *> wet lease.*

dry grassland   *See savannah.*

dry suit   A diving suit which keeps its wearer dry by means of neck, wrist and possibly ankle seals.

DST   *See daylight saving time.*

duchy   The territory of a duke or duchess. Where the term survives it is mainly honorific.

dude ranch   (US) A ranch converted to a holiday centre.

duke   (**duchess** when feminine) A noble of high rank and, in the past, at times independent (such as the Dukes of Normandy). Where the term survives it is mainly honorific.

dumb terminal   A VDU connected to a mainframe computer, that has no intelligence of its own.

dune   A hillock or mound formed of sand. Sand dunes can move with the wind and have been known to engulf large features.

dune-buggy   *See beach-buggy.*

duplex   A hotel suite with two floors.

Dutch   1. Of or relating to the Netherlands. 2. (US) The region of Pennsylvania, mainly Lancaster County, settled by Amish people and others originally from Germany. 'Dutch' is, in this case, a corruption of 'Deutsch'.

duty   The tax levied on certain goods, especially alcohol and tobacco.

duty manager   A person in charge of an establishment at a given time.

duty-free   Goods bought in a place where duties are not levied, such as ships or aircraft in transit in international waters or airspace.

duty-free allowance   The number, amount or value of goods, bought duty-free, that may be brought into a country without payment of duty.

duty-free shop   A retail outlet, usually at an airport, selling goods free of its country's duties and taxes.

DVT   *See deep vein thrombosis.*

DVW   Damage-to-vehicle waiver. Similar to collision damage waiver (CDW). *> vehicle rental insurance.*

DWT   Dead-weight tonnage. The total weight of everything carried on a vehicle or ship, equal to the difference between the laden and the unladen weight.

dyke   (or **dike**) A long wall or bank built to prevent flooding.

D

Ee

E

EANx   *See nitrox.*

ear clearing   The process of equalising the pressure inside the ear with the outside pressure caused by increased depths. Also called Valsalva Manoeuvre.

earl   (**countess** when feminine) A noble of high rank. Where the term survives it is mainly honorific.

earldom   The territory of an earl or countess. Where the term survives it is mainly honorific.

earlybird   Originally a proprietary term used to describe advance booking discounts offered by certain principals. Now often used as any form of advance purchase product attracting a discount, especially package holidays.

easement   1. A right of passage over another's land.
2. A relaxation in routing restrictions, especially on local rail journeys.

east   One of the four cardinal points of the compass, 90° clockwise from north and 180° from west; on the right of maps where (as is normal) north is at the top.
> *north.*

East China Sea   The area of the Pacific Ocean between China, Korea, Taiwan and Japan.

East Greenland Current   A cold current running down the east coast of Greenland, bringing Arctic waters in the Atlantic.

East Indies   A general geographical term used for the area comprising India and the Malay Archipelago. Not commonly used these days.

Easter   A festival in the Christian religious calendar celebrated in March or April on the Sunday following the first full moon after the vernal equinox.

Eastern & Oriental Express   The luxury rail service which runs between Bangkok and Chang Mai in Thailand; and between Bangkok and Singapore via Kuala Lumpur in Malaysia.

eastern hemisphere   The half of the earth to the east of 0° longitude and to the west of 180° longitude.

Eastern Mediterranean Terms   Yacht charter terms under which the fee includes the charter of the yacht with all equipment; basic consumables for engine-room, deck and cabins; the crew's wages and food; insurance for the yacht itself, for third party claims and employer's liability insurance for the crew; fuel for three to five hours cruising per day (depending on yacht and averaged throughout the charter); half board for the guests (breakfast and lunch); berthing dues and other harbour charges (except Corinthian Canal dues); and water or electricity taken from the shore. Other costs, such as fuel for the ski boats, the client's food and drink, berthing and harbour expenses outside the yacht's normal cruising area, laundry and radio telephone and other communication costs, must be paid by the client. These terms may vary.

Eastern Standard Time 1. One of the time zones used in North America, five hours behind UTC.
2. One of the time zones used in Australia, ten hours ahead of UTC.

eatery A colloquial expression for a restaurant or other eating place, often an informal one.

ebb The movement of the tide back out to sea.

EBTA European Business Travel Association. *See Appendix 5a.*

EC European Community, the previous name for what is now the EU.

echo sounder An instrument which measures the depth of water by timing the echo of a pulse as it bounces back from the seabed.

eclipse The total or partial obscuring of one celestial body by another, and the period of time during which this occurs. A solar eclipse is caused by the moon passing between the earth and the sun; a lunar eclipse is caused by the earth passing between the sun and the moon. A solar eclipse, which is what is mainly meant by the word, results in varying degrees of darkness on parts of the earth's surface. During a total solar eclipse, when the sun appears to be totally obscured, the area in complete shadow is called the umbra; the penumbra is the area of partial shadow surrounding this. An annular eclipse is when the apparent size of the moon is too small to fully cover the sun, resulting in a ring of sunlight remaining round the moon. Timings and locations of eclipses can be predicted with complete accuracy. Total solar eclipses over populated areas are comparatively rare.

ecology The study of the interaction of people with their environment.

economy class Usually the cheapest available class on a service and with the most basic level of comfort.

economy class syndrome *See deep vein thrombosis*

economy of scale The savings that might be made when larger quantities of a product or service are supplied. For example, a 12-coach train will incur the same driver costs as a two-coach one.

ecotourism Tourism that considers or encourages the preservation of the environment. Sometimes called green tourism.

ECTAA Group of National Travel Agents' and Tour Operators' Associations within the EU. *See Appendix 5d.*

eddy A small circular movement of air or water.

educational trip *See familiarisation trip.*

educational *See familiarisation trip.*

EEC European Economic Community, the original name for what became the European Community, and what is now the EU. *See European Union.*

effendi A man of standing and respect in many eastern Mediterranean and Middle Eastern countries, occasionally used as a term of respect to a visitor.

efficiency (US) Accommodation, such as a small apartment, with some cooking facilities.

EFT Elapsed flying time. *See actual flying time.*

EFTPOS *See electronic funds transfer at point of sale.*

Egyptiac The civilisation of the ancient Egyptians (c.4000BC to AD280).

Eid al-Adha A festival in the Islamic

E

E

religious calendar marking the culmination of the Hajj.

Eid al-Fitr A festival in the Islamic religious calendar marking the end of Ramadan.

Eight Degree Channel The marine frontier between the Lackshadweep Islands (India) and the Maldives.

Eire A former name for the Republic of Ireland.

EJT Elapsed journey time. *See actual flying time.*

El Niño A change in the ocean-atmosphere system in the eastern Pacific that contributes to significant weather changes throughout the world. El Niño is characterised by an increase in water temperatures in the equatorial regions of the central and eastern Pacific. El Niño is a recurrent phenomenon, first recorded in 1567 and the most recent occurrence prior to the 1990s was in the early 1940s.

El Transcantábrico A seven-day luxury rail cruise running along Spain's northern coast.

elapsed time The actual time taken to travel between two points, taking local time changes into account.

electric storm A thunderstorm.

electrified A railway line with electrical conductors, using either overhead lines or an extra rail. Electrified railways usually provide a faster and more reliable service than those operated by steam or diesel locomotives.

electronic funds transfer at point of sale A payment system by which funds are drawn electronically from a customer's bank account as soon as a transaction has been authorised.

electronic ticketing (or **e-ticketing**) The system by which passengers can

travel without holding a conventional ticket. Their details are stored on a computer system: on reaching their departure point and identifying themselves, passengers will be given authority to check in. Increasingly, this facility applies to most low-cost airlines and UK ferry companies. Passengers with hand baggage only may sometimes check in at a machine and choose their own seat.

elevator 1. The moveable part of an aircraft's tailplane that controls vertical motion.
2. (US) A lift used for carrying people.

Elizabethan Of or relating to the period of English history during the reign of Elizabeth I (1558 to 1603).

Elsan A British proprietary brand of portable chemical lavatory, sometimes used to describe any such appliance.

embankment An earth or stone bank for carrying a railway or road over a depression. Embankments and other earthworks are necessary for railways since they lose efficiency very rapidly if faced with gradients.

embargo 1. A prohibition preventing suppliers from dealing with a country or organisation.
2. A period during which, or for which, bookings may not be taken.

embark To get on board.

embassy The residence and offices of a ambassador. Embassy staff can often provide assistance to travellers.

Emerald Coast The stretch of coast in north-west Florida. The main resorts are Destin and Fort Walton Beach.

Emerald Isle Ireland.

emigrant A person who leaves their native country permanently.

emigrate To leave one's native country permanently.

émigré An emigrant, particularly a political exile.

emir An independent ruler or chieftain in Islamic countries, and sometimes also a military commander.

emirate The domain of an emir.

empire An extensive group of states or countries under the control of one supreme power (an emperor or empress).

Empire Builder The rail service between Chicago and Seattle/Portland in the USA.

emplane *See enplane.*

empty leg The operation of a journey without passengers on board.

en bloc All together. Sometimes used in travel to denote an action taken for a group. > *group.*

en fête Holding or getting ready for a holiday or celebration.

en route Actually travelling on a journey.

en suite Forming a single unit. Often used to describe a bedroom with a connecting bathroom.

endemic A disease which is generally present in a given area.

end-on construction A fare construction method whereby a fare from point A to point B is added to the fare from point B to point C. Since this type of construction is usually resorted to by those wishing to undercut an advertised through fare, there are many ways by which its use is restricted. > *split ticketing.*

endorsement 1. A signature or other entry on a document to indicate that it has in some manner changed.

2. (UK) A record of a driving conviction entered into a driving licence.

engine A colloquial term for a railway locomotive.

engineer (US) The driver of a railway locomotive.

England One of the constituent countries of the United Kingdom of Great Britain and Northern Ireland. > *Great Britain, United Kingdom.*

English breakfast Full cooked breakfast in the English style.

English Riviera The resort coast of south Devon centred on Torquay, Brixham and Paignton.

enplane To get onto an aircraft.

enriched air *See nitrox.*

ensign 1. A banner or flag, especially one used on a ship.
2. A junior naval officer.

entente cordiale A friendly understanding between nations or states. It is particularly applied to the relationship between the UK and France.

entrain To get onto a train.

entrée 1. (UK) A dish served before the main course.
2. (US) The main course.

entrepôt A warehouse for the temporary storage of goods in transit.

entresol A mezzanine floor.

entry permit 1. A form, often needing completion immediately prior to arrival, which must be presented to the immigration officer.
2. The stamp or other endorsement made in a passport showing the date of the traveller's arrival in the country.

E

E

entry visa *See visa.*

envelope The covering of a balloon or airship.

environment 1. The physical surroundings and conditions of an area, especially as they relate to people's lives. 2. The natural world in general.

environs The area surrounding or in the vicinity of a particular place.

enzootic A disease affecting animals which is generally present in a given area.

EP 1. *See European Plan.* 2. *See extended protection.*

epidemic A widespread occurrence of a disease.

Equator An imaginary line at 0° latitude dividing the earth into its two hemispheres, northern and southern.

equatorial At or near the Equator. > *latitude.*

Equatorial Counter-current The current in the tropics that flows in the opposite direction to the trade winds.

Equatorial Guinea A country in West Africa. Not to be confused with Guinea, Guinea-Bissau, New Guinea or Papua New Guinea .

equinox Either of the two times of the year (around 21 March and 23 September) when the sun passes directly over the Equator and when days and nights throughout the world are of equal length. The equinox which occurs in that hemisphere's autumn is known as the autumnal equinox: the one that occurs in that hemisphere's spring is known as the vernal equinox.

ERA European Regional Airlines Association. *See Appendix 5d.*

escalator A staircase powered by a motor consisting of an endless chain of steps continuously ascending or descending.

escarpment A steep slope at the edge of a plateau.

escort 1. *See tour guide.* 2. A person hired by an individual to provide company for an agreed period of time. The term can also refer to a prostitute.

escorted tour A tour, often on a coach, that is accompanied by a tour leader or guide.

escrow account A bank account established to hold a customer's payment to a supplier until such time as specified goods or services have been delivered or performed.

ESITO Events Sector Industry Training Organisation. *See Appendix 5a.*

Eskimo Of or relating to the peoples inhabiting northern Canada, Alaska, Greenland and Siberia. > *Nunavut, Inuit, Inupiat, Inupiak.*

Eskimo civilisation (Also **Inuit civilisation**) The civilisation that started in the Aleutian Islands around 1100BC and lasted until around AD1850.

esplanade A long level area for walking, usually between the beach and road.

estaminet A French term for a small café selling alcoholic drinks.

estate car (UK) A car with an extended rear luggage area.

estuary The mouth of a river that is relatively long and wide. Estuaries are considered to begin at the upstream point where the tidal effect can be detected.

ETA Estimated time of arrival.

ETC English Tourism Council. *See BTA, Appendix 5a.*

ETC European Travel Commission. *See Appendix 5d.*

ETD Estimated time of departure.

Etesian Wind A wind blowing from the north and north-west in the eastern Mediterranean and the Aegean, often creating rough seas.

ethnic Belonging to a group, region or nation having a distinctive cultural tradition.

ethnic minority An ethnic group living in a country or area where they are significantly outnumbered by the majority of the population.

ethnocentric The evaluation of the culture and traditions of other races by criteria relating to one's own.

e-ticket *See electronic ticketing.*

ETOA European Tour Operators Association. *See Appendix 5a.*

Etruscan Of or relating to ancient Etruria in Italy, especially its pre-Roman civilisation.

EU *See European Union.*

Eurasian Of mixed European and Asian parentage.

euro The currency now used by 12 member states of the EU, but not currently the UK. It was introduced in January 2002 and replaced the previously used local currencies. Each country issues its own notes and coins, all of which are legal tender in all 12 countries.

Europe 1. One of the world's continents. As with most continents, opinions differ as to its exact composition and area. > *continent.*

2. Sometimes used, generally in a political or economic context, to refer to the European Union. *See European Union.*

European City of Culture An initiative run by the European Union since 1985 to reflect, promote and celebrate Europe's wide cultural diversity. Until 1999, only one city a year was selected, but the millennium year of 2000 there were nine (Avignon, Bergen, Bologna, Brussels, Cracow, Helsinki, Prague, Reykjavik and Santiago de Compostela), and two in both 2001 (Oporto and Rotterdam) and 2002 (Bruges and Salamanca). The 2003 European City of Culture is Graz: in 2004 it will be the turn of Genoa and Lille. The UK's only representative to date has been Glasgow in 1990.

European Community The former name, replacing European Economic Community (EEC), for what is now known as the European Union (EU). *See European Union.*

European Plan A hotel rate including accommodation only and no meals.

European Union An economic and political association currently comprising the countries of Austria, Belgium, Denmark, Finland, France, Germany, Greece, Ireland, Italy, Luxembourg, the Netherlands, Portugal, Spain, Sweden and the United Kingdom. Many other countries are scheduled to join in the future. For more information, see the Columbus *World Travel Atlas.*

Eurostar The high-speed train service that links London with Paris, Lille and Brussels via the Channel Tunnel. Seasonal services also operate to southern France and to the Savoy area for winter sports.

Eurotunnel The rail shuttle service that carries cars, lorries, coaches and motor cycles, and their passengers, through the Channel Tunnel. This was formerly called Le Shuttle.

E

E

Eustachian tube The passageway which connects the middle ear and the back of the throat.

even keel When a ship is in an upright position.

ex gratia A payment or reimbursement made as a favour, rather than by legal obligation.

exceptions and exclusions An insurance term that refers to the risks that an insurance policy does not cover. Certain exclusions are common to most policies: for example radioactive contamination. Others will depend on the insurance company's business decisions: for example, some cover motorcycling, some do not. Many companies will cover sports such as scuba diving and skiing only if an additional premium is paid.

excess An amount that may be deducted from an insurance claim prior to payment by the insurer. For example, if a baggage cover section had an excess of £35, then a claim for £100 would be reduced to £65 on settlement. This discourages policyholders from making very small claims.

excess baggage Baggage that is larger or heavier than the baggage allowance. On airlines, where space is at a premium, passengers carrying excess baggage generally have to pay extra. Traditionally the standard charge was set at 1% of the first class one-way fare for each kilo of excess, but some carriers have now changed their charging structure.

exchange coupon The coupon or coupons of a ticket or voucher that are exchanged for the service provided.

exchange order *See voucher.*

exchange rate The rate at which money can be converted from one currency to another.

excise duty The tax payable on certain goods, typically alcohol and tobacco.

exclusive Originally accommodation or other facility the use of which is restricted to a select few. Now frequently used as a marketing term implying that a particular offer is special and restricted, even though this may not always be strictly true.

excursion 1. A trip taken as an extra while on holiday, often to a place of special interest.
2. A short trip away, usually for a day or less.

excursion fare A discounted fare with restrictions designed to discourage its use by business travellers.

executive floor A hotel floor reserved for business travellers, usually at a premium rate and often for members of the hotel's loyalty club.

executive lounge The general name given to a room, especially at an airport, that provides extra facilities to those passengers who have paid a premium fare.

exit permit A document or a passport stamp which allows a traveller to leave a country.

exit visa A visa that allows a traveller to leave a country.

exotic A destination, resort or hotel that is strikingly different and glamorous. The term sometimes implies that the destination is also far away.

expatriate A person living in a country other than that of their origin.

expedition A journey made for a specific purpose, such as exploration or scientific research.

exploration A journey made with the intention of discovery.

expo   An abbreviation for exposition.

export   To take or send items out of a country.

exposition   A large international exhibition.

express   A faster than normal method of transport or delivery.

express train   A train stopping at few intermediate stations or none at all.

expressway   (US) An urban motorway.

extended protection   *See vehicle rental insurance.*

extras   Items or services not included in the basic price and which are usually charged for separately.

extreme sport   A generic name given to any sport or activity that involves more than the normal amount of hazard and/or discomfort.

exurb   (US) The district outside a town or city, especially a prosperous area beyond the suburbs.

E

Ff

face-mask A mask with a glass port that fits over the eyes and nose of a diver to facilitate underwater operation.

Fahrenheit The temperature scale in which water freezes at 32° and boils at 212°. A quick way to approximately convert Fahrenheit to centigrade is to deduct 30 and halve the result. Thus, 70°F - 30 = 40. Divide by 2 = 20°C.

fairway 1. A navigable channel.
2. The mown part of a golf course between the tee and the putting green.

fall (US) Autumn.

fam trip *See familiarisation trip.*

familiarisation trip A visit, usually by a group of travel agents, to a resort, hotel, region or other similar organisation body, in order that they can better understand and sell the destination to their clients. They are sometimes called fam trips or educationals.

family cabin A cabin on a ship with sufficient accommodation for a family, usually assumed to be two adults and two children.

family fare A special fare offered to families travelling together.

family plan A special rate for family groups at a hotel or similar establishment.

family room A hotel room with sufficient accommodation for a family, usually assumed to be two adults and two children.

fan jet A type of jet aircraft engine where the incoming air is compressed by a fan.

fantail The overhang at the stern of a ship.

Fantasia A GDS used by some Far Eastern airlines.

Far East A general geographic term describing East and South-East Asia and including Brunei, Cambodia, China, Indonesia, Japan, Democratic People's Republic of Korea (North Korea), Republic of Korea (South Korea), Laos, Malaysia, Myanmar, the Philippines, Singapore, Taiwan, Thailand, Vietnam. Sometimes the definition is taken to include Mongolia and the eastern Siberian region of the Russian Federation.

Far Eastern civilisation The civilisation of the Far East in general, but particularly that of Japan and Korea (c.AD645 to date).

fare 1. The amount that a passenger must pay to be conveyed on a vehicle providing public transport.
2. The range of food and beverages provided in a restaurant.

fare basis The type of fare used for a particular ticket and the code that indicates this.

fare construction point The point where a fare ends or the point of tunraround. This is usually, but not always, the most distant point on the journey.

fast-food outlet An eating establishment that concentrates on providing simple meals, on demand, without delay.

fast-track Any system that allows a more rapid completion of a task. Typically used to describe special airline check-in and airport transit systems that allow more rapid processing, generally for first- and business-class passengers.

fat boys *See carving skis.*

fathom A measure of water depth. A fathom is 6 feet (1.82m).

fathometer A device for measuring the depth of water.

fauna The animal life of a region.

favela A Brazilian shack or shanty town.

FB *See full board.*

FCU *See fare construction unit.*

FE *See foreign exchange.*

federal 1. A system of government in which several states form a unity but remain to a greater or lesser extent independent in their internal affairs, such as Switzerland and the USA.
2. The name commonly given to the central government of a federal country and its agencies.

fee-based pricing *See management fee.*

feeder service A service that carries passengers from a smaller originating point to a main hub, and back.

FEEE The Foundation for Environmental Education in Europe. One of its functions is to administer the Blue Flag Campaign for beaches. *See Blue Flag beach.*

fell A stretch of hills or moorland, especially in northern England.

felucca A small Mediterranean coastal vessel with oars and/or lateen sails. They

are also sometimes seen on the Nile around Aswan.

fen A low, marshy or flooded area of land.

fender 1. A piece of rubber or other resilient substance hung over the side of a ship or boat to prevent damage when mooring or coming alongside another vessel.
2. (US) The wing (or sometimes the mudguard) of a motor vehicle.

ferry 1. A boat, ship or aircraft used for conveying passengers and goods on a regular and relatively short journey.
2. To transfer an aircraft between two points without passengers.

FHA Family Holiday Association. *See Appendix 5a.*

FIAVET Federazione Italiana Associazioni Imprese Viaggi e Turismo. *See Appendix 5c.*

fiesta A public holiday, usually in Latin countries, often associated with a particular saint or other religious figure.

fifth freedom *See freedoms of the air.*

fin The vertical control surface of an aircraft, usually at the rear, that governs its side to side motion.

firm up To make definite.

first class One of the best categories for transport or accommodation, exceeded in comfort only by de luxe.

first floor 1. (UK) The floor above the ground floor of a building.
2. (US) The ground floor of a building.

first quarter 1. The phase of the lunar cycle, seven days after the new moon, when the moon appears as a half-circle.
2. The first quarter of any type of year (such as calendar, financial or accounting), usually beginning on the

F

F

first day of a month. Quarters are commonly used periods for measuring company performances.

first sitting   The earlier of two meal times on a train or cruise ship.

firth   An inlet or estuary.

FIT   Fédération de l'Industrie du Tourisme. *See Appendix 5c.*

Five Pillars of Islam   The five central tenets of the Islamic religion: the profession of faith; the turning towards Mecca five times a day for prayer; the giving of alms; the fasting during the month of Ramadan; and the pilgrimage to Mecca.

fixed wing aircraft   The traditional type of heavier-than-air aircraft, where the wings project from the fuselage and do not move.

fjord   A narrow sea inlet, usually bounded by high cliffs.

flag   A graphic device, usually rectangular and colourful, used to represent a country, state, county, city, town, international organisation or other body. Many countries have more than one flag – some have as many as six – which are generally more ornate variations on a simple basic theme, each of which is used for specific civil, military, ceremonial or governmental purposes. The designs of flags are subject to variation from time to time. Even in official usage, the colours of the same flag may vary considerably from one example to the next, particularly where these appear on different materials or are printed by different processes.

flag alpha   *See A flag.*

flag carrier   The name given to the national airline of a country or state.

flag of convenience   The practice whereby ship owners will register their ships in a country other than their home country where the taxes, wage rates, standards and other aspects may be more favourable.

flagpole   *See flagstaff.*

flagship   The most prestigious hotel, ship or service of a supplier.

flagstaff   1. Any pole set up to fly a flag. 2. On a ship, the pole at the stern that flies the flag of the ship's country of registry. Also known as a jackstaff.

flaps   Extendible, hinged surfaces on an aircraft's wings that control the amount of lift generated.

flat light   A condition common in skiing resorts after the sun has gone down. At this time it is difficult to make out the conditions of a run because the various shades all blur to grey.

flight attendant   A member of an aircraft's cabin crew.

flight code   The unique code that is allocated to every flight and which identifies it throughout the duration of the journey. Flight codes are made up an airline identifier (such as BA for British Airways) and a number that denotes the route. > *airline code.*

flight coupon   An exchange coupon from a ticket that is valid for a flight.

flight deck   The name used for the cockpit on larger aircraft.

flight path   The course of an aircraft.

flight recorder   An automatic device fitted to all commercial passenger aircraft that records the technical data recorded or received during a flight. In the event of an accident this data can help establish the cause. Popularly known as a 'black box' although they are usually painted bright orange.

float plane *See seaplane.*

floatel A hotel that is on a boat, or built over water.

flood tide An exceptionally high tide.

floodplain A low lying flat area of land around a river that is subject to flooding.

flora The plant life of a region.

flotilla A collection of boats sailing together.

flotilla charter An arrangement whereby a group of chartered boats leave one harbour and sail to another, following a pre-arranged itinerary but their own time-table, with support, assistance and ground arrangements being provided by the charter company.

flotsam Wreckage and other objects found floating on water. Often used in conjunction with jetsam.

fly-cruise A package holiday that includes flights and a cruise.

fly-drive A package holiday that includes flights and car hire.

flyer A printed sheet containing advertising or promotional information.

flying boat A large aircraft designed to operate from water. Prior to the widespread construction of airports, flying boats maintained many of the longer distance services.

flying wing An aircraft with little or no fuselage and containing its passenger and cargo accommodation within the wings. Although aircraft of this configuration have flown, none has yet entered regular service.

fo'c'sle *See forecastle.*

FOB Free on board. Delivered without charge to a carrier's vehicle (typically a ship or railway wagon).

FOC Free of charge. Issued or provided without charge.

fog Any cloud of moisture touching the ground that reduces visibility to less than one kilometre.

Föhn 1. A hot, southerly wind on the northern slopes of the Alps.
2. A warm dry wind on the lee side of a mountain.

folklore The traditional customs, beliefs, stories, songs and other cultural traditions of a group of people, usually passed down orally over many generations.

foot A unit of measurement in the imperial system equal to 12 inches (0.305 m). Usually abbreviated ft or '. (Note that the latter symbol is also used to denote a minute of a degree.)

foot passenger A passenger without a vehicle travelling on a car-carrying ferry service.

footfall A marketing expression that refers to the number of people entering a place. It does not indicate the numbers who spend, only those who enter. > *footprint.*

foothill A small hill or range of hills around the bottom of a mountain or range of mountains.

footpath 1. (UK) A path for pedestrians, especially between buildings.
2. A track, generally in the countryside.

footplate (UK) The cab of a railway locomotive.

footprint A marketing expression describing the evidence that a person leaves after having visited a place. Thus the footprints of an international visitor might include visa applications, air

F

F

tickets, credit card payments, hotel registrations, landing cards and currency transactions, all of which can be used to help build up a statistical picture of travel patterns. > *footfall.*

ford A shallow point in a river or stream where it may be crossed by wading or by driving through.

fore Towards the front of an aircraft or ship.

forecastle Pronounced 'foke-sul'.
1. The forward part of a ship where the crew has its quarters.
2. A raised deck at the bow of a ship.

foreign Of, from or situated in a country other than one's own.

foreign exchange A term used to refer to any commercial transaction relating to the supply, exchange or purchase of currency other than that of one's own country.

Foremost West, Four Corners A US regional marketing organisation covering the states of Wyoming, Utah and New Mexico. > *US regional marketing organisations.*

foreshore That part of the shore that lies between high and low water.

forest A large area covered with trees and undergrowth. In tropical areas forests can be extremely dense and inhospitable.

form of indemnity An airline form which a passenger must complete to indemnify a carrier against loss. It is often used in the case of a lost ticket, where the carrier may replace the ticket without charge providing the passenger agrees to repay any loss incurred by the airline should the lost ticket later be fraudulently used.

formal dress 1. Clothing appropriate to an occasion bound by set, usually

traditional, rules and standards.
2. (US) Evening dress.

former GDR *See Germany.*

former Soviet Union The countries of Armenia, Azerbaijan, Belarus, Estonia, Georgia, Kazakhstan, Kyrgyzstan, Latvia, Lithuania, Moldova, Russian Federation, Tajikistan, Turkmenistan, Ukraine and Uzbekistan. The term has no current political or administrative significance, but is sometimes used to describe these countries collectively.

former Yugoslavia *See Yugoslavia, Macedonia.*

Formosa *See Taiwan.*

fortnight (UK) Two weeks.

Four-thousander A term used to describe a mountain of over 4,000m. Normally used in the Alps.

foyer The main lobby or entrance hall of a hotel or theatre (or sometimes a cruise ship).

FP Full pension. *See full board.*

Franc Zone Those countries whose currencies were linked to the French franc at a fixed exchange rate, and are now linked to the euro. The member countries are: Benin, Burkina, Cameroon, Central African Republic, Chad, Comoros, Congo, Côte d'Ivoire, Equatorial Guinea, Gabon, Guinea-Bissau, Mali, Niger, Senegal and Togo.

franchise A formal authorisation granted to an individual or organisation (the franchisee) by another (the franchisor), that gives the former right to sell the latter's products or services and to use its brand name. Many catering outlets, especially fast-food ones, are run as franchises.

franchisee *See franchise.*

franchisor *See franchise.*

Francophile A person who is well disposed towards France or the French.

Francophobe A person who dislikes or distrusts France or the French.

Frank A member of the Germanic peoples who invaded and occupied Gaul in the sixth century. The term was used throughout the Middle Ages by eastern Europeans and Muslims to describe western Europeans generally.

frank An official mark or stamp put on a document, usually the stamp on an envelope, to record payment; and the act of so doing.

free ascent When a diver ascends towards the water's surface without the use of additional air supply.

free house (UK) A drinking establishment, usually a pub, not owned by a brewery which is thus free to sell beers from several suppliers. > *tied house.*

free port A port where goods in transit are not subject to taxes or duties.

free trade The philosophy of allowing trade between nations without governmental regulations, controls or duties.

freeboard The space between the lowest open deck and the waterline of a vessel.

freedoms of the air In the Chicago Convention on Civil Aviation of 1944, it was agreed that airlines would have five 'levels' of freedom under which they could operate. The higher the level of freedom afforded, the greater the level of flexibility the airline will enjoy. A sixth freedom has since been added. The levels are:
• 1. The right to fly over a country.
• 2. The right to land in a country for technical reasons such as refuelling.
• 3. The right to off-load freight, mail or passengers from an aircraft of the country from which they originated.
• 4. The right to load freight, mail or passengers onto an aircraft of the country from which they originated or for which they are destined.
• 5. The right to load or off-load freight, mail or passengers onto or from an aircraft other than that of the country for which they are destined.
• 6. The right of an airline of one country to carry passengers between two other countries, providing it travels via its home country.

freesale A system whereby an agent can sell a facility without reference in advance to the principal. Reservations made in this way will have to be reported to the principal in accordance with specified procedures.

freeskiing A term adopted to cover the increasingly wide range of options available to skiers since the late 1990s. This includes skis of different shape and length (but always shorter and wider than traditional skis) and different types of skiing, such as on terrain parks.

freeway (US) An express highway, the equivalent of a motorway.

freighter In shipping, a vessel operating line services for freight. Some of these vessels carry a limited number of passengers, rarely more than 12.

French Antilles The Caribbean islands of Martinique; and Guadeloupe and five smaller islands. Each forms a Départements d'Outre-Mer (Overseas Department) of France.

French Overseas Possessions The various former French colonial possessions which now enjoy varying degrees of autonomy. There are four Départements d'Outre-Mer; three Territoires d'Outre-Mer; two Collectivités Territoriales; and one overseas country. For more information, consult the

F

F

Columbus *World Travel Guide.*

frequent flyer programmes Incentive loyalty clubs operated by airlines on behalf of customers who use their services regularly. Travellers accumulate points in proportion to the number and value of their journeys and these can be exchanged for gifts of various types, including free flights.

fresh breeze *See Beaufort scale.*

front of house The reception area of a hotel.

frontier The border between two countries, state, province or any other significant administrative division.

fruit machine *See one-armed bandit.*

FSU *See former Soviet Union.*

FTI Federatie van de Toeristische Industrie. *See Appendix 5c.*

FTO Federation of Tour Operators. *See Appendix 5a.*

full board A hotel rate including three meals daily. Also called American Plan.

full foliage (US) The time in the fall when the colours of leaves of trees, especially in New England, are at their most vivid.

full house Originally from the theatre and meaning that all seats are taken. Now often applied in a casual manner to any other accommodation that has been fully taken up.

full moon The phase of the lunar cycle, 14 days after the new moon, when the moon appears as a complete circle.

full pension *See full board.*

full-face mask A face-mask that covers the whole face, including the mouth, eyes and nose.

fumarole An opening in or near a volcano from which hot gases emerge.

funicular A mountain railway, usually one operated by cable.

funitel *See gondola (3).*

funnel The smokestack on a ship. Originally it carried the large quantities of smoke and steam from the engines but these days is more likely to carry diesel exhaust.

furlong An unit of measurement in the imperial system equal to one eighth of a mile. Now rarely used, except for when describing the length of horse races.

furlough (US) A temporary laying-off of employees.

fuselage The main body or an aircraft to which the wings and tailplane are fitted.

FX An abbreviation for foreign exchange. *See foreign exchange.*

Gg

Gaelic Any of the Celtic languages spoken in Ireland, Scotland and the Isle of Man.

gale *See Beaufort scale.*

Galileo A multi-national GDS used by a number of European airlines and travel agents.

galley A ship's or aircraft's kitchen.

game lodge Accommodation in a game reserve or safari park.

game reserve An area in which game animals, especially large ones, are kept in protected but natural environments. Usually they may be viewed by visitors under controlled conditions.

gangplank A movable plank, often with cleats, used to board a vessel.

gangway 1. (UK) A passage between rows of seats.
2. A bridge laid from ship to shore to enable embarkation and disembarkation.

Garden Route A scenic stretch of the South African coast stretching from Mossel Bay in the west to Storms river in the east. The main resorts are Knysna and Plettenberg Bay. Other attractions include Tsitsikamma National Park and the Wilderness Lakes.

garden side A room in a hotel or similar establishment on the same level as the garden and which opens onto it.

garden view A room in a hotel or similar

establishment that overlooks the garden but which has no direct access to it.

Garúa A heavy mist on the Pacific slope of the Andes in a normally very dry part of the coast.

gasthaus A small hotel or inn in German-speaking countries.

gasthof A hotel or inn in German-speaking countries, larger than a gasthaus.

gate The exit from an airport that leads to an aircraft.

gateway A point of access to a country or region. A gateway will usually be an airport or seaport, although certain frontier points and railway stations can be given the designation. In general a gateway is the point served most directly from the originating point, which usually implies that it accepts international traffic.

gauge The distance between the rails of a railway track. In most countries of the world this is the British-invented gauge of four feet eight and a half inches (167 cm).

GAVL Groupement des Agences de Voyages du Grand-Duché du Luxembourg. *See Appendix 5c.*

gazetteer A geographical index or dictionary.

gazpacho A Spanish vegetable soup, served cold.

G

GB See Great Britain.

GBCO Guild of British Coach Operators. See Appendix 5a.

GBTA Guild of Business Travel Agents. See Appendix 5a.

GBTAI Guild of Business Travel Agents Ireland. See Appendix 5d.

GDS See global distribution system.

GEBTA Guild of European Business Travel Agents. See Appendix 5d.

geisha A Japanese hostess trained to entertain male guests with dancing, songs and conversation. Can also refer to a Japanese prostitute.

general sales agent The authorised representative of a principal, particularly in cases where a principal does not have its own office in a country and wishes to appoint a GSA to handle its promotion, sales and enquiries. A GSA may represent several principals.

gentle breeze See Beaufort scale.

gentlemen's agreement An unwritten understanding between two parties, the observance of which is more a matter of honour than of legal obligation.

geographic pole See poles.

geographical county One of the original counties of England, Wales and Scotland (such as Rutland, Pembroke and Buteshire), many of which have been in existence for over a thousand years. Some have seemed to disappear as a result of administrative reforms since the 1880s, although they still exist for some ceremonial, touristic, sporting and other purposes, > administrative counties.

geographical mile See nautical mile.

geography The study of the earth's physical features, resources and climate as well as aspects of its population and their activities.

geology The study of the earth's structure and composition.

George A colloquial term for the automatic pilot on an aircraft.

George Town The capital of the Cayman Islands. Not to be confused with Georgetown, the capital of Guyana, or St George's, the capital of Grenada.

Georgetown The capital of Guyana. Not to be confused with George Town, the capital of the Cayman Islands, or St George's, the capital of Grenada.

Georgian 1. Of or relating to the period of English history during the reigns of the first four Georges (1713 to 1830). 2. Of or relating to the country of Georgia. 3. Of or relating to the state of Georgia in the USA.

Germany A country in central Western Europe, officially the Federal Republic of Germany. Between 1945 and 1991, it was divided between the Federal Republic of Germany (West Germany) and the German Democratic Republic (East Germany). The term 'eastern Germany' generally refers to the eastern part of the country in the present, generally co-extensive with the former GDR. The term 'East Germany' generally refers to the former GDR in the past, or to its legacy today. The distinction is often made when referring to the infrastructure, which in East Germany is in many cases still of a lower standard than that in the former West Germany. > Berlin.

geyser A volcanic phenomenon causing the eruption of hot water and steam, often at regular intervals.

Ghan The rail service in Australia between Adelaide and Alice Springs and (from 2004) Darwin.

ghetto   Part of a town or city (usually a rundown area) occupied by a minority or deprived group.

Ghibli   The local name for the Sirocco in Libya. *See Sirocco.*

ghost town   A deserted town or settlement, usually found in areas that have experienced a short-lived boom. (such as from mining).

gig   A light, two-wheeled horse-drawn carriage.

gimbals   A device to keep something horizontal on a ship, regardless of any pitch or roll.

GIT   *See group inclusive tour.*

gîte   A French expression meaning a holiday dwelling, usually situated in the countryside and rented on a self-catering basis.

glacier   A slowly moving sheet of ice. Some glaciers can be several kilometres wide.

Glacier Express   A spectacular alpine rail service in Switzerland, running between St Moritz and Zermatt.

Glass Country   An area in south-east Småland, Sweden, famous for glass-making.

glen   A narrow valley.

glider   An engineless heavier-than-air aircraft, often one that is towed by a powered aeroplane to assist take-off.

global distillation   The phenomenon whereby cold areas, such as the Arctic, are polluted by emissions produced far away. Such emissions can be carried far from their source and not be deposited until they condense in the colder atmosphere.

global distribution system (GDS)   The generic name given to a range of computer systems that enable agents to make bookings with principals. They were formerly known as computerised reservations systems (CRS). The earliest of these were developed during the mid-1970s, and thus have claim to be the first functioning e-commerce systems in the world.

global indicator   A code shown against the fare on an air ticket that indicates the general route of a long distance flight.

global price tickets   Tickets, often rail, that include a package of facilities, for example, travel, sleeping accommodation and a meal.

globe   The planet earth or a representation of it.

glühwein   Mulled wine popular in Switzerland, Austria and Germany. It is often served in ski resorts.

GMT   Greenwich Mean Time. The former name for Universal Time Co-ordinate (UTC). *See UTC.*

goggles   1. A device used as an aid to seeing under water. Unlike the face mask, goggles cover the eyes only and are for use by surface swimmers.
2. A device used by skiers to protect their eyes against wind, sun and snow.

Gold Coast   1. Australia's largest resort area, situated to the south of Brisbane. The main resorts include Southport, Surfers Paradise and Coolangatta.
2. The section of the Florida coastline around Palm Beach and Miami with numerous resorts.
3. The coastal strip of Ghana, originally named after the gold mined in the area.
4. *See Kona Coast.*

Golden Coast   The coastal region in south-west Sweden stretching from Strömstad in the north to Laholm in the south. The main centres are Gothenburg and Halmstad.

G

G

Golden Horseshoe The area around the western end of Lake Ontario containing over 20% of Canada's population. The main towns are Oshawa, Toronto, Hamilton and St Catharines.

Golden Ring The area to the north-east of Moscow with many towns of great historical, architectural and spiritual significance, including Suzdal, Vladimir and Yaroslavl.

Golden Triangle 1. An area in northern India with many ancient sites and important monuments, with Delhi to the north, Agra to the south-east and Jaipur to the south-west.
2. A region in South-East Asia on the borders of Laos, Myanmar and Thailand. Notorious for the production of opium.

Golfo de California The long gulf in the Pacific Ocean separating the Baja California from the Mexican mainland.

gondola 1. A traditional vessel used on canals, especially in Venice.
2. The passenger-carrying cabin on an airship or balloon.
3. A type of lift common in larger ski resorts and in some other large leisure facilities in hilly or mountainous areas. It is sometimes known in the UK by its French name of *télécabine*. Gondolas differ from cable cars in that they normally contain several dozen cabins, each holding two to eight passengers, that connect to a continually moving cable. Larger gondolas have appeared recently that can hold more than 20 people in each cabin, often standing. Some of these are known as funitels and are suspended from two parallel cables for added stability.

gondolier The oarsman of a gondola.

Good Friday A festival in the Christian religious calendar, celebrated two days before Easter.

gorge A deep, narrow canyon.

gorge-walking The pastime of travelling down streams and along water filled gorges in mountain areas without the aid of boats. The method of progress may require various types of equipment including that used for climbing and caving. Unless experienced in this it is usual to be part of a guided party. Also known as canyoning.

go-show A passenger who arrives for a flight without a reservation.

Goth A member of the Germanic tribe that invaded the Roman Empire in the 3rd to the 5th centuries.

Gothic An architectural style common in Europe in the 12th to 16th centuries.

gourmand A glutton.

gourmet A person who appreciates the finest things, especially food and drink.

gourmet meal Food and drink prepared to exacting standards.

GPU *See ground power unit.*

grade crossing (US) A level crossing.

gradient The slope of a road or railway. Gradients can be measured in percentages or as a ratio. A slope of 10% is equivalent to a ratio of 1 in 10, whereby for every ten feet of progress forward a vehicle would gain one foot in height.

Grain Coast The coastal strip of West Africa situated in Liberia.

Granada A city in Andalucia in southern Spain. Not to be confused with the Grenadines or Grenada.

Grand Tour A historical term given to the practice of sending wealthy young aristocrats on a circuit of the major cultural centres of Europe. The fashion started in the 17th century and is one of the foundations of modern travel.

graticule The intersecting lines of latitude and longitude which are usually used as a basis for drawing a map. These will usually be described as representing progressive increments of degrees north or south, and east or west. Depending on the map projection and the scale, these will appear as straight lines or curves. These may be also be used as a map reference. > *longitude, latitude, map, map projection, map reference.*

gratis Free of charge.

gratuity A tip for service. Theoretically for service over and above that expected but now often demanded as a right by many providers. It is often added to a bill in a restaurant or on a ship, usually at a rate of 10 or 15%.

greasy spoon (UK) A slang expression meaning a cheap, often inferior, restaurant.

Great Barrier Reef A coral reef, the largest in the world, off the north-eastern coast of Australia.

Great Britain The political unit comprising England, Scotland and Wales. Some organisations, such as travel insurance companies, may use a slightly different definition of the term 'Great Britain'. > *United Kingdom.*

great circle The shortest distance between two points on a sphere. A piece of string stretched between two points on a model globe will follow the great circle route and this route will often be significantly different from a straight line on a map projection.

Great Dividing Range The main mountain range in Australia, extending along almost the entire eastern part of the continent.

Great Lakes A group of five lakes in central North America: Lakes Superior, Huron, Erie, Ontario and Michigan. The first four are divided by the border between the USA and Canada; Lake Michigan is entirely in the USA.

Great Lakes of North America A US regional marketing organisation covering the states that border the Great Lakes, and Ontario in Canada. > *US regional marketing organisations.*

Great Plains The area of the USA to the east of the Rocky Mountains.

Great Rift Valley The most extensive and dramatic rift in the earth's surface, creating a chain of mountains, volcanoes and escarpments extending from Syria to Mozambique, but most strongly associated with Kenya and Tanzania.

Greater Antilles The group of Caribbean islands comprising the Cayman Islands, Cuba, Hispaniola, Jamaica and Puerto Rico.

Greek Terms Yacht charter terms under which the fee includes the charter of the yacht with all equipment; basic consumables for engine-room, deck and cabins; the crew's wages and food; insurance for the yacht itself, for third party claims and employer's liability insurance for the crew; sufficient fuel and lubricants for four hours cruising per 24 hours; harbour dues and pilotage within Greek waters; and water and ship's laundry. Other costs, such as the client's food and drink, Corinthian Canal dues where applicable and port taxes and harbour dues outside Greek waters must be paid by the client. These terms may vary.

green card 1. A certificate issued by an insurance company that provides evidence of cover (especially of motor insurance) outside the UK.
2. A work permit issued to residents of the USA who are not US citizens.

green channel See *customs clearance.*

green circle trail (US) The easiest ski run

G

G

in North American resorts. > *green run, blue run.*

green fee   The cost of playing a round of golf. Green fees are charged per person playing and are usually quoted for a round of 18 holes. All-day green fees may also be available.

green run   The very easiest ski run category in Italy, France and French-speaking Switzerland. Rarely used in other parts of Europe where blue run is the easiest category. In North America defined as 'green circle' trail. > *blue run, green circle trail.*

green tourism   *See ecotourism.*

Greenwich Mean Time   The former name for Universal Time Co-ordinate (UTC). *See UTC.*

Greenwich meridian   The meridian of longitude that passes through Greenwich in London from which all the meridians are calculated. Generally this appears in or near the centre of a typical world map. It is also known as the prime meridian or the zero meridian. > *UTC, time zones, GMT, British Summer Time, Daylight Saving Time, International Date Line.*

Grenada   The southernmost of the Windward Islands in the Caribbean. Not to be confused with the Grenadines or Granada.

Grenadines, the   The string of islands between St Vincent and Grenada in the Windward Islands in the Caribbean, politically part of St Vincent and the Grenadines. Not to be confused with Grenada or Granada.

gringo   A slang expression used in Spanish-speaking countries for a foreigner, especially one from North America.

gross registered tonnage   A measure of the capacity of a ship. One GRT is equivalent to 100 cubic feet of enclosed space. The expression derives from the word tun (a type of barrel) and has nothing to do with weight. > *tonnage.*

grotto   A cave, often one part filled with water.

ground arrangements   The additional facilities such as airport connections, accommodation and excursions that may be required by air travellers when they arrive at their destinations.

ground content   The part of a travel arrangement, such as a package holiday, that comprises services provided after arrival at the destination, such as airport transfers, accommodation and guided tours.

ground floor   (UK) The lowest floor of a building.

ground handling agent   A provider of ground arrangements.

ground operator   *See ground handling agent.*

ground power unit   A small engine, separate from the main engines, that maintains an aircraft's air conditioning and other services while it is on the ground.

ground speed   An aircraft's speed relative to the ground.

ground staff   The members of the staff of an airline who are responsible for ground duties such as check-in and ticketing as well as general passenger welfare.

group   A party of travellers whose travel arrangements as regards departure point, transport details, arrival point and ground arrangements are identical or broadly similar and have been arranged en bloc. Economies of scale, for the travellers in terms of cost and for the various travel organisations in terms of convenience, often result from group arrangements.

group desk A counter or office, usually at an airport, for facilitating the processing and onward arrangements of groups.

group inclusive tour Travel arrangements made in bulk for a group.

groyne A low wall built out into the sea to help prevent erosion of the shore.

GRT *See gross registered tonnage.*

GRTG The Guild of Registered Tourist Guides. *See Appendix 5a.*

GSA *See general sales agent.*

GSM Grams per square metre, the most common measurement of paper weight outside North America.

GTOA Group Travel Organisers Association. *See Appendix 5a.*

GTT The Guild of Travel and Tourism. *See Appendix 5a.*

guarantee An agreement by a principal to provide accommodation, even though the exact type, reference or category cannot be advised at the time.

guaranteed reservation Usually applicable to hotels, where a client or agent will guarantee payment for the accommodation booked, even if the client is a no show.

guaranteed upgrade An arrangement whereby passengers of major commercial importance to an airline or hotel are offered a complimentary upgrade to higher class of accommodation than that paid for.

guard (UK) A railway employee who rides on a train and is responsible for passenger safety, reservation and ticket inspection, timely departure from stations and sometimes luggage. Many trains no longer have guards as such, and their various functions are now discharged by other officials before, during or after the journey.

guard's van (UK) The coach or compartment on a train occupied by the guard.

guardianed hut A mountain hut that is owned or managed by a person or a family. Food is purchased from the guardian and self-catering is not permitted.

guest A person resident in a hotel or other accommodation.

guest house A more modern term for boarding house.

guide 1. A person who guides or escorts groups. The duties of the various types of guide vary considerably and the official definitions, where they exist, are shown under their respective headings.
2. A book or other reference manual that gives details of an attraction, resort, country or other place or area.

Guinea Current An extension of the Equatorial Counter-current that flows southwards down the north-west coast of central Africa.

Guinea Monsoon A warm humid wind blowing from the southwest in West Africa between April and September, associated with the rainy season.

Guinea A country in West Africa. Not to be confused with Guinea-Bissau, Equatorial Guinea, New Guinea or Papua New Guinea.

Guinea-Bissau A country in West Africa. Not to be confused with Guinea, Equatorial Guinea, New Guinea or Papua New Guinea .

gulch (US) A ravine.

gulet (Also *gulett, gullette*) A beamy Turkish sailing vessel built mainly of wood on traditional lines. Commonly used for flotilla type holidays.

Gulet Terms Yacht charter terms, mainly

G

G

used in Turkish waters, under which the fee includes the charter of the yacht with all equipment; basic consumables for engine-room, deck and cabins; the crew's wages and food; insurance for the yacht itself, for third party claims and employer's liability insurance for the crew; sufficient fuel and lubricants for four hours cruising per 24 hours; harbour dues and pilotage in Turkish waters; and water and ship's laundry. Other costs, such as the client's food and drink and port taxes and harbour dues outside Turkish waters, must be paid by the client. These terms may vary.

gulf   Similar to a bay, but generally larger.

Gulf Coast   The stretch of coastline on Florida's west coast between Cedar Key in the north and Marco Island in the south. Developed as a resort area separately from Miami's Gold Coast.

Gulf of Aden   The gulf between the Red Sea, the Indian Ocean, Somalia and Yemen.

Gulf of Alaska   The area of the North Atlantic Ocean to the south of Alaska.

Gulf of Guinea   The area of the South Atlantic Ocean between the southern coast of West Africa and the coast of Central Africa.

Gulf of Mexico   The area of the Atlantic Ocean between the USA, Mexico and Cuba.

Gulf States   Any of the countries with a coastline on the Persian Gulf.

Gulf Stream   A warm-water current that moves from the Gulf of Mexico to the North Atlantic. The warmth of the Gulf Stream has a moderating effect on British winters.

Gulf, the   *See Persian Gulf.*

gunnel   *See gunwale.*

gunwale   Pronounced (and sometimes spelt) 'gunnel'. The very top of a ship's sides. Thus, 'full to the gunwales' means there's no more space whatsoever.

Guru Gobind Singh's Birthday   A festival in the Sikh religious calendar, celebrated in December.

Guru Nanak   A festival in the Sikh religious calendar, celebrated at the time of the full moon in July.

Gypsy   A member of the nomadic people of central Europe, of Hindu origin, speaking a language related to Hindi.

gyrocompass   A non-magnetic compass working by the action of a gyroscope. A gyrocompass can be set to indicate true north.

gyroplane   An aeroplane deriving its lift from a freely spinning overhead rotor. > *autogiro.*

gyrostabiliser   A stabiliser using the steadying effect of a gyroscope to maintain the stability of a ship or other vessel.

Hh

habitat   The indigenous or actual location of a plant or animal species. Destruction or modification of habitats is a frequent consequence of tourism development.

habitué   A regular visitor or resident.

HACE   *See High Altitude Cerebral Edema*

hachures   The parallel lines shown on some maps to indicate the steepness of gradients.

hacienda   In Spanish-speaking countries, an estate or plantation with accommodation.

hackney carriage   (UK) The original term for a taxi. No longer in common use but still the official term for a licensed taxi in the UK.

ha-ha   (UK) A dry ditch, usually with a wall on its inner side, used as a boundary that does not spoil the view.

hairpin bend   A sharp U-shaped curve in a road.

hajj   (or **hadj, haj**) The Islamic pilgrimage to the Sacred Mosque at Mecca in Saudi Arabia.

hajji   (**hajja** when feminine) A Muslim who has undertaken the hajj.

halal   Food and drink prepared in accordance with Islamic law.

half pipe   Originally a horizontal, semi-circular structure used for skateboarding, but now a common feature at ski resorts. They are particularly popular with snowboarders, but also with skiers using the latest short skis. A half pipe is built from snow on a ski slope and is typically around 100m (350 feet) long and 5m (16 feet) wide.

half round trip   A fare construction based on the sum of half the two return fares to a destination. This type of construction is useful when, for example, a passenger travels outward on a peak date and returns off peak.

half-board   *See demi-pension.*

half-pension   *See demi-pension.*

hall porter   (UK) The member of hotel staff in charge of messages, passing of information and baggage. > *concierge.*

halo   A ring of light that appears around the sun or moon under particular meteorological conditions. Haloes differ from coronæ, appearing very much further away from the object they surround. > *corona.*

halocline   The boundary between waters of differing salinity.

halt   (UK) A minor station on a railway line.

hamlet   (UK) A small village, usually one without a church.

hand baggage   Bags and other items, usually those of airline passengers, that are carried on board rather than being

H

checked in. All carriers have strict limits on the size and weight of hand baggage, which must usually be able to be stored under a seat or in an overhead locker. Sometimes referred to as 'carry on' baggage. > *baggage allowance, excess baggage.*

hand luggage   *See hand baggage.*

hand spear   A spear, used for catching fish, which does not include any form of propulsive gun.

handicap certificate   The official proof of the golfer's handicap. Some golf courses will require to see a golfer's official handicap card before allowing them onto the course. > *handicap.*

handicap   An official rating of a golfer's ability. The lower the handicap the better the player. Maximum handicaps (the handicaps given to beginner golfers) are usually 28 for men and 36 for women. In continental Europe, it is not uncommon for clubs to allocate handicaps above 28 and 36. Travel agencies should be prepared to provide golf clubs with the handicaps of their client golfers. Many clubs have a handicap limit whereby only golfers of a certain standard will be allowed to play. > *handicap certificates.*

handle tow   A simple form of ski lift comprising a continually moving cable that skiers simply catch hold of.

handling agent   1. An organisation that provides services to incoming visitors on behalf of a travel agent or tour operator. The rates for such services are contained in a confidential tariff.
2. A company that looks after the needs of passengers and their baggage at an airport on behalf of an airline.

handling fee   A fee paid to an agent for working on a ticket that is sold by another and on which no further commission may be earned.

hangar   A large building used to house aircraft.

Hanoverian   1. Of or relating to the kings and queens of England between 1714 and 1901, or to that period generally.
2. Of or relating to the city of Hanover in Germany.

Hanseatic League   A medieval political and commercial league of north German towns.

hansom   A two-wheeled, horse-drawn cab. The term is still in use in some areas to denote a horse-drawn sightseeing vehicle.

Hanukah   *See Chanukah.*

HAPE   *See High Altitude Pulmonary Edema.*

Hapsburg   (or **Habsburg**) Of or relating to the most widespread, successful and long-lived royal family in medieval and early modern Europe, branches of which provided, amongst numerous other rulers, the kings of Spain (and much of the New World) between 1516 and 1700, the Holy Roman Emperors (rulers of Germany) between 1438 and 1806, and the emperors of Austria from 1804 until 1919; also to those periods of the history of those countries and regions generally.

harbour   A bay or other protected area where ships can anchor in safety.

hard currency   A currency that is sought after and has a relatively high rate of exchange.

hard shoulder   (UK) An emergency stopping area along the edge of a motorway.

hard-top   A car with a hard but detachable roof.

Harmattan   A dry, dusty land wind of the West African coast, occurring from December to February.

HATA Hong Kong Association of Travel Agents. *See Appendix 5c.*

hatch An opening, usually covered when at sea, on a ship's deck that gives access to the holds.

hatchback *See coupé.*

HATTA Hellenic Association of Travel and Tourist Agencies. *See Appendix 5c.*

haute cuisine A French expression meaning food of the highest quality, usually, but not invariably, served in expensive and elegant surroundings.

haven A harbour or port, often considered a refuge.

Hawaiian Sling A hand-held diver's spear with an additional tube-like device and rubber band which enables the user to propel the spear in a catapult fashion.

hawker A person who sells unsolicited goods or services. In some places, the authorities have tried to control the number of hawkers by enforcing a system of licenses or tickets.

hawse That part of a ship's side where the hawse holes are situated.

hawse hole The opening in a ship's side through which the anchor chain passes.

hawser A cable used to tow or secure a ship.

hazardous activity *See dangerous activity.*

HBAA Hotel Booking Agents Association. *See Appendix 5a.*

HCA Holiday Centres Association. *See Appendix 5a.*

head office location An IATA-accredited agent's place of business that is also an approved location.

heading A direction or bearing.

headland A promontory.

headline city The main city of entry in a timetable, beneath and following which services to other places are listed.

headwaters The streams flowing from the source of a river.

headway The rate of progress of a ship.

health precautions The preventative measures which a traveller should take before embarking on a foreign trip. Travellers need to be aware of the possible dangers of disease or other health hazards. Details of risks are published by several organisations, and under the terms of the EU Directive on Package Travel, travel agents are obliged to inform their customers of them.
Travellers abroad are at risk from a range of unfamiliar situations and infections. Changes in food and water and insects and insect-borne diseases are probably the two most important problems a traveller will encounter, but other issues including heat, stress, jet-lag and excessive alcohol consumption can also be significant. Many of these risks can, with the right advice and precautions, be minimised or eliminated. Specific advice on which diseases are present in countries to be visited is likely to be complicated. A practical starting point for the traveller seeking advice is to consider which diseases can be prevented by immunisation, prophylactic tablets, or other measures, and decide whether it is appropriate to do so in each case.
An unpredictable environment is a particular problem for overland travellers who plan their own journeys, and who need greater knowledge of disease prevention and management than the air or sea traveller whose environment, food and drink are largely in the hands of the operator. Unforeseen changes in timetables may lead to stays in accommodation not of the expected

H

H

standard. Delays at airports, particularly out-of-the-way ones, can take place in overcrowded and unhygienic conditions where the facilities have not kept pace with increased demand. Jet-lag and exhaustion may prompt a traveller to take risks with food and drink. More experienced travellers tend to have fewer health problems. Better planning, immunisations and experience in prevention may all play a part, as well as salutary lessons learnt on previous occasions.

A recent survey of returning travellers (most of whom had been to Europe, especially the Mediterranean countries) showed that half had had diarrhoea or respiratory symptoms while abroad. Excessive alcohol, sun and late nights can add to the problems. About 1% of package holidaymakers who take out a health insurance policy make a claim. Diarrhoea and sunburn are principal reasons, but accidents are also common. Injuries occur especially in and around swimming pools, to pedestrians forgetting on which side of the road the traffic drives, to motorists on unfamiliar roads, and to users of unfamiliar equipment such as gates on lifts. Sexually transmitted diseases may be contracted and may require urgent treatment.

Long-stay travellers may adapt to these initial problems, but then find themselves suffering from diseases endemic in their chosen country, such as malaria, hepatitis, diarrhoea and skin problems.

The traveller should be insured against medical expenses and most policies include the cost of emergency repatriation when appropriate. Such insurance, however, rarely covers a service overseas similar to that available at home. Language and administrative differences are likely to present problems. Reciprocal arrangements between countries differ and money may have to be paid and then reclaimed in the visited country itself, which can be time-consuming. Extra provision should be made for such emergencies.

Brief information on the major diseases and other health risks are given under individual entries elsewhere in this Dictionary. For more detailed information, please consult the Health appendix of the latest edition of the Columbus *World Travel Guide*, which includes listings of specialist sources of further advice.

heartland The central or most important part of an area.

heat-stroke A feverish sickness caused by over-exposure to high temperatures.

heave The up and down motion of a vessel at sea.

heave to To stop in the water without anchoring or mooring.

heavier-than-air Of an aircraft, one that weighs more than the air it displaces. Such aircraft can only remain in the air through the power of their engines.

Hebrew 1. Of or relating to the Semitic people originally from ancient Palestine. 2. The official language of Israel.

hectare An area equal to 10,000 sq m (2.47 acres).

hedging The act of entering into forward-buying arrangements for foreign currency in order to offset the effect of subsequent unfavourable movement in exchange rates.

HEDNA Hotel Electronic Distribution Network Association. *See Appendix 5b.*

heel When a vessel at sea tilts to port or starboard.

helicopter An aircraft with rotating wings. Helicopters can take off and land vertically and are thus often used for flights to destinations where there are no runways. Helicopters are slower than planes and so are mainly used for short journeys.

heliport The equivalent of an airport, but used for helicopters. As they need no runways, heliports are much smaller than ordinary airports.

heli-skiing A holiday arrangement where skiers are taken to the skiing area, frequently on a mountaintop, by helicopter. This has obvious advantages for those who wish to ski in areas not served by lifts.

helium An inert, light gas used these days to give buoyancy to lighter-than-air aircraft.

Hellenic The civilisation of ancient Greece (c.1300BC to 146BC).

helm The mechanism by which a ship is steered. Originally this was a wheel directly connected to the rudder. Nowadays it is often a small computer-controlled wheel.

hemisphere In geography, one half of the earth's surface, each separated from the other by the Equator or by the line of 0°/180° longitude.

hepatitis A potentially fatal infection of the liver causing jaundice. There are two main types of infectious hepatitis, A and B. A is caused eating contaminated food or drink; B by contaminated blood products or sexual contact. Apart from the obvious precautions, short-term immunity can be obtained by a pre-journey injection. > *health precautions*.

heritage A general expression that describes anything that has a link with some past event or person.

heritage attraction An attraction that capitalises on its connection with heritage.

heritage tourism Holidays taken with the sole or principal aim of exploring the history and culture of the region being visited. The phrase is sometimes used pejoratively.

herringbone seating plan A common configuration at meetings, conferences or seminars whereby the delegates are seated in rows of chairs separated by a central aisle which slants in a V-shape, with the speakers' table at the open end of the V.

Hibernian Of or relating to the island of Ireland.

Hibiscus Coast The coastal area in South Africa near Port Shepstone, the main resort of which is Margate.

hidden city ticketing The discouraged practice of issuing a ticket to a more distant point with a lower fare than the intended change point and suggesting that the passenger end the journey at the change point.

High Altitude Cerebral Edema (HACE) High Altitude Cerebral Edema (sometimes spelled Oedema). A very serious condition caused by swelling of the brain due to fluid accumulation as a result of high altitude exposure. It is characterised by blinding headaches and loss of co-ordination (ataxia), and requires immediate descent and medical attention. > *HAPE*.

High Altitude Pulmonary Edema (HAPE) High Altitude Pulmonary Edema (sometimes spelt Oedema). A very serious condition caused by liquid collecting in the lungs as a result of high altitude exposure. It is characterised by extreme shortness of breath (even after rest) and gurgling or bubbling sounds in the lungs, and requires immediate descent and medical attention. > *HACE*.

high latitudes The areas of the earth near the poles.

high road A main road.

high seas The open seas, not within the jurisdiction of any state or country.

high season The busiest time for the use of a travel facility.

H

H

high tide See *high water*.

high water The tide at its fullest.

high water mark An indicator showing the level reached at high water.

higher intermediate points An airline fare construction principle that applies if a multi-sector journey passes through a point to which, from the point of origin, the fare is higher than it is to the ultimate destination. In such cases, an adjustment to the fare may need to be made.

highway A public road.

hijacking The taking control by force of a vehicle, usually an aircraft.

hill A raised area of ground, less high than a mountain.

hill station A government settlement, originally used for officials' holidays during the summer, in the higher areas of India, Malaysia and Sri Lanka.

hill walking grades See *climbing grades*.

hill walking The activity which involves exploring countryside, moorland, wilderness or mountain terrain by foot, generally following established pathways and making use of equipment such as hiking boots and waterproofs and skills such as navigation and route planning.

Himalayas The mountain range in Asia that separates the Indian sub-continent from China.

Hinduism The religion of the Hindus, based on the belief in Brahma as the absolute, all-embracing spirit, mainly followed in the Indian sub-continent. > *religion*.

hinterland 1. The geographical area beyond a coast or river banks.
2. An area served by a port or other transport hub.

Hispaniola An island in the Greater Antilles in the Caribbean, divided between the Dominican Republic and Haiti.

historical attraction Any attraction that derives interest from its historical significance.

hitchhike To travel by soliciting lifts in passing vehicles. This is against the law in some places.

Hittite The civilisation of ancient Turkey (c.2000BC to c.1200BC).

HIV A complex, infectious and often fatal viral disease, endemic worldwide but particularly prevalent in parts of sub-Saharan Africa, passed on by sexual intercourse and contaminated blood. > *health precautions*.

HMA Hotel Marketing Association. *See Appendix 5a.*

HMS When placed in front of a ship's name means Her/His Majesty's Ship: used for vessels in the Royal Navy.

hold The area in a ship or aircraft where the baggage or cargo is stored.

hold baggage Baggage that is checked in by an air passenger and generally placed in the hold.

Holi A festival in the Hindu religious calendar, also known as the Carnival of Colour, celebrated at the time of the full moon in March.

holiday Any time away from the normal working environment, or a trip taken away during such time.

holiday camp Now usually referred to as holiday centres. Mainly a UK phenomenon which developed after the 1935 Holiday Pay Act. Holiday camps or centres now offer a high-grade product, with many entertainment and other facilities included.

Holiday Care *See Appendix 5b.*

holiday centre *See holiday camp.*

holiday complex *See holiday camp.*

holidaymaker A person on holiday.

Home counties The counties immediately surrounding London.

home port The port from which a ship originates.

home town The town of one's birth, early life or fixed residence.

homeland A person's native land.

Hong Kong A Special Administrative Region of the People's Republic of China since 1997, although it is still often regarded as a separate travel destination.

horizon The point at which the earth and sky appear to meet.

horizontal integration The expansion of an organisation by its move into associated areas of activity, but not those areas connected with the work done by its suppliers or distributors. In travel, for example, an airline might decide to buy a hotel chain.

Horn of Africa The part of north-eastern Somalia which protrudes into the Gulf of Aden, and which is the easternmost part of the African mainland.

hors d'oeuvres The first course of a meal.

horse latitudes The two regions of calm located at 30° north and at 30° south of the Equator.

hospitality 1. Those people and organisations that are involved in the accommodation and catering sectors. 2. The business of entertaining others, generally for commercial gain.

hospitality suite A hotel room used for entertainment or meetings, rather than sleeping.

host location A head office or branch office to which a satellite ticket printer is connected and controlled.

hostal A Spanish term for a small hotel or guest house.

hostel A form of comparatively basic and generally non-serviced accommodation available throughout the world. The sleeping arrangements are usually in dormitory-style. Self-catering facilities may also be available. > *youth hostel.*

hostelry 1. (UK) A colloquial term for a pub. 2. (US) A small inn.

hotel 1. An establishment providing accommodation and meals. A hotel would be expected to provide a greater and/or superior range of facilities than establishments such as guest houses. 2. (Australia & New Zealand) A public house.

hotel register The list of guests who are staying or have stayed at a hotel. These days it is usually computerised, although written ledgers still exist.

hotel representative An organisation that represents a number of hotels. This enables travel agents and independent brokers to obtain information and make bookings more easily.

hotelier A hotel manager, operator or owner.

hourglass skis *See carving skis.*

house limit The maximum amount of credit that will be extended to a guest at a hotel or similar, or a casino, before full or partial payment of the amount owing is requested.

H

H

house wine Wine, often of average quality and usually the cheapest on the restaurant's list, sold in bottles or carafes.

houseboat A boat fitted out as living accommodation.

house-flag The flag indicating to which company a ship belongs.

hovercraft Otherwise known as an air cushion vehicle (ACV). A vehicle that travels on a cushion of air, constrained by a flexible skirt, rather than being in contact with ground or water. Although hovercraft are considered to be flying vehicles, they are only able to travel at a maximum height of a few feet, as determined by the skirt depth.

hoverport A port for hovercraft.

hovertrain A tracked air cushion vehicle.

HTF *See SSC, Appendix 5a.*

hub and spoke The use of a central base (the hub) from which connecting transport links operate to outlying areas (the spokes). > *interchange point.*

Hudson Bay 1. A large bay in north-eastern Canada.
2. The previous name for the rail service between Winnipeg and Churchill in Canada.

hull The body or frame of a ship or aircraft.

human geography The branch of geography that deals with the effects of human activity on the earth's surface and vice versa.

Human Immunodeficiency Virus *See HIV.*

Humboldt Current A cold current flowing north along the west coast of South America and cooling the coastal region as far as the Equator.

humidity A measure of the amount of moisture in the air. Higher levels of humidity are uncomfortable since sweat is less able to evaporate from the skin and its cooling effect is therefore reduced. The relative humidity of the air is expressed as a percentage, with 100% being the maximum amount of moisture the air can hold at a given temperature. As hot air can hold more moisture than cold air, 100% humidity at 30°C contains more moisture than 100% at 15°C. Various medical bodies have described the comfort level for an average person as being between 30 and 70% relative humidity, within which range many places (both indoor and outdoor) comfortably sit. A notable exception is the passenger cabin of a typical aircraft at cruising altitude, where the relative humidity can fall to as low as 1%.

hummock A small hill.

hurricane A storm with winds in excess of 64 knots. Hurricanes usually occur in tropical areas, since they need plenty of sun to provide their power. > *Beaufort scale.*

hydraulic test The process of pressure-testing a diving cylinder in order to assess its suitability for further use as a container of high pressure gas.

hydrofoils 1. The foils or wings attached to the hull of a specially designed vessel. Once sufficient speed has been attained, the vessel rises until its hull is clear of the water and is supported on the wings.
2. A ship or boat fitted with hydrofoils. Such vessels can travel at much higher speeds than conventional ships.

hydrogen A light, highly inflammable gas that was originally the first choice for giving buoyancy to lighter-than-air aircraft. Accidents caused by fire were common and hydrogen is no longer used for this purpose.

hydrography The science of surveying the

waters of the earth and the adjacent land area, usually for the purpose of producing navigational maps and charts.

hydroplane A light, fast motorboat designed to skim over the water.

hypersonic Over five times the speed of sound.

hyperventilation Unusually deep or rapid breathing, often a result of panic.

hypothermia Reduced body core temperature.

hypoxia Reduced levels of oxygen within the body. A risk to travellers at extreme altitudes or in certain diving situations.

H

Ii

IAGTO   International Association of Golf Tour Operators. *See Appendix 5a.*

IATA Traffic Area   *See Area.*

IATA   International Air Transport Association. *See Appendix 5d.*

IATAN   International Airlines Travel Agent Network. *See Appendix 5b.*

IATM   International Association of Tour Managers. *See Appendix 5a.*

Iberia   The peninsula in Western Europe occupied by Andorra, Gibraltar, Portugal and Spain.

Iberian   Of or relating to Iberia.

ICCA   International Congress and Conference Association. *See Appendix 5d.*

ICE   The high-speed inter-city train services connecting many of the major cities in Germany.

ice axe   A tool used to assist climbers. There are 'walking', 'climbing' and 'general mountaineering' axes. Walking axes are usually longer than the others and are used more as a walking stick is used and provide added security when travelling on snow or ice. The others are shorter and not suitable for walking on level ground, and need some instruction to be used safely.

ice climbing   The ascent of cliffs, crags, icefalls and mountains by means of climbing steep sections of snow, ice (and sometimes rock), requiring the use of specialist tools like ice axes and crampons. Usually regarded as more dangerous than rock climbing due to instabilities in snow or ice, winter weather conditions and lack of 'gear' placements.

ice gully   A gully that has become frozen and can now only be accessed with appropriate climbing tools.

ice-boat   A boat-like vessel mounted on runners and able to travel on ice.

ice-climbing grades   *See climbing grades.*

IDL   *See International Date Line.*

IFTO   International Federation of Tour Operators. *See Appendix 5a.*

IFTTA   International Forum of Travel and Tourism Advocates. *See Appendix 5b.*

igloo   A dome-shaped house made of ice, as built by the Inuit (Eskimo) peoples.

IIT   Independent inclusive tour. A tailor-made arrangement put together to meet the specific needs of a customer.

ILAM   Institute of Leisure and Amenity Management. *See Appendix 5a.*

immigrant   A person living or working in a country other than their own.

immigration   1. The act of entering a country with the intention of settling there permanently.
2. The area in an airport or other

international transport terminal where passengers show their identity and travel documents and are given permission to enter or leave the country.

imperial 1. Of or relating to an empire or similar state.
2. Of or relating to the non-metric system of weights and measures, a form of which is still officially used in the USA. Some aspects of it (such as pints and miles) are still officially used in the UK; unofficially, so are many others. > *Appendix 6.*

implant A business travel agency employee working in the customer's own location, usually to undertake that customer's business travel exclusively.

import To bring items into a country.

inaugural The first time of use of a new aircraft, route or similar product, service or vehicle.

inboard Within the sides or towards the middle of a ship, aircraft or other vehicle.

inbound 1. A flight or other travel service arriving at an airport, port or other transport terminus.
2. The return leg of a package holiday flight.

inbound tour operator *See incoming tour operator.*

Inca Of or relating to the South American Indian people whose empire, centred on Peru, lasted from c.1100 to the 1530s.

incentive commission A bonus commission paid to an agent in order to encourage extra sales. Usually such commission will be paid once an agreed sales target is reached

inch A unit of measurement in the imperial system equal to approximately 2.5 cm. Usually abbreviated to in. or ". (Note that the latter symbol is also used to denote a second of a minute of a degree.)

incidentals Minor items of expenditure that are too small to be worth detailing.

inclusive rate A tariff for a hotel room, meal or similar in which all costs such as taxes, gratuities and cover charges are included.

inclusive resort An accommodation and leisure complex which aims to satisfy as many of the requirements of its visitors as possible on the one site.

inclusive tour *See package holiday.*

inclusive tour excursion fare A fare designed to be part of an inclusive package which would, in theory, also include accommodation.

incoming tour operator A tour operator that specialises in supplying services, such as ground arrangements, for visitors to a country.

incoming tourism Tourism coming into a country from another country.

Indaba A Zulu word for a gathering. Now also used as the name for an annual tourism marketplace held in South Africa.

indemnify To make good a loss.

indemnity Compensation for a loss. > *travel insurance.*

indemnity basis A principle used by the insurance business for valuing a lost or stolen item, and generally regarded as the replacement cost less wear-and-tear.

independent 1. (UK) A travel agency group with less than five outlets.
2. A traveller who makes his own ground arrangements rather than travelling as part of a package or tour.
3. A hotel or other property not a member of or affiliated to a group pr chain.

index An alphabetical list of entries in a book.

Indian Ocean   *See oceans.*

Indian Pacific   The rail service between Sydney and Perth in Australia.

Indic   1. The civilisation of the region around the Indus and Ganges rivers (c.3000BC to c.AD500). 2. The language of this group.

indicator   *See global indicator.*

indigenous   Belonging to or originating from a country or region.

indirect routing   A routing going via a point or points that it need not necessarily take. Indirect routings may be made necessary through lack of suitable services or through passenger inclination.

Indochina   The geographical region comprising Cambodia, Laos, peninsular Malaysia, Myanmar, Singapore, Thailand and Vietnam.

industrial attraction   A tourist attraction that capitalises on its connection with industry, usually historical.

ineligible   Not entitled or allowed.

infant   A child who has not yet reached the age at which child fares will be charged and who may be allowed to travel free. This will vary from service to service, but for most airlines an infant is anyone under two years old. > *child.*

inflatable   (or **inflatable dinghy**) A small boat made from rubber or a similar material that can be easily carried and is inflated when needed for use.

in-flight catering   The food and beverage services provided on board an aircraft. On most airlines the cost is included in the fare, but on some no-frills airlines an extra charge is made.

in-flight entertainment   Those services, such as films, music and magazines which are available to passengers during a flight.

informal   Without ceremony or formality. When referring to an event it usually refers to the style of dress expected.

information display   Any system for making information available to a customer or an audience.

information technology   The use of computers for recording, storing, analysing and displaying information.

infrastructure   The underlying, man-made framework of a place, such as buildings, roads, railways, telecommunication lines, sewers, and water and power supplies.

inhabit   To dwell in or occupy.

inhospitable   Uninviting or otherwise unwelcoming.

in-house   Provision of goods or services from within a company or institution.

inland   Situated in the interior of a country or state.

inlet   A small arm of water penetrating the land.

inn   (UK) A public house which may also provide accommodation.

inoculation   An alternative name for vaccination.

in-plant   *See implant.*

insalubrious   Of a climate or place, unhealthy.

inshore   At sea, but close to the shore.

inside cabin   A ship's cabin that has no window or porthole and thus no natural light.

insular   Like or relating to an island.

insurable interest The insurance principle that states that a person cannot insure against a risk in which they have no direct interest.

insurance premium The sum taken by an insurance company from a proposer in order to accept the risk. As a rule, the higher the risk the greater the sum required.

interchange point Any point on a public transport network where passengers may change services. > *hub and spoke.*

inter-city Existing or travelling between cities. Sometimes used as a generic term for transport services offering rapid conveyance between major points.

intercontinental Existing, involving or conducted between two or more continents.

interior Inland and remote from the coast or frontier.

interline A co-operative administrative arrangement between two or more carriers. This facilitates more streamlined ticket sales, flight connections, check-in and baggage handling.

internal Existing, involving or conducted within a single nation or state.

internal combustion engine An engine, using petrol or diesel fuel, that develops its power by means of controlled burning of the fuel in enclosed cylinders. Most cars and motorcycles are driven by internal combustion engines.

international Existing, involving or conducted between two or more nations.

International Date Line (IDL) An imaginary line, based on the line of 180° longitude, which runs through the Pacific Ocean, on the east side of which the date is one day earlier than on the west. The IDL does not follow the line of 180° exactly but deviates to avoid cutting through certain countries, in the same way that the other time zones do. > *UTC, time zones, Greenwich meridian, GMT.*

international departures *See international outbound tourism.*

International fare expenditure A term defined by the WTO as being 'any payment made to carriers registered abroad by any person resident in the compiling country'.

International fare receipts A term defined by the WTO as being 'any payment made to the carriers registered in the compiling country of sums owed by non-resident visitors, whether or not travelling to that country.'

international outbound tourism (Also **international departures**) A term defined by the WTO as being 'the visits that each person makes from their country of usual residence to any other country for any purpose other than exercising a remunerated activity in the country visited'. Note that the term 'tourism' refers to travellers generally, rather than those travelling purely for pleasure. > *tourism, international visitors.*

international tourism *See tourism.*

international tourism expenditure A term defined by the WTO as being 'expenditure of outbound visitors in other countries including their payments to foreign carriers for international transport.' This is normally expressed in US$. For various reasons, fare payments are often expressed as separate items on many travel and tourism statistics. Each country may have different ways of calculating expenditure. Note that the term 'tourism' refers to travellers generally, rather than those travelling purely for pleasure. International tourism expenditure is classed as an export by the country concerned. > *tourism.*

international tourism receipts A term defined by the WTO as being 'expenditure of international inbound visitors including their payments to national carriers for international transport. They should also include any other prepayments made for goods and services received in the destination country'. This is normally expressed in US$. For various reasons, fare receipts are often expressed as separate items on many travel and tourism statistics. Each country may have different ways of calculating receipts. Note that the term 'tourism' refers to travellers generally, rather than those travelling purely for pleasure. International tourism receipts are classed as imports by the country concerned.

According to the WTO, US$463 billion international tourism receipts were recorded worldwide in 2001 (a fall of 2.6% over 2000). > *tourism.*

international tourists See *international visitors.*

international visitors (Also **international tourists**) The official distinction between 'visitors' and 'tourists' is problematic for many reasons and open to many different interpretations. The WTO defines an international visitor as being 'any person who travels to a country other than that in which she/he has her/his usual residence but outside her/his usual environment for a period not exceeding 12 months and whose main purpose of visit is other than the exercise of an activity remunerated from within the country visited'. The distinction between people who visit wholly for pleasure, those who visit wholly for business and the people who mix both cannot easily be separated by this definition. Where they bother to do so, different countries will have different ways of attempting to record these differences. The WTO subdivides international visitor into: a) a tourist (overnight visitor) – a visitor who stays at least one night in collective or private accommodation in the country visited; and b) a same-day visitor – a visitor who does not spend the night in a collective or private accommodation in the country visited. For some countries, same-day visitors will be particularly numerous, and may therefore inflate the arrival statistics out of proportion to the amount of time or money actually spent by visitors in the country in question.

In addition, it must be remembered that WTO figures relate to the number of arrivals and not to the number of persons. The same person who makes several trips to a given country during a given period will be counted as a new arrival each time, while a person who travels through several countries on one trip is counted as a new arrival at each frontier crossing. Due to the different methods used by different countries to collect data, international visitors may sometimes be determined by international arrivals at frontiers (including or excluding same-day visitors), or by international tourist arrivals at hotels and similar establishments. The abolition of frontier controls as a result of such developments as the Schengen Agreement (affecting, amongst others, France, Italy and Spain, three of the four most visited countries in the world) has made the problems of statistical calculation more acute. According to the data released in June 2002 by the WTO Secretariat, international tourist arrivals amounted to 693 million in 2001 (a fall of 0.6% compared to 2000). > *tourism.*

Internationale Tourismus-Börse See *ITB.*

interoceanic Between or connecting two or more oceans.

interprovincial Existing, involving or conducted between two or more provinces.

interstate 1. (US) A motorway crossing a state boundary. In the USA, interstates that have a two-digit even number tend to run east-west; those that have a two-digit

odd number tend to run north-south; and those that have a three-digit odd number are beltways around cities.
2. Existing, involving or conducted between two or more states.

Inuit   Of or relating to the Eskimo people, particularly those of northern Canada, and their language.

Inupiaq   The Eskimo-Aleut languages spoken in northern Canada, Alaska and Greenland.

Inupiat   Of or relating to the Eskimo people of Alaska.

invalid   1. Not valid for use (pronounced in-*valid*).
2. A person who is less able through disease or injury and will need special help or care when travelling (pronounced *in*-valid).

invalidate   To make a document invalid for use.

invisible exports   Items, such as services, that require the transfer of funds into a country but that do not involve the actual movement of goods. Incoming tourism is an example of an invisible export since such tourists bring funds into the country.

invisible imports   Items, such as services, that require the transfer of funds out of a country but that do not involve the actual movement of goods. Outgoing tourism is an example of an invisible import since such tourists take funds out of the country.

involuntary change   An alteration to an airline passenger's journey that has been brought about by circumstances beyond their control. The passenger should not lose the benefit of any special fares or concessions granted, even if the involuntary change results in the ticket being invalidated.

IPA   International phonetic alphabet. *See* *phonetic alphabet.*

Ireland   1. An island situated in the west of the British Isles, which includes the Republic of Ireland and the six counties of Northern Ireland, politically part of the United Kingdom.
2. The Republic of Ireland.

Irminger Current   The northernmost arm of the Gulf Stream.

Iron Curtain   The name given to the division of Europe along ideological grounds which existed between 1945 and the early 1990s.

Islam   The religion of the Muslims, based on the teachings of the Prophet Mohamed. > *religion.*

island   A piece of land, other than a continent, entirely surrounded by water.

island-hop   To travel from island to island.

Isle of Man   An island in the Irish Sea between Great Britain and Ireland. It is a British Crown Dependency and not part of the United Kingdom, although close ties are maintained.

islet   A small island.

isobar   A line drawn on a weather map that joins points of equal barometric pressure.

isolated   Remote or cut off.

isopleth   A line on a weather map joining points with an equal incidence of a particular meteorological feature.

isotherm   A line drawn on a weather map joining points of equal temperature.

Israeli   Of or relating to the modern state of Israel.

issue   Of documents, to prepare by writing or printing, ready for handing over to a customer.

issuing carrier The airline or other operator whose ticket is issued, or in whose name it is issued.

isthmus A narrow strip of land joining two larger land masses.

IT 1. *See inclusive tour.*
2. *See information technology.*

ITAA Irish Travel Agents Association. *See Appendix 5c.*

ITB Internationale Tourismus-Börse, one of the most important travel exhibitions in the world, held in Berlin in March each year. Attendance is generally restricted to persons connected with the travel industry.

itinerary 1. A journey.

2. The details of a customer's travel arrangements such as modes of transport, dates, times and destinations.

ITM Institute of Travel Management. *See Appendix 5a.*

ITMA Incentive Travel & Meetings Association Ltd. *See Appendix 5a.*

ITOA Irish Incoming Tour Operators Association. *See Appendix 5a.*

ITT Institute of Travel & Tourism. *See Appendix 5a.*

ITX *See inclusive tour excursion fare.*

Ivory Coast 1. The coast of Côte d'Ivoire, formerly popular with traders in ivory.
2. The former name of Côte d'Ivoire.

Jj

jack A ship's flag, especially one flown from the bow. It generally indicates the ship's nationality.

jackstaff A small mast set at the bow of a ship on which a jack is hoisted.

jackstaff The staff at the bow of a ship that carries the jack.

Japan Current A warm-water current in the Pacific Ocean, the equivalent of the Atlantic's Gulf Stream.

Japanese encephalitis A viral disease transmitted by mosquitoes and endemic in certain parts of Asia. > *health precautions.*

JATA Japan Association of Travel Agents. *See Appendix 5c.*

jeepney A small bus especially common in the Philippines. Many were originally built from old US Jeeps.

Jerusalem One of the three holy cities of Islam (Mecca and Medina being the others), and also of central importance to both Christianity and Judaism, situated between the Mediterranean Sea and the Dead Sea.

jet aircraft An aircraft powered by jet engines. The first jet airliner was the De Havilland Comet, introduced in the 1950s, but it was the adoption of larger jets like the Boeing 707, and the rapid increase in runway length and airport facilities to accommodate them, that created a dramatic increase in worldwide air travel.

jet engine An engine that relies on the continuous burning of fuel to provide thrust and/or power to drive a propeller. The jet turbine engine was invented in the 1930s but the first jet aircraft did not fly until the end of the Second World War.

jet lag A temporary discomfort suffered by passengers who fly across a number of time zones in one journey. Dehydration, disruption of sleep patterns, lack of exercise and daylight, too much food and too many diuretics such as tea, coffee and alcohol can all contribute to this.

jet set A colloquial term for groups of wealthy and socially prominent people who supposedly travel from place to place by jet in search of enjoyment.

jet ski A water vehicle designed to carry one or two persons and propelled by a jet of water. These are usually controlled by handlebars similar to those on a motorcycle, and are thus often referred to as 'wet bikes'. Since they have no wheels, this expression is obviously nonsensical.

jet stream A high-speed air current. Pilots often take advantage of jet streams to increase the speed of their aircraft without having to burn extra fuel.

jetfoil A hydrofoil vessel, powered by water jets.

jetsam Discarded material thrown overboard at sea, especially when deliberately jettisoned to lighten the vessel. Normally used in conjunction with flotsam.

J

jetty 1. A pier or breakwater. A landing jetty is one that passengers can use for embarkation and disembarkation.
2. The extensions at airports where aircraft park and load. These are sometimes called bridges.

Jew A person of the Jewish faith.

jib A triangular sail extending from the outer end of the bowsprit to the top of the mast of a boat or ship.

John O'Groats The north-easternmost point of mainland Britain, in Caithness, Scotland.

jolly-boat A type of ship's boat, smaller than a cutter.

journey To travel from one place to another for any reason, and the act of so travelling.

joystick A colloquial name for the control column of an aircraft.

Judaic Of or relating to Jews or Judaism.

Judaism The religion of the Jews.
> *religion*.

jumbo jet The colloquial term applied to large, wide-bodied aircraft, in particular the Boeing 747.

jump jet A jet aircraft that can take off vertically.

jump seat An aircraft seat, often foldaway, used by crew members during take-off and landing.

junction A point where a road or railway meet, join or cross.

jungle An area of very dense vegetation, especially in tropical areas.

jungle fever Severe malaria.

junior suite Accommodation usually with one room with a sitting area at one end.

junk A flat-bottomed sailing vessel typically used in China.

junket A slang expression for a trip offered at the expense of a principal to thank its customers and hopefully gain new business.

junta A political or military group or faction that takes power after a revolution or coup d'état.

J

Kk

kala-azar A tropical parasitic disease transmitted by sandflies.

Karoo (or **Karroo**) An elevated, semi-desert, plateau in South Africa.

kasbah The Arab quarter surrounding a North African castle.

kayak Originally an Eskimo canoe, but now used to describe any similar type of vessel.

keel A horizontal structure, usually of steel, that runs the length of the bottom of a ship. It could be considered the ship's backbone and is the base from which all other parts are built.

keelboat 1. A yacht with a permanent keel.
2. (US) A large flat riverboat

keelson A line of timber fastening a ship's floor-timbers to the keel.

Kelvin A scale of temperature with the same graduations as those used in centigrade, but with absolute zero (minus 273°C) used as its starting point. The freezing point of water is 273°K.

kerosene 1. (US) Paraffin, as used in some domestic heaters.
2. The fuel used by jet aircraft.

key *See cay.*

key card A small card, similar to a credit card, used instead of a room key in some hotels.

Khamsin An oppressive, hot, south or south-easterly wind occurring in the eastern Mediterranean which can contribute to dust storms.

Kharif The rainy season in northern India and Arab countries.

Khmer 1. The civilisation of ancient Cambodia (c.AD100 to 1432).
2. A native of modern Cambodia.

kibbutz A communal settlement in Israel.

kilo- A prefix commonly mound in the metric system, meaning one thousand times. Thus a kilowatt is 1,000 watts.

kilogram (or **kilo**) A weight of 1,000 grams, or approximately 2.2 imperial pounds.

kilometre A length of 1,000m or approximately 0.62 of a statute mile.

king *See monarch.*

king room A hotel room with a king-sized bed.

kingdom A country with a monarch as its head of state.

Kingston The capital of Jamaica. Not to be confused with Kingstown, the capital of St Vincent & the Grenadines.

Kingstown The capital of St Vincent & the Grenadines. Not to be confused with Kingston, the capital of Jamaica.

K

klong A canal in Thailand.

kloof A steep-sided ravine in South Africa.

knap The summit of a hill.

knoll A small hill.

knot Nautical miles per hour. 20 knots is approximately 23 mph.

Kona Coast Part of the south-west coast of the island of Hawaii, also known as the Gold Coast.

Korea, Democratic People's Republic of North Korea.

Korea, Republic of South Korea.

korridorzuge A term used in German-speaking countries for a type of train service in that travels through another country in a special 'corridor' of track, within which it may not stop to pick up or set down passengers. This type of routing will avoid the circuitous journey that would otherwise be necessary, such as that from Innsbruck to Salzburg.

kosher Food and drink prepared in accordance with the Jewish law. The term is often used loosely to describe anything that is true or genuine.

kremlin A citadel within a Russian town.

Kremlin The seat of the Russian government in the centre of Moscow.

Kurds The Aryan peoples living in parts of Iraq, Iran, Turkey and Syria.

Kuroshio A warm current that brings tropical waters northward past Japan. Almost the equivalent of the Atlantic's Gulf Stream.

kyle A Scottish name for a narrow channel between an island and another island or the mainland.

K

Ll

La Niña The opposite phenomenon to El Niño that also causes significant global climatic changes. La Niña is characterised by unusually cool water temperatures on the equatorial regions of the central and eastern Pacific.

La Palma One of the Canary Islands. Not to be confused with Las Palmas de Gran Canaria, capital of the island of Gran Canaria, also in the Canary Islands.

Labrador Current A current bringing cold water and icebergs down from Baffin Bay. Where it meets the Gulf Stream of Newfoundland, the mixing of the waters gives rise to the fogs that affect the Grand Banks for around 120 days each year.

Labrador Sea The area of the North Atlantic Ocean between southern Greenland and Labrador in Canada.

ladder The form of fare construction box on airline tickets in which the calculations are shown vertically.

lagoon An enclosed body of water, usually sea, such as the centre of an atoll.

lake A large body of fresh water surrounded by land.

Lake Shore Ltd A train service in the USA running between Chicago, and New York and Boston.

lanai A Hawaiian term for a room with a balcony or patio, usually overlooking water or gardens.

land arrangements Another name for ground arrangements.

land breeze A breeze blowing off the land onto the sea.

land bridge A neck of land joining two land masses.

land mass A single large body of land, such as a continent.

Land of the Midnight Sun *See Lapland.*

land yacht A vehicle with wheels and a sail used for recreational purposes on beaches and sand flats. Sometimes called a sand yacht.

Land's End The south-westernmost point of mainland Britain, in Cornwall, England.

landau A four-wheeled enclosed horse-drawn carriage with a rear hood that can be lowered.

landfall The first sighting of land after a sea journey.

landing card A document which sometimes needs to be completed by passengers before arrival at a foreign destination to facilitate progress through immigration.

landing gear The wheels of an aircraft. Also known as the undercarriage.

landing stage A platform, often floating, onto which passengers may disembark

L

from a vessel.

landing strip An aircraft runway, often small and away from an airport and possibly grass-covered.

landlocked A country or region with no coastline.

landmark A conspicuous building or topographical feature that is easily recognised from a distance.

landscape The natural scenery or view of an area.

landside That part of an airport open to any legitimate visitor; the area before customs and other controls.

landward Towards the land.

langlauf Cross-country skiing.

Lapland A region of Northern Europe mainly within the Arctic Circle, traditionally the home of Father Christmas. It consists of the northern parts of Norway, Finland, Sweden and the Russian Kola Peninsula. Also sometimes known as the Land of the Midnight Sun.

Lapp A member of the nomadic Mongol peoples of northern Scandinavia. The term Sami is now the preferred name.

Las Palmas (Las Palmas de Gran Canaria) The capital of the island of Gran Canaria in the Canary Islands. Not to be confused with the nearby island of La Palma.

Lassa fever A serious viral disease of tropical Africa.

last quarter 1. The phase of the lunar cycle, 21 days after the new moon, when the moon appears as a half-circle.
2. The last quarter of any type of year (such as calendar, financial or accounting), usually beginning on the first day of a month. The term fourth quarter is often used for this. Quarters

are commonly used periods for measuring company performances.

last seat availability The facility available on GDSs to give information regarding limited availability of airline seats.

late booking A vague term that means any booking that is made only a short while before travel. The period will vary according to the service booked. For example, an inclusive holiday booked a week before departure would probably be considered late; an air ticket from London to Paris booked by a business traveller at similar notice would probably not.

lateen sail A triangular sail on a long yard at an angle of 45° to the mast. Commonly used on Arab dhows.

Latin 1. The language of the Roman Empire, medieval Europe and still, for some purposes, of the Roman Catholic church.
2. A general description of anything relating to the peoples or countries using languages which developed from Latin.

Latin America All of the Americas south of the USA. The term sometimes excludes the few countries in this area where Spanish or Portuguese are not the official languages.

latitude, lines of (or **parallels of**) Any of the imaginary circles drawn around the earth at right angles to earth's axis. The lines of latitude are expressed in relation to the Equator, which runs around the globe at its widest point and is approximately 40,076 km (24,902 miles) in length. This is said to be at 0° latitude: the other lines of latitude run parallel to the Equator and are numbered in degrees north or south. Both the northern and southern parallels end at the poles at 90° north and 90° south respectively. Lines of latitude are parallel to each other, but are not all of equal length. Each division of one degree (divided into 60 minutes) is 60 nautical miles (approximately 110 km or 69 miles) apart; their lengths progressively diminish as they approach the poles. > *longitude, lines of.*

launch   A motor boat, sometimes used to carry passengers from ship to shore.

lavatory   Another name for a toilet or rest-room.

lay-by   (UK) An area by a road where vehicles may stop.

layover   A period of rest or waiting time between one part of a journey and the next.

LCA   Leading Cruise Agents of the UK. *See Appendix 5a.*

LDW   *See vehicle rental insurance.*

Le Shuttle   *See Eurotunnel.*

le surf   A French expression for snowboarding.

league   1. A group of people, cities, nations or other organisations combining for a particular purpose.
2. An old-fashioned measure of distance equal to three miles.

lee   The direction away from the wind. Sometimes referred to as leeward.

leeward   *See lee.*

Leeward Islands   The group of Caribbean Islands that includes: Anguilla, Antigua and Barbuda, Dominica, Guadeloupe, Monserrat, Saba, St. Eustatius, St. Kitts & Nevis and St. Maarten/St Martin.

leeway   1. The sideways drift of a ship to the lee of its desired course.
2. An allowable deviation or freedom of action.

left luggage   (UK) Luggage temporarily deposited in a storeroom or locker specially designated for that purpose.

left, driving on the   The practice followed by traffic in the UK, the Channel Islands, the Isle of Man, Ireland, Malta, the English-speaking states of the Caribbean Sea, the Indian Ocean and the Atlantic Ocean, Surinam, Guyana, most of East and Southern Africa, the Indian sub-continent, Australia, New Zealand, Hong Kong, Macau, Japan, parts of South-East Asia, and most of the states of the South Pacific; over 60 countries, territories and dependencies in all. Traffic elsewhere drives on the right.

leg   The journey between two consecutive scheduled stops.

legal advice and expenses insurance   *See travel insurance.*

legend   1. An event or story which has no provable basis in fact.
2. A panel on or near a map or chart which provides explanations of any symbols and abbreviations used.

lei   A Polynesian garland of flowers, traditionally placed around the necks of visitors to these Pacific islands.

leishmaniasis   Any one of a number of parasitic diseases cause by the bite of sandflies.

leisure   Free time or time at one's disposal.

leisure travel agent   A travel agent dealing mainly with holidaymakers, rather than business travellers. > *travel agent.*

leisure traveller   A traveller who is not travelling on business or for some other obligatory reason.

Lent   A period of 40 weekdays between Ash Wednesday and Easter Eve, traditionally a time of fasting and self-denial among Christians.

L

leprosy A slightly contagious disease that affects the nerves causing loss of sensation and consequent damage and disfigurement through unfelt injury. Still common in some Third World countries although easily treatable.

Lesser Antilles The group of Caribbean Islands comprising the Leeward Islands, the Virgin Islands, the Windward Islands and the small chain of Venezuelan islands east of Bonaire, and also the islands of Aruba, Barbados, Curaçao and Trinidad & Tobago.

Levant A former name for the area of the eastern Mediterranean now occupied by Syria, Lebanon, Israel and Palestine NAR.

Leveche A hot, dry and dusty wind in southern Spain which blows from the Sahara. > *Sirocco.*

levee (US) An embankment alongside a river, or surrounding a field that is to be irrigated.

level crossing An intersection where a railway crosses a road on the level.

levy A tax or toll.

LGV The dedicated high-speed lines (*lignes à grande vitesse*) on which French high-speed trains operate some of their services. (Some are also run on normal track). >*TGV.*

liability insurance supplement *See vehicle rental insurance.*

licensed premises (UK) A place such as a pub that is permitted to sell alcoholic drinks.

lido deck The deck of a ship that contains the swimming pool and sunbathing area.

lien A right over another's property in order to protect a debt.

life jacket A buoyant outer garment that keeps the wearer afloat in water.

lifebelt (UK) *See lifebuoy.*

lifeboat A small boat carried on board a ship to evacuate passengers in the case of serious emergency. It is a maritime regulation that all ships must carry enough lifeboats to accommodate all those aboard.

lifeboat drill An obligatory demonstration of the safety procedures on board a ship.

lifebuoy A buoyant support, often a ring, that will keep a person afloat in water.

lifeline A line which connects a diver to a point on the surface.

life-raft A raft carried on board a ship to provide an alternative or additional safety measure.

life-support systems The systems of air-conditioning, pressurisation, heating and the like that allow passengers to survive in a hostile environment, such as at a high altitude.

lift 1. The force generated by an aircraft's wings that enables it to fly.
2. (UK) An elevator, used for people or goods.

lift pass *See lift ticket.*

lift ticket (or **lift pass, ski pass**) (US) A ticket that allows the holder to use some or all of the lifts at one or more ski areas for an agreed period of time, sometimes for the entire season. Lift tickets are increasingly sophisticated and the latest versions electronically open turnstiles to allow access to a lift without needing to be removed from the user's pocket. Some act in the same way as credit cards and can be used in mountain restaurants, recharged with credit, sometimes using the internet or a mobile telephone. The terms lift pass and ski pass are more widely used in the UK and Europe.

light air *See Beaufort scale.*

light breeze *See Beaufort scale.*

light railway A railway, often narrow gauge, constructed to less demanding standards than normal and designed to cope only with light traffic.

lighter A small boat used to transfer goods between ships or to the shore.

lighter-than-air An aircraft that weighs less than the air it displaces: in other words, one that can float in the air. Such aircraft can remain in the air indefinitely without the need for engine power.

lightning A high-voltage, naturally occurring electrical discharge between clouds and other clouds or the earth.

limited 1. Of accommodation generally, when only a small amount of space remains available for sale.
2. A service, often rail, where the number of passengers is restricted to the amount of seating or other accommodation available. Usually such services require advance reservation. In the US the name is sometimes given to any long-distance luxury rail service.
3. A common form of company incorporation whereby the liability of the directors for the company's debts is limited to the extent of their investment.

limited mileage A car rental tariff whereby a certain number of miles or kilometres is included in the cost of the rental, each additional mile or kilometre thereafter being charged for at a fixed rate.

limo A colloquial term for limousine.

limousine An enclosed motor car, originally one with a division between driver and passengers, but the term is now often used casually to refer to any luxurious vehicle.

liner A large passenger ship, traditionally used for long-distance voyages.

link span A type of complex loading bridge used at ports and harbours which can be adjusted to allow for tidal height variations, such as occur in the Channel ports of Dover and Calais.

liqueur A spirit, usually sweetened and highly flavoured, traditionally drunk after meals.

liquor 1. (US) Alcoholic drink.
2. The broth, sauce or gravy in which meat has been cooked.

lithosphere The scientific name for the earth's crust or surface.

live-aboard A sea-going craft, designed for or adapted for use by scuba divers with facilities for guests to eat and sleep on-board. Also called safari boat.

live-in A person who sleeps at their place of employment.

live-out A person who sleeps away from their place of employment.

livery The distinctive colour scheme used by a carrier to identify its vehicles.

llano A treeless plain, especially in South America.

load factor The percentage of occupancy of seats or other accommodation. A 100% load factor means full occupancy.

load line *See Plimsoll line.*

lobby An entrance or reception area of a hotel, typically of a hotel.

local 1. Belonging to a particular place or region.
2. Of or belonging to the neighbourhood.
3. (UK) A colloquial term for a pub.

L

local service A transport service operating in and around the local area.

local time The time as reckoned in a particular place. Most timetables are expressed in local times, even where a journey spans more than one time zone.

locality A district or neighbourhood.

location The place or position where something is situated.

locator A unique reference number given to a travel reservation in order that it may be accessed quickly at a later date.

loch A Scottish expression for a lake or arm of the sea.

lock A separate section of a canal or river fitted with gates to control the flow of water, thus allowing vessels to change levels.

lockjaw *See tetanus.*

locomotive A vehicle designed to haul a train or (more rarely) another form of transport.

lodge card A charge card 'lodged' in the care of an agent (usually a business travel agent) against which travel facilities may be charged. This system allows the cardholder a credit facility without the necessity for opening an account directly with the agent.

log The official record of the progress and happenings on board a ship or aircraft.

log cabin A hut or similar dwelling built from tree trunks.

loggia An open-sided extension to a building.

long vacation (UK) The extended summer holiday taken by students at British universities.

long weekend A weekend holiday extended by a day or days on either side.

longboat The largest boat used on a sailing ship.

long-haul An inexact term that is usually applied to journeys between continents.

longitude, lines of (or **meridians of**) Any of the imaginary great circles drawn around the earth from pole to pole. The meridians of longitude are expressed in relation to the 'Greenwich (or 'prime', or 'zero') meridian' which runs through Greenwich in London. This is said to be at $0°/180°$ longitude: the other lines of longitude also form great circles from pole to pole and are numbered in degrees east or west of it. Meridians of longitude are all equal in length, but not parallel to each other. At the Equator each division of 1 degree (divided into 60 minutes) is 60 nautical miles (approximately 110 km or 69 miles) apart: the distance between them gets progressively less as they get closer to the poles. > *latitude, lines of.*

loss damage waiver *See vehicle rental insurance.*

lounge A seating area designed to accommodate people for a short period while they are waiting to move to another area or facility.

Low Countries The geographical region comprising Belgium, Luxembourg and the Netherlands.

low latitudes Regions at or near the Equator.

low season The period during which there is the least demand for a product or service.

low tide *See low water.*

low water The tide at its lowest.

lower deck Generally the lowest deck of

a ship, immediately above the hold.

loyalty club　An incentive programme for frequent users of a supplier's services.
> *frequent flyer programmes and frequent stay programmes.*

luau　A Hawaiian outdoor feast with entertainment.

lubber line　A line marked on a compass showing a ship's forward direction.

luggage　Another term for baggage.

lugger　A small ship with two or three masts with a lugsail on each.

lugsail　A four-sided sail.

lunar　Of or relating to the moon.

lunar eclipse　*See eclipse.*

lunar month　A period of 28 days reckoned from the new moon.

lunar year　A period of 12 lunar months, about 354.3 days.

L

Mm

Macau Part of the People's Republic of China since 1997, although it is still often regarded as a separate travel destination.

Macedonia 1. A division of northern Greece.
2. A district in south-western Bulgaria.
3. One of the former constituent republics of Yugoslavia, now independent. Officially known as the Former Yugoslav Republic of Macedonia. > *Yugoslavia.*
4. An ancient kingdom in northern Greece, ruled most famously by Alexander the Great in the 4th century BC.

Mach number A measure of speed as compared to the speed of sound. Mach 1 is the speed of sound; Mach 2 is twice the speed of sound, and so on.

Madeira An island in the Atlantic off the north-west coast of Africa and politically part of Portugal.

magic carpet A simple ski lift in the form of a moving walkway. Often used on beginners' and children's ski slopes.

maglev From magnetic levitation. A train supported slightly clear of its track by magnetic repulsion.

magnetic compass A compass that indicates direction in relation to a magnetic pole by means of a magnetised pointer.

magnetic pole Either of the two variable points of the earth's surface, near to but not exactly corresponding to the geographical North and South Poles, where the lines of force of the earth's magnetic field are vertical. According to which hemisphere one is in, the needle of a magnetic compass will indicate the north or the south magnetic pole. Magnetic poles move slowly around the geographic poles and a constantly varying adjustment must be made to a magnetic compass reading if a true bearing is needed. > *poles.*

Magyar Of or relating to the Ural-Altaic peoples now predominant in Hungary.

maiden voyage The first journey of a new ship, traditionally after some form of ceremony.

main course The principal course of a meal.

main deck The upper deck between the forecastle and the poop of a merchantman.

main line A primary railway line, generally with express as well as stopping services. Dedicated high-speed lines are often shown separately on timetables and maps.

main mast The principal mast on a vessel.

main road A major highway, generally including motorways.

main sail The sail fixed to the main mast of a vessel.

Mainland 1. The largest island in Orkney and in Shetland in the UK.

2. A colloquial term for the South Island of New Zealand.

mainland A large continuous piece of land, excluding its associated islands.

mainplane The main wing of an aircraft.

mainsheet A line that controls and secures the mainsail.

maître d'hôtel A French term describing the head waiter in a restaurant. Used world-wide and often abbreviated to maître d'.

mal de mer Seasickness.

Malabar Coast The coastal region of the states of Karnataka and Kerala in south-west India. The main ports are Calicut, Cochin and Trivandrum.

malaria Formerly known as marsh fever. One of the most common diseases to which travellers are exposed. It is prevalent in many areas of Asia, Africa and Latin America. It is caused by plasmodium parasites that live inside the anopheles mosquito. It is difficult to cure and travellers should protect themselves by avoiding mosquito bites and by taking suitable anti-malarial drugs. Mosquitoes have developed resistance to some drugs in some parts of the world. > *health precautions.*

Malay Archipelago The largest island group in the world, off the south-east coast of Asia and between the Indian and Pacific Oceans. Major islands in the group include Borneo, Sulawesi (Celebes), Jawa (Java), New Guinea and Sumatera (Sumatra). The countries within the archipelago are Brunei, Indonesia, Malaysia (East), Papua New Guinea and the Philippines.

management fee An amount paid by a corporate customer to a business travel agent. There are two main systems:
1. A management fee is agreed for a

specified period, regardless of the number of transactions taking place.
2. A fee is charged for each transaction, regardless of the period over which they are completed. Occasionally the two systems may be combined. Management fees have now become the normal way of trading between travel agents and corporations rather than relying on commission from suppliers. > *travel agent.*

management information system A term used to denote the statistical and other data supplied by business travel agents to their customers in order to monitor spend and travel trends.

mañana An expression of Spanish origin meaning literally tomorrow, but implying later or possibly never.

manifest The official list of passengers or cargo being carried on a vehicle, ship or plane.

manifold A connecting pipe between two or more sources of high pressure gas.

manual issue A document which is hand-written, rather than computer-processed and printed.

manufacturing One of the three types of profession (agriculture and services being the others) into which economic activity is generally divided for statistical purposes.

Manx Of or relating to the Isle of Man.

Maori The inhabitants of New Zealand and the Cook Islands before the arrival of European settlers.

MAP *See modified American plan.*

map A flat representation of all or part of the earth's surface generally showing political and/or physical features, or illustrating a particular theme.
Two important features of maps are their scale (determining how much detail can

M

M

be included); and their function (determining what kind of features are concentrated on). Only maps of very small areas can clearly display all the physical and man-made features. A map produced for motorists will show roads more prominently and comprehensively than railways, while one illustrating diving sites will be more concerned with bathometric (sea-depth) contours than with the altitude of the land. Also, local significance can be of more importance than absolute size. A mountain of 2,000m in the Himalayas or a town of 50,000 people near Paris would probably not merit inclusion on many maps of those areas: the same sized feature in a comparatively flat or under-populated area (like England or central Australia) probably would.

Maps which have been designed to display one theme exclusively may have no consistent scale or may distort the shape of the area being covered and the relative positions of the places marked on it. A good example of this is the map of the London Underground. In the same way, a map showing ferry services in Europe might distort land shapes in order to maximise the length of the coastlines and the area of the sea.

map projection The method by which all or part of the world's surface can be represented in two dimensions. The term is also used to describe the name of the particular projection used.

Because the earth is spherical, displaying its surface in two dimensions requires some distortion, the effects of which become greater as the area of coverage increases. In the case of town plans and maps of small countries or regions, this distortion is insignificant; on maps of large countries, continents or the entire world, it is very significant indeed. Different projections address this problem in different ways and, as a result, the shape and respective sizes of landmasses may vary from one map to another. To a greater or lesser extent, on most world map projections the further a place is from the Equator, the larger it will appear

to be. Greenland, for instance, is roughly two-thirds the size of India; yet because of their respective positions on the earth's surface Greenland appears on many maps to be considerably bigger. For this reason, scale bars are often omitted from maps showing very large areas, as a fixed distance (say 1cm) on the page will, in different parts of the map, represent a different distance on the ground.

As a general rule, the more similar the latitude between two places (whether north or south of the Equator), the more accurate their respective sizes will be. Thus two places, one at 40° north and one at 40° south will be in proportion: two places, one at 10° north and one at 55° north, will not.

map reference Two sequences of numbers and/or letters, one running along the horizontal edge of a map and one along the vertical, which together help locate a particular place or feature. On some maps, the graticule lines will fulfil this function. > *graticule*.

Maple Leaf The rail service running between Toronto in Canada and New York in the USA.

Mardi Gras 1. Shrove Tuesday in many Catholic countries.
2. The celebration often associated with this, most famously in Nice, Rio de Janeiro and New Orleans.

marina A harbour, often specially constructed, with moorings and, generally, associated facilities for small boats and yachts.

marine Of or relating to the sea or shipping.

mariner A seaman.

market 1. A public place, often in a town centre, where goods are bought and sold.
2. A group of people or a place with a demand for a certain service or commodity.

marketing The business of promoting and selling a product or service.

mark-up 1. The amount added to a net price to arrive at a selling price.
2. The act of correcting a proof.

Marlin Coast An area of coast in northern Queensland, Australia, centred on Cairns.

maroon To abandon or leave stranded in a place, generally abroad.

marsh fever *See malaria.*

marsh Low land flooded for much of the year.

Mascarene Islands The group of volcanic islands in the Indian Ocean, east of Madagascar, that includes Réunion and Mauritius.

mask clearing An underwater process whereby the mask is held firmly to the forehead whilst the diver exhales through the nose. The exhaled air rises to the top of the mask and forces water out at the bottom thus clearing the mask.

massif A compact group of mountains.

mast A tall pole, usually fixed to the hull of a ship. On sailing vessels masts will be high and substantial to take the weight and thrust of the sails. On powered vessels, they may carry little more than the ensigns and wireless aerials.

masthead The highest point of a mast.

maximum permitted mileage The maximum number of miles that may be flown within each IATA fare component. The MPM is usually about 20% greater than the actual ticketed point mileage (TPM). For example, the ticketed point (or flown) mileage from London to New York is 3,458 but the MPM is 4,149. The mileage concept often permits a traveller to make stopovers at intermediate points without having to pay a higher fare.

Mayan The civilisation of ancient Mexico and Guatemala (c.2500BC to c.AD1550), one of the longest surviving civilisations in history.

mayday The standard international radio distress call.

MC Master of ceremonies.

MCO *See miscellaneous charges order.*

MCS Mountaineering Council of Scotland. *See Appendix 5a.*

MCT *See minimum connecting time.*

MDR-TB Multiple Drug Resistant Tuberculosis. An increasingly common and very serious disease with mortality rates in excess of 50%. > *health precautions.*

meadow An area of grass and small flowers.

M

mean sea level The level of the sea midway between high and low tides.

meander 1. A section of a river that has a series of curves or bends.
2. A slower or less direct route taken by planes to satisfy air traffic restrictions, or by ships to avoid rough seas or to arrive in port at a specific time.

Mecca (Also **Makkah**) One of the three holy cities of Islam (Medina and Jerusalem being the others), 80 km from the Red Sea in Saudi Arabia. > *hajj.*

media The collective term for the various methods of mass communication, including the press, television, radio and the internet.

medical expenses insurance *See travel insurance.*

medieval (or mediæval) Of or relating to the Middle Ages (broadly speaking from the 10th to the 15th centuries).

M

Medina   One of the three holy cities of Islam (Mecca and Jerusalem being the others), 338 km north of Mecca.

medina   The old Arab quarter of a North African town.

Mediterranean   1. The sea between Southern Europe, North Africa and Western Asia.
2. Of or relating to the islands of the Mediterranean Sea and the countries bordering it.
3. A type of climate. *See climate zones.*

Mediterranean Yacht Brokers Association   An organisation which represents and regulates yacht charter companies in Europe, and which has developed standard terms and contracts for yacht chartering in various parts of the world.

meet and greet   The provision of a service to meet and assist passengers on arrival at their destination port, station or airport. This term is often used by car parking companies who meet their customers at the airport and park their car for the duration of a trip.

megalopolis   A very large city or conurbation.

Melanesia   The collective name given to the group of islands in the south-west Pacific Ocean, south of the Equator and north-east of Australia. It includes Fiji, Nauru, New Caledonia, Papua New Guinea (excluding the New Guinea mainland), Solomon Islands and Vanuatu.

melt water   Water formed from the melting of ice, especially from a glacier.

Meltemi   *See Etesian Wind.*

member   A term used to describe an airline, travel agent or tour operator which subscribes to an association such as IATA, ABTA or AITO. *A list of many travel-related bodies may be found in Appendix 5.*

memsahib   A polite form of address used in India when referring to a woman.

menagerie   A collection of wild animals for exhibition, generally privately owned.

meningitis   A potentially fatal disease caused by inflammation of the brain or spinal cord. Meningoccal meningitis is endemic in certain parts of the world, including the southern fringes of the Sahara and the Indian sub-continent. > *health precautions.*

menu   1. A list of food and drink available in a restaurant.
2. A list, on a computer screen, giving a choice of actions that may be taken.

Mercator projection   A type of map projection, designed originally for navigation purposes, in which lines of latitude and longitude are shown as parallel intersecting straight lines. > *map projection, latitude, longitude.*

merchant marine   (US) *See merchant navy.*

merchant navy   (UK) A nation's commercial shipping fleet.

merchantman   A ship used for merchant (or passenger and mixed cargo) purposes, as opposed to military or tanker use.

meridian   *See longitude, lines of.*

mesa   A high, steep-sided plateau.

Meso-American   Of or relating to the area stretching from Central Mexico to Nicaragua or the various pre-Columbian civilisations which flourished there.

mestizo   A Spanish expression meaning a person of mixed parentage, especially Spanish or Portuguese and Native American (Indian).

meteograph   An instrument that records a number of different meteorological phenomena simultaneously.

meteorology   The science of the study of weather.

metric   The decimal-based system of weights and measures, used throughout most of the world except for the USA. > *Appendix 6.*

metro   A name used in many parts of the world to describe an urban railway system in general, and that of some cities in particular. Apart from Paris (see below), the urban railways of Madrid, Barcelona, Lisbon, Washington DC and Moscow (as well as many others) are known as the Metro. Names for other systems include BART in San Francisco, DART in Dublin, U- and S-Bahn in many German cities including Berlin, MRT in Singapore, MTR in Hong Kong, and Subte in Buenos Aires.

Métro   The underground railway network in Paris. It is sometimes taken also to include the RER, the city's deep-level express network.

Metroplex   The metropolitan area of Dallas-Fort Worth in Texas. The cities between Dallas and Fort Forth are described as the Mid-Cities: the largest of these is Arlington.

metropolis   The main town or city in a region.

mezzanine   A low storey between two others in a building, usually the first and ground floors.

MIA   Meetings Industry Association. *See Appendix 5a.*

mic   (pronounced 'mike') An abbreviation for microphone.

Micronesia   A collective name for the islands in the west part of the Pacific Ocean, north of the Equator and east of the Philippines. It includes Guam, Kiribati (western part), the Marshall Islands, Federated States of Micronesia, Northern Mariana Islands and Palau.

Micronesia, Federated States of   One of the island countries in the area known generally as Micronesia.

Middle America   1. Mexico, Central America and the Caribbean 2. The middle classes in the USA.

Middle East   A general geographic term describing a loosely defined area comprising the countries of the Arabian Peninsula, Egypt, Iran, Iraq, Israel, Jordan, Lebanon, Palestine NAR and Syria. It is often extended to include Algeria, Morocco, Sudan, Tunisia, Cyprus, Libya and Turkey.

Midnight Sun Coast   The eastern coast of Sweden from Gavle to the Finnish border.

midnight sun   The sun as seen in polar regions, at midnight during that hemisphere's summer.

midships   *See amidships.*

midtown   (US) That part of a town or city midway between the uptown and downtown districts, particularly where this forms a distinct area.

migration   The movement of people or animals, either temporarily or permanently, from one place to another.

mike   An abbreviation for microphone.

mile   *See statute mile, nautical mile.*

milli-   A prefix commonly found in the metric system, meaning one thousandth part of. Thus a millimetre is one thousandth of a metre.

millibar   The international unit for measuring atmospheric pressure.

millimetre   A unit of measurement in the

M

metric system, one-tenth of a centimetre.
> *centimetre.*

mini-bar A small cabinet or fridge found in a hotel room containing drinks and snacks. A charge is usuually added to the room bill for those used.

minibus (UK) A small bus, usually for fewer than twelve passengers.

minicab (UK) A car available for hire which cannot by law be hailed in the street but which must be ordered by phone. They are less tightly regulated than taxis.

minivan 1. (US) See minibus.
2. (UK) A small van.

minimum connecting time (MCT) The minimum amount of time that a passenger may allow between flights or any other mode of transport. Every major airport in the world has set MCTs

minimum rated package A UK term for an inclusive tour by air that provides 'nominal' accommodation in order to comply with regulations. > *seat only.*

minimum stay The shortest time a passenger can stay before using the return portion of a ticket. Return before this time will usually involve a surcharge. The most used minimum stay requirement is the 'Sunday Rule' whereby travellers may not return from their point of turnaround until after 0001 on the Sunday following the day of arrival.

miniple (UK) A travel agency group with between five and 20 outlets.

Minoan Of or relating to the civilisation, language and people of Crete (c.3000BC to c.1200BC).

minute 1. One sixtieth of an hour; sixty seconds.
2. One sixtieth of a degree of arc.
> *nautical mile*

mirage An optical illusion, most commonly seen in deserts and other very hot places, usually caused by the refraction of light in warm air.

MIS *See management information system.*

miscellaneous charges order (MCO) An airline voucher that can be used for almost any type of service. For example, a passenger might choose to have an MCO issued to cover excess baggage charges. Nowadays replaced by MPDs (multi-purpose documents).

Mississippi River Country A US regional marketing organisation covering the states that border the Mississippi river.
> *US regional marketing organisations.*

mist Water vapour near the ground limiting visibility to between one and two kilometres.

mistral A cold, northerly wind that blows down the Rhone valley and southern France into the Mediterranean.

mixed route A climbing route from one point to another that involves differing types of terrain. Normally used to denote that one will encounter rock as well as snow and/or ice while ascending this route.

mobile home 1. A large caravan permanently parked and used as a residence.
2. (US) A recreational vehicle (RV).

moderate breeze *See Beaufort scale.*

modified American plan Also known as half-board or *demi pension*. A hotel rate which includes room, breakfast and one other meal.

Mogul (or **Mughal**) 1. An alternative form of *Mongol*
2. Of or relating to the dynasty which ruled an empire in India from the 16th to 19th centuries.

M

mogul   1. A bump on a ski slope.
2. An influential or important person.

momentarily   1. (UK) Lasting for a very short time.
2. (US) Shortly.

monarch   A king or queen ruling as a head of state, often by right of hereditary succession, with powers ranging from the absolute to the purely ceremonial.

monarchy   1. A country with a monarch as its head of state.
2. A general collective term for the role and office of a monarch and its associated dignities, traditions, constitutional status and functions.

Mongols   The peoples of Central Asia who made considerable conquests in the 13th century under Gengis Khan and Kublai Khan. > *Mogul.*

monitor   A computer screen.

mono-hull   A vessel with a single hull. Most vessels are constructed in this way.

monolingual   1. A person who can speak only one language.
2. Something that is written in, or spoken in, only one language.

monoplane   An aeroplane with one pair of wings, the conventional arrangement for modern aircraft.

monorail   A railway whose track consists of a single rail.

monoski   A single, straight ski, used with both feet locked to it in a parallel position.

monsoon   1. A wind in southern Asia blowing from the south-west in summer and from the north-east in winter.
2. The rainy season associated with the monsoon.

monument   A structure generally intended to commemorate a person or event. For descriptions of a selection of the more notable monuments throughout the world, consult the Columbus *Tourist Attractions & Events of the World.*

moor   1. To secure a vessel to the land, or to a buoy at sea.
2. A tract of open, uncultivated land.

Moor   A member of the Muslim peoples of mixed Berber and Arab descent.

mooring   A place where a vessel can be moored.

moraine   An area of rocks and other debris deposited by a glacier. The ground is often loose and stony and can be uncomfortable to walk on.

Moresque   Architecture in the Moorish style.

Morse code   An early communications system using a combination of dots and dashes to represent the different letters of the alphabet. The increasing power and sophistication of modern communication systems has rendered it obsolete.

mosque   A Muslim place of worship.

motel   Originally a hotel designed for overnight stays by car travellers, often with limited facilities. The name is also given to more traditional types of hotel, whose guests arrive by other means.

motion sickness   Nausea caused by the movement of any form of transport.

motor bike   *See motor cycle.*

motor boat   A boat powered by an engine, usually internal combustion.

motor coach   1. (US) A large passenger-carrying road vehicle, generally equipped with toilet facilities.
2. A passenger coach on an electrified railway which has its own motor.

M

motor cycle A cycle, usually with two wheels, powered by an engine.

motor scooter A small motor cycle with additional weather protection.

motor ship A ship powered by internal combustion engines, usually diesel. Usually denoted by the abbreviation MS in front of its name.

motor yacht A yacht powered by a motor.

motorail Originally a proprietary term for the vehicle-carrying services operated by the former British Rail. Now often used to denote any such service.

motorway (UK) A high-speed multi-carriageway road with special regulations.

motu A term used in the South Pacific for a very small island or islet.

mountain hut A refuge available in areas popular with climbers designed for overnight accommodation. They can be anything in size from places that sleep half a dozen people to those that can accommodate over one hundred.

mountain sickness *See altitude sickness.*

Mountain Standard Time One of the time zones used in North America, seven hours behind UTC.

mountain A large elevation of the earth's surface, taller and generally steeper than a hill. Mountains generally occur in ranges, of which the three largest in area are the Himalayas (Asia), the Rockies (North America) and the Andes (South America). Traditionally a mountain has to be over 1,000 feet (305m) in height to be considered as such. The world's ten tallest mountains are all to be found in the Himalayas. For a list of the tallest mountains in each continent, consult the Columbus *World Travel Atlas.*

mountaineering The ascent of mountains (normally with the aim of reaching the summit) by a combination of hill walking, trekking, scrambling, via ferrata, rock climbing or ice climbing. As well as the obvious risks, additional dangers result from practising the above techniques in remote areas subject to extreme weather conditions and altitude problems. > *altitude sickness and acclimatisation.*
2. A type of climate. *See climate zones.*

mouth 1. The opening of a cave.
2. The point where a river enters the sea.

mouthpiece That part of the aqualung or snorkel which enters the mouth and through which the wearer may breathe.

Mozambique Channel The area of the Indian Ocean between Mozambique and Madagascar.

MPD Multi-Purpose Document. *See MCO.*

MPM *See maximum permitted mileage.*

MS When placed in front of a ship's name means Motor Ship.

mudéjar A style of architecture found in Iberia dating from the late middle ages, a blend of Gothic and Arabic styles.

Mughal *See Mogul.*

MUISZ Association of Hungarian Travel Agencies. *See Appendix 5c.*

mull The Scottish word for a promontory.

multi-hull A vessel with several hulls.

multi-lateral agreement An agreement between three or more parties.

multi-lingual 1. A person who can speak three or more languages fluently.
2. Something that is written in, or spoken in, three or more languages.

multiple dives More than one dive taken

within a relatively short space of time.

multiple entry visa A visa valid for several visits.

multiple (UK) A travel agency group with a large number of branches, generally accepted to be 20 or more. A company with five to 20 outlets is generally referred to as a miniple and smaller groups as independents.

multiplier effect The term used to describe the way in which expenditure by tourists affects the local economy by a greater amount than the value of the initial expenditure might suggest.

multi-sector A journey that involves several separate legs.

municipal golf course A golf course open to the public. A municipal or public golf course is usually open to all visitors, although some of the world's top municipal courses have special booking procedures.

municipality A town or area having its own local government.

mural A painting executed directly onto a wall or, less commonly, a ceiling, usually part of some larger scheme of decoration.

Muslim (also **Moslem**) Of or relating to the Islamic religion, its followers or the customs and culture associated with it.

MV When placed in front of the name of a boat or ship means Motor Vessel.

MY When placed in front of the name of a boat or ship means Motor Yacht.

MYBA See Mediterranean Yacht Brokers Association.

Mycenaean Of or relating to the late Bronze Age civilisation of ancient Greece.

mystery client One of the terms used to describe a person who visits a retail outlet such as a travel agency pretending to be a client, but whose real purpose is either to discover pricing or other information for a rival company, or to assess the levels of knowledge and service for a feature in a trade publication.

mystery tour (UK) A coach excursion on an unknown route to an unknown destination.

M

Nn

N/A   1. Not available.
2. Not applicable.

NACOA   National Association of Cruise Oriented Agencies. *See Appendix 5b.*

NACTA   National Association of Commissioned Travel Agents.

nadir   The lowest point. Typically used to describe the fortunes of a person or organisation.

NAITA   National Association of Independent Travel Agents. *See Appendix 5a.*

named driver   A person, specified on a rental agreement or an insurance document, who is permitted to drive a particular vehicle.

Napoleonic   Of or relating to the period when Napoleon I was Emperor of France (1799 to 1815).

narks   A colloquial term for nitrogen narcosis.

narrow boat   A vessel used on a canal, mainly in Great Britain, these days for leisure although there are a few commercial services. Often incorrectly referred to as a barge.

narrow gauge   A railway track gauge of less than the standard four feet eight and a half inches.

narrow seas   (UK) The English Channel and the Irish Sea.

narrow-bodied   When applied to aircraft, means the traditional design with a single centre aisle.

nation   A community of people of mainly common descent, history, language and culture, generally when organised within a political state.

national   1. A person who has a citizen of the country or state in question.
2. Of, belonging to or conducted within a nation.

national park   An area of natural beauty or interest protected by a state for the use and enjoyment of the general public.

national tourist office   An government-run organisation which exists to promote tourism that country to the consumers and the travel trade, both directly and through their network of overseas branches.

nationality   The status of belonging to a particular nation.

native   A person born in or living in a particular place.

natural attraction   A tourist attraction that is not man-made.

naturalise   To admit a person to the citizenship of a country.

nature reserve   A tract of land left in its natural state to preserve its fauna and flora.

nature trail A signposted track through an area of countryside, whose natural attractions it is designed to show off.

nautical Of or relating to the sea, sailors or navigation.

nautical mile The length of one minute of an arc of a great circle round the Earth, equal to 1,852m (2,025 yards, or approximately 1.15 statute miles). > *statute mile.*

navigable A river or other stretch of water that allows the passage of vessels.

navigation 1. The act of plotting the course of a vehicle and ensuring that it keeps to it.
2. A river artificially modified to improve its ability to convey commercial traffic such as barges or narrow boats.

NEA National Exhibitors Association. *See Appendix 5a.*

neap tide A tide occurring just after the first and third quarters of the moon, when there is the least difference between high and low water and when the tidal streams run least strongly.

Near East A general geographical term, now rarely used, that describes an area of south-west Asia that includes the Arabian Peninsula, Cyprus, Israel, Jordan, Lebanon, Syria and Turkey. Often extended to include Egypt and the Sudan.

near gale *See Beaufort scale.*

negative buoyancy The state of being heavier than water, and therefore prone to sinking in it.

neighbourhood 1. The region in or near to a place.
2. A district in a built-up area.

net fare Any non-commissionable fare to which an agency must add its own consultancy fee.

net rate A wholesale rate to holiday organisers who would be expected to add their own mark-up.

net registered tonnage A measure of the capacity of a ship. As with GRT, it is the measure of the enclosed space in a ship, but the calculation is made after spaces such as crew quarters, engine room have been deducted. In other words, it is a measure of the space that can be used for paying passengers' accommodation.

Netherlands Antilles Those islands of the West Indies administered by the Netherlands. They comprise Bonaire, Curaçao, Saba, St Eustatius and St Maarten. Aruba was a part of the Netherlands Antilles until it became a separate dependency of the Netherlands in 1986.

neutral buoyancy The state of being the same weight as water, and therefore neither sinking in it nor rising to the surface.

neutral unit of construction An artificial currency used to construct IATA air fares and to exchange funds between airlines. It is necessary to have one unit of currency (NUC) against which each actual currency has an exchange rate. As a result, IATA can pass funds between members by use of NUCs, rather than a multitude of local currencies.

New Guinea A large island north of Australia, divided between the Indonesian state of Irian Jaya and Papua New Guinea.

new moon The phase of the lunar cycle when the moon appears as a thin crescent, or not at all.

new tourist A recent term describing tourists who exhibit a number of travel characteristics including independence, experience, environmental awareness, flexibility, health-consciousness and a demand for quality.

N

New World   North and South America collectively, as regarded by the Old World.

Newfoundland Standard Time   One of the time zones used in North America, three and a half hours behind UTC.

nimbostratus   Low, dense, grey cloud from which rain often falls.

NITB   Northern Ireland Tourist Board. *See Appendix 5a.*

nitrogen narcosis   A condition sometimes experienced by divers where sufferers become insensible, in a manner similar to being drunk. It is caused by the effects on the body of nitrogen when under pressure. Symptoms vary with each individual.

nitrox   An abbreviation taken from the words nitrogen and oxygen and used in relation to the contents of a gas cylinder containing a mixed gas for breathing underwater where the oxygen content has been increased beyond 21%, thus reducing the Nitrogen content in order to reduce susceptibility to DCS. Also termed enriched air and enriched air nitrox (EANx).

nitrox course   Formal training in the use of nitrox.

nitrox diving   Scuba diving using nitrox instead of ordinary breathing air.

no show   The failure to use a confirmed hotel room or airline seat reservation without having cancelled. On many short flights the proportion of no-shows can reach 20%, which explains why airlines overbook.

no-frills   A basic service or product providing the minimum to meet a customer's requirements.

no-go area   (UK) An area to which access by unauthorised people is forbidden.

no-man's land   An area assigned to no particular owner. Often used to describe the stretch of land between the frontiers of adjoining territories, particularly (as in Korea and Cyprus) where there is a strong military presence.

non-aligned   A state that does not side with any other particular state or country or international alliance.

non-commissionable   A product or service that carries no agent's commission.

non-op   Non-operational or not operating.

nonref   An airline code that officially means 'refund restricted' but that is often and incorrectly assumed to mean non-refundable.

non-resident   1. Someone who is not permanently domiciled in a particular country.
2. Someone who is not staying at a particular hotel or other accommodation. In many cases, some facilities are not available to non-residents, or are only available if paid for.

non-smoking   A compartment or area where smoking is not permitted.

non-stop   A trip that is continuous from beginning to end.

non-transferable   A ticket, voucher, reservation or other travel service that can only be used by the person for whom it was originally provided.

normal fare   A fare carrying no special restrictions of validity or use.

Norman   1. A native or inhabitant of Normandy.
2. Of or relating to the peoples of Scandinavian origin who settled in Normandy in the 10th century and invaded England in 1066 (ruling until 1154). They also founded states in Sicily and the Middle East.

N

3. The style of Romanesque architecture introduced to Britain by the Normans.

north   One of the four cardinal points of the compass, 90° clockwise from west and 180° from south. Most maps have north at the top, although in some cases the orientation might be twisted slightly (for example, to show all of a given land mass at a suitable scale). In such cases, the direction of north will be illustrated with a compass arrow.

North America   One of the world's continents. As with most continents, opinions differ as to its exact composition and area. > *continent.*

North Atlantic Drift   The northern extension of the Gulf Stream that warms the coasts of Iceland, Norway and Spitzbergen.

North Pacific Current   The Pacific equivalent of the North Atlantic Drift. It brings the warm waters of the Kuroshio to the north-west coast of North America.

North Pole   The northernmost point of the earth.

North Sea   The sea between the British Isles, Scandinavia and the Netherlands.

northern hemisphere   That part of the earth north of the Equator.

Northern Ireland   One of the constituent countries of the United Kingdom of Great Britain and Northern Ireland. > *Great Britain, United Kingdom.*

northern lights   *See aurora borealis.*

nose   The projecting front of an aircraft or other vehicle.

nose wheel   The front landing wheel of an aircraft.

nouvelle cuisine   A style of cooking that avoids traditional heavy sauces in favour of lighter and fresher ingredients and pays particular attention to the presentation of the food.

NRT   *See net registered tonnage.*

NT   National Trust. *See Appendix 5a.*

NTO   National Tourist Office. *See tourist office.*

NTS   National Trust for Scotland. *See Appendix 5a.*

NUC   *See neutral unit of construction.*

null and void   Invalid, not binding.

nullify   To invalidate.

N

Nunavut   The new name for the eastern (Inuit) part of Canada's Northwest Territories, from which it was separated in 1999. Nunavut is an Inuit word meaning 'Our Land'. It covers an area of around one million square miles (2,560,00 square kilometres), approximately 20% of Canada's land area.

nursery slope   A gentle ski run used to teach the art of skiing or snowboarding.

nursery   *See ski kindergarten.*

Oo

OAG   A publisher of airline and other travel-related information derived from the original Official Airline Guide.

OAP   (UK) *See old age pensioner.*

oasis   A fertile spot in a desert, often around a pool of water.

observation car   A carriage on a train built to allow a good view. Also known in the US as a bubble car or dome car.

occidental   Of or relating to the western nations and culture.

occupancy   The number of people using a particular facility.

occupancy rate   1. The number of people occupying a room in a hotel. If one person stays in a double room, they may be charged a low occupancy rate.
2. A measurement of the percentage of the total number of beds in a hotel that are actually occupied on a given night. Thus an occupancy rate of 50% suggests that the hotel is half full.

ocean   A large sea. There are five oceans: Arctic; Atlantic (sometimes split into North and South); Indian; Pacific; and Southern. For obvious reasons, the boundaries between them are not always easy to define. Many oceans contain areas that are known as seas, bays, gulfs or similar (such as the South China Sea, the Bay of Biscay and the Gulf of Mexico) a selection of which have their own entries elsewhere in this book. Roughly 70% of the surface of the world is covered by oceans.

oceanarium   A large seawater aquarium.

ocean-going   Of a ship. One designed to cross large stretches of water.

Oceania   1. One of the world's continents. As with most continents, opinions differ as to its exact composition and area.
> *continent.*
2. Sometimes used to describe the world's oceans and seas generally and collectively.

oceanic   Of, relating to or near an ocean.

octopush   A form of underwater hockey played in a swimming pool.

off season   Another name for low season.

off-line carrier   A carrier whose flights are being booked on another carrier's reservation system.

off-line point   A city not served by a particular carrier.

offload   To remove a person from, or refuse to carry a person on, a flight or other means of transport. This may be a result of overbooking, although there are other reasons, such as unacceptable behaviour.

off-peak   A period of low demand for a product or service.

off-piste   Away from the prepared ski-runs. Many travel insurance policies do not cover off-piste skiing due the sharply increased level of risk.

off-season   *See off-peak.*

offshore   At sea some way from the shore.

OK   The official abbreviation on most travel documents for a confirmed seat, room or other booking.

old age pensioner   (UK) An elderly person. This expression tends to be considered derogatory these days and terms such as senior citizen are often preferred. Persons of pensionable age can usually obtain discounts on most forms of travel.

Old World   Europe, Asia and Africa.

omnibus   *See bus.*

on board   When a person has boarded a ship or other vessel.

one-armed bandit   A coin- or token-operated slot machine used for gambling.

one-class   A means of transport where all passengers have access to all facilities and public areas. On one-class ships there may still be significant differences between the quality of sleeping and eating accommodation, but the communal areas (such as spas, restaurants, bars and decks) will be available to everyone.

one-way rental   A car rental that terminates at a location other than that at which it started. In many cases an additional one-way rental charge will be payable by the hirer. One-way rentals may not always be offered at a particular vehicle rental location.

one-way rental charge   *See drop-off charge.*

one-way trip   A journey from origin to destination with no return booking.

on-line carrier   The carrier whose system is being used to make a booking.

on-line connection   An arrangement of flight connections between services of the same carrier.

on-line marketing   The promotion of goods or services using the internet or other electronic media.

onshore   1. On land, rather than on water. 2. A wind blowing from the sea to the land.

open   A booking for which confirmed reservations have not yet been made. > *open-ended, open date, ticket (1), reservation.*

open bar   A catering arrangement whereby drinks are not charged to those who consume them (but may be to the organiser of the event).

open date   Any date on a booking that is awaiting a confirmed reservation. > *open-ended, open, ticket (1), reservation.*

open sea   An expanse of sea away from the land.

open skies   The philosophy or policy of total deregulation allowing unrestricted access to airspace by any carrier.

open-ended   A booking with a return portion that is awaiting a confirmed reservation. > *open, open date, ticket (1), reservation.*

open-jaw   A return journey that has different originating and terminating points, or with different turnaround points. For example, London to Montreal, returning to Manchester; or London to Montreal, then returning from Vancouver to London.

option   (UK) A provisional booking, usually for a holiday, held without payment while a customer decides whether to go ahead with the purchase.

option date   The deadline by which a whole or partial payment must be made,

O

a contract signed or a reservation confirmed in order to secure the product or service in question.

optional extra Anything bought by a customer that is additional to the basic holiday or other arrangement. This has the same meaning as the term 'add on', which is more common in North America.

Ordnance Survey maps (UK) A series of very detailed maps produced by the Ordnance Survey, an official survey organisation.

organiser Under the EC (now EU) Package Travel Regulations, anyone who organises, other than 'occasionally', a package holiday. This does not have to be a commercial organisation; an individual, even if arranging a package on a purely voluntary basis, is still bound by the regulations.

Orient Express The rail service which, between the 1880s and 1977, operated services from London to Istanbul via Paris, Milan, Venice, Belgrade, Sofia and Athens. Today it is an ordinary train running between Paris and Venice. The name may be dropped in the near future. > *Venice-Simplon Orient Express.*

oriental Of or relating to the eastern nations and culture.

origin 1. The starting point for a journey. 2. The place from where a person initially comes.

Orthodox Of or relating to the family of Christian churches (including Russian, Greek and Romanian) which originated in Eastern Europe and Western Asia and separated themselves from the Roman Catholic church in the 11th century.

orthodox A person who strictly adheres to the forms and observances of a particular religion, such as Judaism.

ÖRV Österreichischer Reisebüro- und Reiseveranstalter Verband. *See Appendix 5c.*

Ottoman Of or relating to the Turkish dynasty founded in 1300 and lasting until 1922, and the empire that it ruled.

outback The remote bush country of Australia.

outboard A motor attachable to the outside of the stern of a boat.

outbound 1. A flight or other mode of transport leaving from an airport, port or other terminus. 2. The outward sector of an air package holiday.

outcrop A stratum of rock emerging from the surface of the soil.

outfall The mouth of a river, stream, drain or other waterway where it empties.

outing A short trip or excursion, especially from one's home.

outlying Remote.

out-of-date A document whose validity has expired.

outrigger 1. A beam or spar projecting from the side of a ship or boat to add stability. 2. A boat fitted with outriggers. 3. A part of a map which projects beyond the frame in order to show an outlying part of the area being considered. Maps of the UK, for example, may require an outrigger to show the whole of the Cornish mainland.

outside cabin A cabin on a ship with a window or porthole. A cabin on the outside of a ship without a porthole or window is not considered to be 'outside'.

overbooking The situation in which

more people with reservations for a flight turn up for it then there are seats available. This is known as overselling in the US.

over-capacity   A surplus of seats or beds or other accommodation above what is needed to meet the needs of customers.

Overland   The rail service between Melbourne and Adelaide in Australia.

overpass   A road or railway that passes over another by means of a bridge.

overriding commission   (or **override**) Officially, the extra commission paid by principals to their general sales agents to enable them to pay full commission to other agents. The term is often used to describe any commission paid in excess of the 'standard' amount.

overseas   Foreign or abroad.

overselling   (US) *See overbooking.*

Oyashio   The Pacific's equivalent of the East Greenland Current, flowing south through the Bering Strait.

O

Pp

Pacific Ocean *See oceans.*

Pacific Rim Those countries and regions surrounding the Pacific Ocean, especially the eastern Asian nations.

Pacific Standard Time One of the time zones used in North America, eight hours behind UTC.

package holiday The term is generally used to describe a travel product that includes transportation, usually by air, and accommodation. However, it now has a strict definition in EU legislation, as follows: 'The pre-arranged combination of not fewer than two of the following when sold or offered for sale at an inclusive price and when the service covers a period of more than 24 hours or includes overnight accommodation: (a) transport; (b) accommodation; (c) other tourist services not ancillary to transport or accommodation and accounting for a significant proportion of the package'. In simple language, any arrangement that includes something more than just travel is likely to be a package. It can also be referred to as an inclusive tour.

Package Travel, Package Holidays & Package Tours Regulations 1992 The regulations, made under the EC Council Directive 90/314 and colloquially known in the trade as the 'EU Directive', were introduced in an attempt to harmonise consumer protection throughout the EC. The legislation is backed up by UK law and contravention of its provisions is a criminal offence.

Padania A name claimed for the area of Italy from Umbria and Tuscany northwards. A local political party, the Northern League, would like to see the area become an independent country within the EU.

paddle steamer A vessel propelled by paddles, either on its side or at its stern.

page To call for someone in a hotel or similar environment. Originally done by means of a page who called the person's name, nowadays it is usually done by means of a public address system.

pagoda A Hindu or Buddhist temple or sacred building, usually a tower with many tiers, most common in Far Eastern countries.

PAI (personal accident insurance) *See travel insurance.*

painter A short length of rope used to tie up a boat.

pairings The names of golfers who wish to play together. A maximum of four golfers can play together at one tee-time. The golf club may request to know the names of the golfers playing at each tee-time. These are referred to as the pairings. > *tee-time.*

Palace on Wheels The luxury rail service in India which provides services between Delhi and major tourist centres in Uttar Pradesh and Rajasthan, including Agra and Jodhpur.

palatial 1. Of or relating to a palace.

2. Very luxurious.

pampas   A large treeless plain in South America.

Pampero   A strong, cold wind in South America, blowing from the Andes to the Atlantic.

Panama Canal   The canal that connects the Atlantic Ocean with the Pacific Ocean, running through Panama.

pandemic   A disease prevalent throughout a given region.

panhandle   (US) A narrow strip of land projecting from one state into another.

panorama   An unbroken view of the surrounding area, usually from a high point.

Papal States   The territories, mainly in Central Italy and at times very extensive, which were for many centuries under the political control of the Papacy. All that now remains of these is the Vatican City.

Papua New Guinea   A country occupying the eastern part of the island of New Guinea. Not to be confused with Guinea, Equatorial Guinea or Guinea-Bissau.

par of exchange   The official term to denote the recognised value of one currency in terms of another.

parador   A Spanish hotel owned by the government. Often converted from castles or other old buildings, they offer a high standard of accommodation, frequently in areas where normal commercial provision might not be feasible.

paragliding   An sport in which participants jump from a height with a parachute-like canopy strapped to their backs.

parallel   *See latitude, lines of.*

paramotoring   An aerial sport in which

the user flies wearing a paraglider canopy and is propelled by a pusher propeller.

parasailing   An aerial sport in which participants, wearing parachutes, are towed though the air by a motor boat.

parascending   A generic term for the main parachuting sports. *See parasailing, paragliding, paramotoring.*

paratyphoid   A disease resembling typhoid, caused by different but related agents. > *health precautions.*

parish   1. A district having its own church and clergy.
2. A district constructed for the purposes of local government.

parkway   (US) An open, landscaped highway.

part charter   An arrangement whereby a tour operator contracts some of the seats on an aircraft, rather than booking the whole aircraft.

partial pressure   The pressure exerted by any single constituent gas within a mixture of gases.

partner fare   A special fare issued to an accompanying partner at a reduced rate.

partnership   A business, owned and operated by two or more people, without limited liability. > *limited.*

party   An alternative term for group.

pass   1. The lowest passage between two mountain tops.
2. A permit, usually free, giving access to an amenity.

passage   An alternative term for journey, particularly one by sea.

passenger   A person, other than the driver or crew, travelling in or on some form of vehicle.

P

P

passenger coupon   The coupon or coupons of a ticket or voucher that are retained by the passenger. Passenger coupons will usually give outline details of the conditions of carriage and occasionally also act as a baggage check.

passenger mile   One passenger carried for one mile. When the number of passengers carried is multiplied by the number of miles travelled, a total passenger mile figure is obtained for that carrier.

passenger name record (PNR)   A unique code used by an airline to store and recognise a booking.

passenger sales agent   A travel agent appointed to sell passenger (as opposed to freight or cargo) tickets and services.

passenger space ratio (PSR)   A shipping term for the GRT divided by the passenger capacity of a vessel. The lower the number the higher the density and the less space there is likely to be for each passenger. A vessel with a PSR of 20 is likely to be more crowded than one with a PSR of 40. Only the most luxurious ships would have PSRs in excess of 50.

passenger transport authority   A public organisation set up to control public passenger transport services.

Passover   A festival in the Jewish religious calendar, lasting for eight days in March or April.

passport   An identity document that allows its bearer to travel abroad.

passport control   The point at an airport, port or border where travellers have to show their passports. This may also be known as immigration control.

PATA   Pacific and Asian Travel Agents Association. *See Appendix 5d.*

path   1. A small track or trail.
2. A determined route along which something moves (e.g. flight path).

patio   1. A paved area adjacent to a house   2. An inner courtyard in a Spanish or Latin American house.

patois   The dialect or slang of the locals in an area, that might differ significantly from the official language of the country.

patriality   Having the right by birth to live in the UK.

pavement   1. (UK) The area on one or both sides of a road reserved for pedestrians. Referred to as a sidewalk in the USA.
2. (US) The roadway or its surface.

pax   A common abbreviation for 'passengers'.

payload   The proportion of the total weight of a vehicle that can produce revenue. Payload can be of passengers, cargo or both.

PC   1. Any desktop computer.
2. A desktop computer running on the Windows, rather than the Macintosh (Mac), operating system. Transferring data between these two platforms is now far less troublesome than was once the case. In general, PC-to-Mac poses fewer problems than does Mac-to-PC. Macs are particularly common in the print and design industries.

PDF file   A widely used format for supplying designed pages electronically to clients or to printers which does not require their having the programme in which the document was created.

peak season   Another name for high season.

ped Xing   (US) Abbreviation for 'pedestrian crossing'.

pedalo   A small, pedal-operated pleasure boat.

pedicab A pedal-operated rickshaw.

pedometer An instrument, carried or worn by a walker, that measures the distance travelled.

pedway (US) A route built for pedestrians in an urban area.

pelican crossing See zebra crossing.

penalty fare A fare charged, often with a surcharge, to a passenger on board public transport without a valid ticket or authority to travel in the class and/or on the route travelled.

peninsula An area of land surrounded by water or projecting into the sea and connected to the mainland by a relatively small area.

peninsular Of or relating to a peninsula.

pension A European term for a small hotel. Some grading systems require certain minimum facilities from establishments before they can be categorised as hotels and in cases where these standards are not met, a pension designation may be given.

penthouse An apartment on the roof of a building. Often used by hotels to denote their highest (and usually best) accommodation.

penumbra See eclipse.

peoples Persons making up a community, tribe, race, nation or similar.

per diem See diem.

perestroika A Russian expression meaning the practice of restructuring or reforming a political system. Its application in the former Soviet Union has lead to the emergence of many new or revived states and countries.

perishability Anything that is perishable will deteriorate if it is not used. In travel, an unsold seat or room or an unhired car perishes as soon as bookings close.

permafrost Subsoil that is permanently frozen, as found in extreme northern and southern latitudes.

permanent way (UK) The completed track of a railway.

Perpendicular A form of Gothic architecture, popular in England in the 15th and 16th centuries, characterised by the vertical tracery in the larger windows.

Persian Gulf (or **the Gulf, Arabian Gulf**) The gulf which separates the Arabian peninsula from Iran.

personal accident insurance (PAI) See travel insurance.

personal liability insurance See travel insurance.

personal money insurance See travel insurance.

personal money Currency carried for an individual's use. Depending on the context, this can refer to cash only, or also to other forms of exchange such as travellers' cheques and vouchers, and even admission or travel tickets. Most insurance policies can offer cover against loss of personal money while travelling. The conditions under which such a claim can be made will be set out in the small print and will vary from policy to policy.

personal possessions insurance See travel insurance.

Peru Current See Humboldt Current.

pet passport See Pet Travel Scheme.

Pet Travel Scheme (PETS) Introduced in 2000, this allows cats and dogs to travel between the UK and a number of European and long-haul destinations

P

(though currently not North America) without the need for a six-month stay in quarantine on arrival in the UK. In order to comply with the scheme, pets must be micro-chipped, be issued with an appropriate pet passport, and have a valid vet's certificate certifying vaccination against rabies.

PETS *See Pet Travel Scheme.*

PEX A promotional excursion fare which carries a number of restrictions regarding dates and times of flights.

phaeton 1. An open four-wheeled horse-drawn carriage.
2. (US) A vintage touring car.

Phoenician Of or relating to the Semitic peoples of ancient Phoenicia in southern Syria and the Lebanon.

phonetic alphabet An officially defined list of words starting with successive letters of the alphabet for confirming the spellings of words. Each major language has at least one, but for travel and tourism by far the most important is the English one, as that is the industry's language. The most widely used English phonetic alphabet is as follows: Alpha, Bravo, Charlie, Delta, Echo, Foxtrot, Golf, Hotel, India, Juliet, Kilo, Lima, Mike, November, Oscar, Papa, Quebec, Romeo, Sierra, Tango, Uniform, Victor, Whisky, X-ray, Yankee, Zulu. *For a list of phonetic alphabets in French, Spanish, German and Italian, and a pronunciation guide for the alphabets and numbers in these languages, please see Appendix 7.*

physical feature Any feature that is a part of the landscape, either created naturally (such as a mountain) or man-made but seeming to be natural (such as a canal).

physical geography The branch of geography that deals with physical features.

piazza A public open square, especially in Italy.

pick-up *See check-out (2).*

picnic A meal eaten out of doors, often without tables or chairs.

picnic site A place where travellers may stop to have a picnic.

pictogram An informative sign or symbol created by means of a stylised image rather than words, and generally internationally recognised irrespective of language.

pictograph 1. *See pictogram.*
2. Ancient hieroglyphic writing in picture form.

pidgin A simplified language, often containing words from several languages, used to communicate between people having no common language.

pidgin English A pidgin, the main language of which is English.

piece concept The airline baggage system where the free allowance is based on the size and number of items, rather than their weight.

pied-à-terre A dwelling. kept for occasional use.

piedmont A gentle slope leading from the foot of the mountains to a region of flat land.

pier 1. A bridge-like structure, raised on piles and leading out over water.
2. A projection from an airport terminal building leading towards an aircraft stand.

pilgrim A person who visits a sacred place for religious reasons.

pilgrimage A journey taken by a pilgrim or group of pilgrims.

pillar valve The valve attached to one end of a high pressure diving cylinder used to gain access to the contents.

P

pilot   1. A person who flies an aircraft.
2. A person licensed to navigate ships into and out of ports and harbours who will join a ship to advise the captain on its handling during these procedures.

pinnace   A ship's small boat, usually motor-driven.

Pioneer Club   A body of specialist UK travel agents who have undertaken a USTTA (subsequently Visit USA) training programme.

PIR   *See property irregularity report.*

piste   (UK) A marked ski run down a mountain. It is usually formed of compacted snow, but some resorts prefer to leave the snow ungroomed.

piste basher   *See piste groomer.*

piste groomer   A large tractor with very wide caterpillar tracks designed to flatten ski runs. Also known as piste basher or snow cat.

piste map   (UK) A map showing all the ski runs and lifts in a ski resort's ski area. Known as a trail map in North America.

piston engine   An internal combustion engine similar to the type used in cars, generally only used by small or old aircraft.

pitch   1. The distance between the front edge of an aircraft seat and the front edge of the seat behind.
2. The fore and aft motion of a ship.

pizza pie   (US) *See snowplough (2).*

plage   The French word for a beach.

plague   Any deadly disease spreading rapidly over a wide area.

plague, the   Bubonic plague, a contagious bacterial disease, usually transmitted by rat fleas.

plain   A level tract of land, especially one with few trees.

Plan Management   The department of IATA responsible for the administration, management and development of the Billing and Settlement Plan.

plane   1. An aircraft.
2. The action of a boat travelling at speed and rising in the water so that the front part of the hull is clear of the surface.

Plantagenet   Of or relating to the kings of England between 1154 and 1399 (some say 1485).

plat du jour   The chef's daily recommendation in a restaurant.

plate   1. A small embossed metal sheet used in a ticket validating machine. Each plate gives details of the carrier and the issuing agent.
2. A large part of the earth's crust. *See plate tectonics.*
3. The sheet metal forming the outer shell of a ship.
4. A polished metal sheet used in offset lithographic printing on which the image has been engraved.
5. (US) The main course of a meal served on one dish.

plate tectonics   The science of the movement of the earth's plates upon its fluid interior that lead to phenomena such as volcanoes and earthquakes.

plateau   A large, flat, elevated area of land.

platform   1. The raised area of a railway station where passengers embark and disembark.
2. A raised area in an auditorium or similar from which a speaker may address an audience.

playa   The Spanish word for a beach.

plaza   A market place or open square in a town in Spanish speaking countries.

P

Plimsoll line A series of lines, painted on the outside of a ship's hull to indicate the various safe levels to which the vessel may be loaded. There are several lines denoting the levels for varying situations such as water salinity and season.

Plimsoll mark *See Plimsoll line.*

ply To travel regularly between two or more points, generally on water.

ply for hire To offer the services of a vehicle, typically a taxi, to members of the public on an ad hoc basis.

PM Post meridiem – used in 12-hour clocks and timetables for the period between midday and midnight. Most transport schedules in the United States are listed using am and pm. Note that IATA regulations require that am and pm be written without full stops.

PNR *See passenger name record.*

podium A raised platform used for public speaking.

point-of-sale display Material used to promote a product or service at the place where it can be bought.

point-to-point air fare A fare that is valid only between a specified pair of plates and which allows no stopover en route.

polar 1. Of, at or relating to the poles.
2. A type of climate. *See climate zones.*

polder An area of land reclaimed from the sea. These are especially common in low-lying countries such as Holland.

pole star A star in the constellation of Ursa Minor that appears in the direction of true north.

poles The most northerly and southerly points of the Earth's surface, at 90° north and 90° south, and the points about which the earth rotates (also known as

geographic poles). True north and true south are calculated from these points. Magnetic north and south are the points towards which compasses point and are not the same as true north and south. > *magnetic poles.*

poliomyelitis (or **polio**) An infectious viral disease that can cause paralysis. > *health precautions.*

political geography The study of the boundaries, divisions and possessions of states.

pollution The spoiling of the environment by the impact of harmful things such as effluents and noise.

polyglot 1. Of or relating to many languages.
2. A multi-lingual person.

Polynesia The collective name for the islands of the central and south Pacific ocean including American Samoa, Cook Islands, Easter Island, French Polynesia, Hawaii, Kiribati (east), New Zealand, Niue, Pitcairn Islands, Tokelau, Tonga, Tuvalu, Wallis and Futuna and Western Samoa.

Polynesian civilisation The civilisation of Samoa and Tonga (c.500BC to c.1775).

Poma One of the world's main lift manufacturers, responsible for the Millennium Wheel in London. Also the common name for a particular type of ski lift. > *drag lift.*

pond 1. A very small, enclosed body of water.
2. A colloquial term for the Atlantic Ocean, particularly used by people who fly across it frequently.

pontoon 1. A floating support for a temporary bridge.
2. A flat-bottomed boat.

pony cylinder A small high-pressure diving cylinder normally strapped to the

P

side of the main diving cylinder capable of providing a small amount of breathing air in an emergency.

pool agreement An arrangement where two or more carriers agree to serve a route and accept each other's tickets. The revenue earned is 'pooled' and divided between the carriers in proportion to the number of seats sold.

pool side A room in a hotel or similar establishment on the same level as the swimming pool and which opens onto it.

pool view A room in a hotel or similar establishment that overlooks the swimming pool but which has no direct access to it.

poop The aftermost and highest deck of a ship.

pooped When a following wave overtakes a boat and breaks over its stern, possibly swamping it.

population The inhabitants of a place referred to collectively.

port 1. An originating, en-route or destination point for a vessel, usually a ship.
2. The left-hand side of a vessel when one is looking towards the forward end. Denoted by a red light.

port of call A scheduled stop on the itinerary of a cruise or line service.

port surcharge A fee charged to rental companies delivering or collecting hire vehicles at a port or airport.

port taxes Charges levied on passengers arriving or departing from a port, similar in principle to airport taxes.

porter 1. A person employed to carry luggage and generally give assistance at an airport or railway station.
2. (US) A sleeping car attendant.

porthole The circular window in a ship or boat.

POS *See point of sale.*

posada A small Spanish roadhouse or restaurant.

positioning The movement of an aircraft, ship or other vehicle from where it is to where it can begin to earn revenue. Positioning is costly and some carriers, particularly cruise lines, seek to defray these costs by offering positioning voyages for which they can sell accommodation at particularly attractive rates.

positive buoyancy The state of being lighter than water, and therefore floating on the surface of it.

positive space A confirmed hotel reservation.

post code (UK) The mail sorting code appearing at the end of the address.

post-date To date a document (such as a cheque) later than its date of issue. Usually done to delay payment to the carrier and usually thus officially frowned upon.

pothole A deep hole or system of caves.

pound 1. A unit of weight in the imperial system, equal to c.454 grams.
2. The unit of currency used in the UK and in some dependant territories, divided into 100 pence. Also known as pound sterling.

pourboire A French term for a tip or gratuity.

pousada A Portuguese government-owned hotel, built in the local style.

pousse-café A French term for a liqueur, taken with or after coffee.

powder snow Light, fluffy snow, often recently fallen, most commonly found in dry climates.

P

powerboat A powerful motor vessel, often used for racing.

powwow A conference or meeting for discussion, originally between North American Indians.

pp In travel, per person. However there are several other meanings so the abbreviation should be used with care.

prairie A large area of treeless grassland, mostly found in North America.

pre-boarding An arrangement by which those with special needs may be allowed onto an aircraft before other passengers.

pre-book To reserve in advance.

precinct 1. An enclosed or clearly defined area, such as a pedestrian precinct in a town (from which vehicles are excluded). 2. (US) A police district.

precipice A steep cliff.

precipitation The falling of rain, sleet, hail or snow.

pre-existing condition An insurance term relating to a condition, such as an illness, that existed before the insurance was contracted. Many companies will not cover claims so arising.

préfect The chief administrative officer of a *departement* in France.

préfecture A district under the control of a préfect.

preferred supplier A principal with which a travel agency has a special agreement. This is usually that it will give extra sales support in return for additional commission or other incentives.

premier First in class, style or importance.

premium The amount payable in consideration for a contract of insurance.

premium traffic The name given to those, such as business travellers, paying the most expensive prices for a service.

prepaid ticket advice A notification to a distant point that a passenger has paid for a ticket. Usually used if a passenger wishes to collect the document from a point other than that of payment (at the airport of departure, for example).

pre-payment Payment made in advance for a service.

president 1. The elected head of a republic. 2. (US) The head of a company or corporation.

pressurisation The stabilisation of the air pressure in an aircraft's cabin. Modern aircraft fly at heights where the air is too thin to be breathed comfortably, and most cabins are thus pressurised to a degree that is safe both for the passengers and the structure of the plane. Generally this is set to the equivalent of atmospheric pressure at around 6,000 to 8,000 feet.

prestige Of a higher class or standard than normal.

prevailing wind The wind direction that occurs most frequently at a place. In the UK, the prevailing winds are generally from the west.

price grid The way in which prices are often displayed in travel literature, such as brochures. Commonly the details of the holiday are listed on one axis of the chart and the departure dates on the other. The intersection points on the grid show the price for that holiday at that time. The same principle is used for timetables where different fares apply at different times.

price-fixing An agreement between suppliers to maintain prices at an agreed level. This is now illegal in many countries, including the the USA and the UK.

P

price-ring *See price-fixing.*

prime meridian The meridian of longitude at 0° that passes through Greenwich. > *Greenwich meridian, longitude, lines of.*

prince (**princess** when feminine) A non-reigning male member of a royal family, or the monarch of a small territory (such as Monaco).

principal An individual or organisation in the travel industry, responsible for organising or providing some sort of facility. This might be transport: airlines, shipping lines, railways, car rental companies and bus and coach operators are examples. Providers of accommodation, such as hotels, motel and holiday centres are also principals. Other principals provide services which may be less obvious, such as travel insurance companies.

principality A country, territory or state governed by a prince (such as Monaco).

priority boarding *See pre-boarding.*

private 1. Accommodation in a private dwelling
2. Individual arrangements made personally by a traveller.
3. Having sole use of vehicle or other travel component, such as a balcony or a swimming pool.
4. A form of company incorporation whereby the company's shares are owned by a small number of people closely connected to it, and not traded publicly.

private facilities The provision of washing and toilet facilities in a hotel room.

private golf club A membership-based golf club. Some private golf clubs only allow club members and their guests access to the course. Others may allow visitors to play for on payment of a green fee, although access may be restricted to certain days of the week or times of the day. > *green fee.*

pro rata In proportion. A pro rata payment would be made in proportion to the rest of the payment.

pro tem For the time being or temporarily.

program 1. (US) A pre-determined series of events.
2. (US) The printed document used to describe this.
3. A piece of computer software, and the act of writing or editing it.

programme 1. (UK) A pre-determined series of events.
2. (UK) The printed document used to describe this.

projection See *map projection.*

promenade (UK) A public walkway along the seafront.

promenade deck An upper deck on a ship that is designed for passengers to walk around.

promontory A piece of high land jutting into the sea.

promotional fare A specially reduced fare designed to attract customers.

propeller A large screw-shaped device that provides thrust for an aircraft or ship. The action of the screw forces water or air to the rear thus creating the thrust.

property irregularity report (PIR) A form used by airlines to record details of a problem with a passenger's property, such as its loss or damage.

propjet An aircraft with propellers that are driven by a jet turbine engine.

protectorate A state that is controlled and protected by another.

province A principal administrative division of some countries. *See Appendix 3 for a list of Canadian Provinces.*

P

provisional booking A reservation that has not yet been confirmed by the agent or passenger and where space is being held pending a decision. > *option.*

provisioned charter The rental of a boat or yacht or similar vessel that includes fuel and provisions but not crew.

prow The pointed or projecting part of the front of a ship.

PSA Passenger Shipping Association Ltd. *See Appendix 5a.*

PSARA Passenger Shipping Association Retail Agents Scheme. *See Appendix 5a.*

PSR *See passenger space ratio.*

PSV (UK) *See public service vehicle.*

PTA 1. *See prepaid ticket advice.*
2. *See passenger transport authority.*

pub (UK) *See public house (1).*

public bar (UK) The name often given to the less well-appointed bar in a pub (the other often being called the 'saloon').

public golf course *See municipal golf course.*

public holiday A day when most commercial premises and government departments are closed. > *bank holiday.*

public house 1. (or **pub**) (UK) A place designed for the sale and consumption of alcoholic drinks, and sometimes food. These often (but not always) are owned by a brewery, and often (but not always) have two bars.
2. In some countries, a brothel.

public service vehicle A vehicle, such as a bus, operated to serve the needs of the public.

public transport Vehicles travelling on fixed routes and offering carriage to the public, usually on payment of a fare.

publican 1. (UK) The keeper of a pub.
2. (Australia) The keeper of a hotel.

published fare The fare shown in a carrier's official tariff.

Pullman Luxury train carriages without sleeping berths. Few now remain except on special services, such as the UK portion of the Venice-Simplon Orient Express. The original Pullman was an American railroad company that ran luxury services with sleeping accommodation.

pullman berth A name sometimes given to an upper berth that can be folded away when not in use.

punt A narrow, flat-bottomed boat used mainly on rivers and generally propelled by means of a long pole.

Purim A festival in the Jewish religious calendar, celebrated four weeks before Passover (in February or early March).

purser The person who looks after the administration of the passengers on board a ship or aircraft.

put about Of a ship or boat, to turn around.

Pyrenees The mountain range in Europe that separates the Iberian peninsula from France.

P

Qq

quad   An abbreviation for quadricycle.
> *cycle.*

quad bike   A small four-wheeled motorcycle used for recreation and sport.

quad chair   *See chair lift.*

quad room   A hotel room suitable for sleeping four people.

quadricycle   1. A four-wheeled cycle.
2. An alternative name for quad bike.

quagmire   A marsh or bog.

quarantine   A period of time during which animals or people, who may possibly have been exposed to a disease, are isolated from others to avoid the chance of transmitting infection. Until recently, animals imported into the British Isles had to undergo a six month quarantine period although the introduction of micro-ships and pet passports means that this is now not always necessary. *See Pet Travel Scheme.*

quarter-deck   Part of the upper deck of a ship, situated towards the stern, usually reserved for officers.

quay   A wharf or pier.

quayside   The land near a quay.

queen   *See monarch.*

queen room   A hotel room with a queen-sized bed (about 5 feet 6 inches wide).

Queenslander   1. A native of the state of Queensland in Australia.
2. The rail service between Brisbane and Cairns in Australia.

queue   1. (UK) A line of people waiting for something.
2. The making available of an item on an agent's computer terminal. For example, if an agent has made a request for a reservation that cannot immediately be confirmed (possibly because the service is full), the request is queued. When space becomes available, the agent's computer is automatically accessed by the principal and the details advised.

quick release   A style of belt buckle that allows for quick removal. It is particularly favoured by divers as it facilitates the swift removal and jettison of weight belts and cylinders. It is also worn by cabin crew on aircraft.

quicksand   Loose wet sand into which an object or person is likely to sink.

quid   (UK) A colloquial term for a pound sterling.

quin room   A hotel room for sleeping five people.

quote   A price calculated for a service and advised to a potential customer so that they may decide whether to accept the offer.

Q

Rr

rabies A contagious and usually fatal virus disease of dogs and other mammals. It can be transmitted to humans through saliva. Endemic in most of the world although not in the British Isles where quarantine (and now the Pets Travel Scheme) has kept it out. > *health protection, Pet Travel Scheme.*

RAC Royal Automobile Club. *See Appendix 5a.*

race Each of the major divisions of humankind, distinguished by variations in physical characteristics.

rack railway *See cog railway.*

rack rates The rates advertised by hotels and other principals before any discounts. So called because these are the prices on the leaflets in the racks.

racking policy The marketing decisions taken by a travel agency as to which brochures it will display and how prominently it will display them.

radar Radio detection and ranging. A system for detecting the range and presence of objects. Now an integral part of all transport systems.

raft A flat, floating construction of timber and other buoyant materials.

rail *See terrain park.*

rail map A map showing the railway routes of a country or area.

railcar A railway vehicle consisting of a single powered carriage.

railcard (UK) One of various types of card that allows its holder discounted rail travel fares.

railhead The start or end of a railway.

railroad (US) A railway.

Railtrack The organisation formerly responsible for running the track and some principal stations on the railways of Britain.

railway A means of transport in which the vehicles run on metal rails.

rain forest Luxuriant and dense jungles growing in tropical areas.

rain shadow A region sheltered from rainfall, usually by mountains.

Raj The period of British rule in India, ending in 1947.

rajah An Indian ruler or dignitary.

rake-off Commission or share on a deal, often an underhand one.

Ramadan The ninth month of the Muslim year, during which fasting is observed from dawn to dusk. As the Islamic calendar is determined by sightings of the new moon, the dates of Ramadan (and all other Islamic months) change each year. Generally, it falls eleven days earlier each year.

R

ramjet A type of jet engine in which the air is drawn in and compressed by the forward motion of the vehicle, rather than by a fan.

ramp *See apron.*

Randstad The most populous part of the Netherlands, including the cities of Amsterdam, Rotterdam and The Hague.

rapid transit A system or vehicle designed for high speed transport of passengers in urban areas.

rapids A section of a river where the water runs very fast, often over rocks.

rappelling *See abseiling.*

rate The charge for an item or service, generally where this involves rental rather than purchase. It is often expressed as a specific amount for a specific period of time.

Rath Yadra A festival in the Hindu religious calendar, celebrated at the time of the first full moon in November.

ravine A deep narrow gorge.

reasonable care The duty placed on an insured person to act in a prudent manner, often defined as behaving as if there were no insurance in place.

rebate A discount or an amount refunded.

re-book To reinstate a booking or to book a passenger again.

receivership A person appointed by a court to handle the affairs of, and realise the assets of, a bankrupt company.

receiving agent *See incoming tour operator.*

reception The area in a hotel or other public building where visitors report on arrival.

receptionist A person working in reception.

receptive agent *See incoming tour operator.*

réchauffé Food that has been warmed up.

recompression The act of re-pressurising a diver, usually in a recompression chamber after the onset of decompression sickness.

recompression chamber Pressurised steel chamber used for the compression, decompression and recompression of the occupants at air pressures which equate to various depths of water.

reconfirmation The requirement that passengers who break an air journey for more than 72 hours may need to advise the airline of their intention of using their next reservation. There are many variations to this procedure, which is now only followed by a small number of airlines, particularly in Asia.

record locator The identification for a file or record in a computer.

recreational vehicle (RV) (US) A general term used to denote any motorhome.

red carpet Preferential treatment afforded to an important visitor or traveller. Traditionally a red carpet was laid for the person to walk upon.

Red Centre The heart of the Australian outback, centred on Alice Springs.

red channel *See customs clearance.*

Red Crescent An international aid organisation, mainly active in Muslim countries.

Red Cross An international aid organisation, mainly active in Christian countries.

R

red ensign   The flag of the British merchant navy.

red run   A ski run of moderate difficulty suited to intermediate or advanced level skiers and snowboarders. Known as a blue square trail in North America.

Red Sea   The gulf that separates the Arabian peninsula from Africa.

red-eye   A colloquial expression for an overnight flight, especially from the west coast to the east coast in the USA.

red-light district   An area of a town or city where brothels and other aspects of the sex industry are located.

reef   A ridge, often of coral, at or just under the surface of the sea.

re-embark   To get back on board a vessel.

re-entry visa   A visa that allows a traveller back into a country.

refuelling service   A service provided by some vehicle rental companies whereby a customer can return a vehicle without a full tank of fuel, the cost of the fuel required being taken from their credit card.

refuelling stop   A stop required en route, generally by a plane, solely for the purpose of taking fuel on board. Passengers cannot join or leave at a refuelling stop.

Regency   Of or relating to the period of English history during the regency at the end of George III's reign (1811 to 1820).

regime   A method or system of government. The term tends to be used in a derogatory way about governments that are not well thought of.

region   An area of land having more or less definable boundaries.

register   The official record, maintained by hotels, of the names and other details of guests.

registered baggage   Baggage that has been put into the care of a carrier who will undertake to handle and convey it until arrival at the passenger's destination.

regulator   Also called demand valve. A valve that reduces the high pressure contained in an aqualung cylinder to a usable pressure so that the diver is able to breathe.

reissue   1. To issue a document again, usually after having made changes to it. 2. A document so reissued.

relative humidity   *See humidity.*

relief map   A map showing the height or depth of physical features by means of bands of colour rather than contour lines.

relief road   (UK) A road taking traffic around a congested area.

religion   Any of the systems of belief in a controlling superhuman power or powers demanding obedience, reverence and worship, often associated with a structured or ritualistic system of organisation, and often professing a comprehensive moral and ethical code intended to guide or govern all aspects of the lives of its adherents.
The number of religions, past and present, and the various denominations and sects within them, are almost beyond count. Most would agree that there are five which have had a particularly profound influence on the world, on other religions, and on each other. These are, in order of antiquity, Hinduism (c.4000BC), Judaism (c.2000BC), Buddhism (c.560 BC), Christianity (c.AD30) and Islam (c.AD622); and, in order of number of estimated present-day adherents, Christianity (c.2 billion), Islam (c.1.3 billion), Hinduism (c.900 million),

R

Buddhism (c.360 million) and Judaism (c.15 million). If one adds Sikhism (which developed in northern India in the 16th century, and which has c.23 million adherents), and the traditional religions of China and Africa (c.225 million and c.95 million respectively), nearly five out of six of the world's population are thus accounted for. Of the 1.1 billion who remain, most (c.850 million) are estimated as being non-religious. Other religions, all of which are estimated to have less than 15 million adherents, include Spiritism, Baha'i, Jainism, Shinto, Cao Dai, Tenrikyo, Neo-Paganism, Unitarian-Universalism, Rastafarianism, Scientology and Zoroastrianism. Finally, there is Juche, the official philosophy of Korea DPR (North), which is for sociological reasons sometimes regarded as a religion. Further information on the main customs and beliefs of the world's major religions can be found in the Columbus *World Travel Guide*.

Two aspects of religion are likely to affect the day-to-day life of the travel trade professional. The first is that many holidays, or excursions within a holiday, are influenced by a desire to witness some aspect of religious life, whether this be a pilgrimage to Lourdes, Puri, Mecca or the Wailing Wall or a recreational visit to Khajuraho, Notre Dame, Thimpu or the Blue Mosque. Some knowledge on the part of the travel arranger of the religious beliefs which underpin the allure of these places will often be useful. Secondly, some religious adherents will have strict views on a number of matters, while others may find themselves needing to avoid the consequences of the strict views of others. The travel arranger may thus find clients specifying unacceptable carriers or transit stops, essential or prohibited days or dates of travel or specific dietary requirements. Brief details for selection of the main religious festivals for a selection of the major religions may be found throughout the text. In most cases, their dates change from year to year.

remark   A note or endorsement on a document to convey a special instruction.

Renaissance   Of or relating to a loosely defined period during the 14th to 16th centuries in Europe during which there was a revival of art and literature using classical models. With a qualification, the term is also used to describe similar artistic revivals at other times and in other places (such as the Carolingian Renaissance in France and Germany or the Celtic Renaissance in Ireland).

rental day   A 24-hour period starting at the time the vehicle was rented, often rounded to nearest hour or half-hour. Any rental period which exceeds the rental day may incur an additional charge.

renter   The person, usually but not always the driver, who is responsible for paying for a vehicle rental agreement and who is liable for any obligations under it.

rep   *See representative.*

repatriation   The bringing home of a traveller from abroad, usually for reasons of sickness or emergency.

representative   Anyone who represents a company or organisation. In travel, the expression usually refers to a tour operator's employee, retained in a resort to attend to the needs of its customers.

republic   A country with an elected representative, rather than a monarch, as head of state.

Republic of China   *See ROC.*

request   1. Where a facility has been asked for but not confirmed.
2. The circumstance of a potential passenger being placed on a waiting list for a flight in case of cancellations. The code RQ is officially used for this. Because of the possible confusion between meanings, some travel clerks use the abbreviation WL for a waiting list, but this is not an official airline abbreviation.

R

request stop (UK) A stop at which a vehicle, usually a bus, will only stop on the instruction of a passenger or potential passenger.

re-route To change the routeing on a ticket or itinerary.

reservation 1. In general, a booking made for a particular accommodation, transport, entertainment or other service. 2. The act of booking, or receiving confirmation for, space on a particular transport service. Although many tickets (such as most air journeys) have reservation and travel details shown on the one document, on some services (such as most rail journeys) a ticket only shows that a passenger has paid for travel and a separate reservation document may be necessary.

reservation system Any system that is set up to control the booking of flights, holidays and other travel products and services. Most reservation systems are now computerised.

reserve To make a booking. > *reservation*.

reserved Space that has been booked or set aside for a customer or group.

resort A city, town, village or other development visited by holidaymakers, often for a specific reason. Since individual preferences vary, almost anywhere can be considered a resort. However, major centres such as London, although attracting large numbers of visitors, are not usually called resorts. In the USA, the term is now often used to describe a large-scale hotel and leisure complex, or even a large hotel with extensive grounds and facilities.

resort complex A concentration of specifically constructed and largely self-contained holiday facilities.

resort condominium A block of separately owned apartments in a North American resort complex.

rest house A place for travellers to rest in, possibly overnight. Typically found in the Indian subcontinent.

restaurant An eating establishment offering a range of food, often with table service.

restaurateur (or **restauranteur**) A person who owns or runs a restaurant.

Restoration Of or relating to the period of English history following the restoration of Charles II after the English Revolution, and generally associated with his reign (1660 to 1685).

restroom (US) A lavatory.

retail travel agent A company or individual which makes and sells travel services. > *travel agent*.

re-time To set a new schedule for a service.

return ticket (UK) A ticket bought for a journey to one or more places, returning to the originating point. It is known as a round-trip ticket in the USA.

revaccination A repeat vaccination to boost or reinforce the original.

revalidation The process of amending a detail of a ticket or reservation. The expression usually refers to airline tickets, on which agents may only change flights or dates of travel.

revalidation sticker A sticker which is attached to a ticket to show that certain details have been amended and recorded.

reverse thrust The system by which the exhaust of a jet engine can be directed forward into the direction of travel. This can be used to reverse an aircraft on the ground or to create a powerful braking effect after landing.

R

RHIB (or **RIB**) A rigid-hulled inflatable boat.

ría A long narrow inlet formed by the submergence of a river valley, especially in north-west Spain.

Richter scale A logarithmic scale that records the severity of earthquakes. Its values range from 0 to 9. The most severe earthquake ever recorded (at Gansu in China in 1920) measured 8.6.

rickshaw A light two- or three-wheeled vehicle usually drawn by a person or people on foot. In some parts of the world, such as southern India, they may be motorised.

ridge A long narrow hilltop or similar.

ridgeway A road or track along a ridge.

rift valley A steep-sided valley caused by subsidence of the earth between two faults. The river Jordan lies at the bottom of the deepest rift valley on dry land.

rig 1. (US) A vehicle, particularly a lorry.
2. The arrangement of sails ands masts on a boat.
3. To make a boat ready for a voyage.
4. To fix, control or manipulate fraudulently.

rigging The arrangement of sails and ropes on a sailing ship.

right of abode (UK) A person's right to take up residence in a country.

right of way 1. A right established to travel across another's land.
2. A path having such a right.
3. The order of precedence of a ship or other vehicle.

right, driving on the See *left, driving on the.*

ring road (UK) A road that encircles a town or city, such as the Périphérique around Paris or the M25 around London.

rip A stretch of rough or fast running water in the sea or a river, caused by the meeting of currents.

river A substantial stream of water, flowing to an ocean or sea (or sometimes to a lake). For a list of the world's longest rivers, consult the Columbus *World Travel Atlas.*

riviera Any coastal region with a sub-tropical climate, especially in southern France and north-west Italy.

Riviera The popular tourist region in south-east France and north-west Italy bordering the Mediterranean Sea. The coastal strip stretches from Cannes to La Spezia. The French Riviera is also known as the Côte d'Azur: main coastal resorts include Cannes, Antibes, Nice and Monte-Carlo. The Italian Riviera is divided into the Riviera di Ponente in the west and the Riviera di Levante in the east. The main resorts include Genoa and La Spezia.

road A generic term for any path or way with a specially prepared surface and intended for the use of pedestrians, animals or vehicles.

road map A map showing the roads of a country or area, sometimes to the exclusion of some other features such as railways.

road train A large road locomotive pulling a number of trailers, commonly used in Australia.

road warrior Marketing jargon for a business traveller, especially one who demands special facilities in hotels.

roadhouse An inn or similar establishment on or near a road.

roadside The strip of land next to a road.

roadway The part of a bridge used for traffic.

R

roaring forties Areas of high wind at approximately 40° to 50° north and south of the Equator.

ROC 1. The Republic of China, or Taiwan. The term Taiwan (ROC) is often used by that country to describe itself. It is not to be confused with the People's Republic of China, the official name for mainland China.
2. A ticketing abbreviation meaning record of change.

rock climbing grades See climbing grades.

rock climbing The ascent of boulders, cliffs, crags and mountains by means of climbing steep sections of rock, requiring the use of hands and feet for progress and technical safety equipment such as a rope, harness and 'gear' – machined metal items that can be temporarily lodged in the rock to safeguard progress.

Rocky Mountains The main mountain range in North America, extending from Alaska to New Mexico.

Rocky Mountaineer A luxury tourist train running between Vancouver and Jasper or Calgary in Canada.

Rocky Mountains International A US regional marketing organisation covering the states of Idaho, Wyoming, South Dakota and Montana. > US regional marketing organisations.

RoE Rate of exchange. Used when calculating prices quoted in foreign currencies into local money or in a bureau de change.

ROH See run of house rate.

roll The side to side movement of a ship.

roll on, roll off The system used on most car ferries that allows vehicles to be driven on and driven off, as opposed to being loaded by crane.

rolling stock 1. The locomotives, carriages, goods wagons and other vehicles used on a railway.
2. (US) The road vehicles of a company.

Roman numerals The system of numbering, often employed for preliminary pages in books, that uses letters and letter combinations. They can be used either in capitals or in lower case. The units are I=1, V=5, X=10, L=50, C=100, D=500 and M =1000. Where a lower number is placed before a higher number, the former is subtracted from the latter: thus IV is 4 and XC is 90. Where a lower number is placed after a higher number, the two are added together: thus VI is 6 and CX is 110. Multiples of 1,000 are sometimes indicated by a vertical line over the letter/s to be multiplied. No zero is used in the Roman numbering system. > Arabic numerals.

Romanesque A style of architecture prevalent in Europe between 900AD and 1200 with massive vaulting and rounded arches.

Romantic Road A tourist route in Germany between Wurzburg and Füssen, passing through areas of great scenic and historic interest.

Romany See Gypsy.

rondavel A round hut or similar simple building, especially in South Africa.

room night One room occupied for one night.

room only Hotel accommodation provided without any meals included.

room service The provision of drinks, meals and other services in a hotel room.

roomette 1. (US) A single compartment in a railway sleeping car.
2. (US) A small room available for letting.

rooming list A list giving details of clients

R

booked, usually when a group is involved.

ro-ro *See roll on, roll off.*

Rosh Hashanah A festival in the Jewish religious calendar celebrating the new Year. It takes place in September or October.

rostrum *See podium.*

rotating wing aircraft An aircraft whose wings rotate in flight to provide lift. This is usually a helicopter or similar.

rough passage A crossing over rough seas.

round the world (RTW) 1. A journey round the world.
2. An air fare using this construction.

round trip 1. (US) A journey to one or more places and then back to the originating point.
2. An airline term meaning a return trip comprising two fare components only, the fares for which are the same, but with different routes. > *circle trip.*

roundabout 1. An interchange where roads converge in a circular junction. in general, the traffic already on the junction has priority over that waiting to enter it, although in many French-influenced countries the reverse is the case. Roundabouts are very rare in the USA.
2. A merry-go-round at a funfair or similar.

rounding The act of adjusting a figure, usually a price, to the nearest convenient or specified unit. Fares for most transport operators are calculated to a nearest whole unit. In the case of UK rail, for example, this is usually five pence. Any calculation must be rounded to the specified unit before the fare is used. Population and area figures for countries are often rounded to the nearest 1,000.

Route 66 The first long-distance paved highway in the USA, immortalised in song and popular legend. It was completed in 1926 and fully paved by 1937, and ran from Chicago to Los Angeles via Springfield, Oklahoma City, Amarillo, Albuquerque and Flagstaff. With the opening of Interstate 40 in 1984, Route 66 was decommissioned, but a Route 66 Association now exists to recall its heyday as 'the main street of America'. As a result, many old road signs and landmarks along the route have been replaced or restored.

routing The way or course taken on a journey. Many fares will be available by a specific route or routes and the restriction as to what route is available for any ticket will be shown somewhere on the document.

rover ticket A ticket allowing unlimited travel in a particular area for a specified time. Usually restricted to the services of one carrier or its commercial partners.

Royal Orient The luxury rail service in India which provides services between Delhi and major tourist centres in Rajasthan, Gujarat and Daman & Diu including Udaipur and Sasan Gir.

Royal Scotsman The luxury rail service running from Edinburgh to various towns in Scotland.

royalty 1. The amount, usually a percentage, of sales revenue paid to the owner of a product or service.
2. Persons belonging to a royal family.

RQ A code used to indicate that a passenger's booking is on request or waitlisted. > *request.*

RT *See round trip.*

RTW *See round the world.*

rubberneck A derogatory term for a tourist or sightseer.

rudder The part of a ship or aircraft that controls its direction.

R

running gear The suspension and wheels of a vehicle.

running lights Sometimes called navigation lights. The lights that a vessel must display when travelling at night.

run-of-the-house rate A reduced price at which a hotel has agreed to offer rooms.

runway A long, straight, flat and wide paved pathway from which aircraft take off and onto which they land.

rural Of or relating to the countryside.

Rust Belt The areas of the north and north-eastern United States characterised by older, heavy industry, particularly the steel and auto industries.

RV *See recreational vehicle.*

ryokan A Japanese term for a traditional wayside inn.

R

Ss

Sabbath   The day of rest and religious observance kept by Jews on a Saturday. Agents should be aware of the possible implications on travel arrangements.

sabbatical   Leave granted at intervals to a university teacher for study or travel, originally every seven years. The term is now often used to denote any extended leave period granted to an employee.

Sabre   A GDS sponsored by American Airlines.

saddle   The lowest passage between two mountain tops.

safari   A trip into a wildlife area, such as a game reserve, for photography or occasionally hunting.

safari boat   *See live-aboard.*

safari park   *See wildlife park.*

safety announcement   Instructions in the use of the safety and evacuation equipment on board a ship or aircraft given by the crew soon after the start of a journey, usually with the aid of a video.

safety deposit   A facility offered by hotels for the safekeeping of their guests' valuables.

sahel   A semi-arid region which forms a transitional area between deserts and more fertile areas such as savannahs and forests

Sahel, the   The area of sahel on the southern borders of the Sahara.

sahib   A polite form of address used in India when referring to a man.

sail   The large piece of material, traditionally canvas, fixed to a ship's mast to catch the wind.

sailboard   A small boat with a mast and sail used in windsurfing.

sailboat   (US) A sailing boat.

sailing boat   (UK) A boat propelled by sails.

sailing list   An obsolete term that meant a shipping line's timetable. Where they exist, shipping lines now call them timetables.

sailing ticket   A passenger or vehicle control document used on some shipping and ferry services that experience very heavy peak demand.

sailplane   An engineless heavier-than-air aircraft used for sustained unpowered flight. Originally sailplanes differed from gliders in that gliders needed a permanent tow and sailplanes could fly using upward wind currents. Nowadays the distinction is rarely made.

sales agency agreement   An agreement for the sale of a principal's services. Most principals will have a specific form or structure for such agreements.

salinity   The concentration of salt in a

S

liquid, typically the sea. The higher the salinity the more buoyant the water.

saloon 1. A public room on a ship.
2. (US) A bar.
3. (UK) The name often given to the better-appointed bar in a pub (the other often being called 'public')
4. (UK) An enclosed motor car with no partition between driver and passengers. *(US: sedan)*
5. (UK) A railway carriage serving as a lounge.

saloon keeper (US) A bartender.

salt A sailor (often 'old salt' to imply knowledge and experience).

salt flat The dried up bed of a salt lake that leaves a plain covered in salt.

salt lake A lake of salt water.

salubrious Of a climate or place, healthy.

salvage The rescue of a ship or other vessel or its property following an accident or similar.

salvage tug A tug designed to rescue disabled vessels.

samovar A Russian urn used for making tea. and at one time a standard provision on Russian long-distance trains.

sampan A small boat used in the Far East.

sample room A room that displays merchandise.

sand yacht *See land yacht.*

sandbank A deposit of sand forming a shallow place in the sea or a river.

sandbar *See bar (2).*

SAR Search and Rescue.

Sargasso Sea An area of the North

Atlantic in which large clumps of sargasso seaweed are found on or near the surface.

SARS Severe Acute Respiratory Syndrome, an air-borne disease caused by the corona virus, linked to the common cold. The first reported case was in Hanoi in February 2003 and it has since spread widely.

satellite printer location The place in which a satellite ticket printer is located. The official IATA definition is: 'An accredited agent's place of business in one country, controlled by a host location in the same country: (a) which is located on the premises of a customer of the agent, such customer not being an agent or tour operator; (b) which is not accessible to the general public; (c) whose sole purpose is the issuance, by means of a satellite ticket printer, of traffic documents to the customer or its employees; and (d) which is entered on the agency list as a satellite ticket printer location.'

satellite state A small country dependent on or controlled by another.

satellite ticket printer A ticket printer located away from an agency that can be used to print out traffic documents in a distant location. Satellite ticket printers can only be controlled by the agency.

satellite town A small town dependent on a nearby larger town or city.

SATH 1. The Society for the Advancement of Travel for the Handicapped (UK). *See Appendix 5a.*
2. The Society for the Advancement of Travel for the Handicapped (USA). *See Appendix 5b.*

satnav Satellite navigation. A navigation system using data from satellites, common on ships and aircraft.

saturation diving Diving for long periods whereby body tissues are saturated with dissolved nitrogen to the maximum extent for the depth in question.

S

savannah (or **savanna**) The tropical grasslands bordering on the equatorial rain forests in both the northern and southern hemispheres. > *climate zones*.

Saxon Of or relating to the Germanic peoples that conquered parts of England in the 5th and 6th centuries.

scale The ratio between the a distance on a map and the corresponding distance on the ground. This is normally expressed in one of two ways: numerically (for example 1:5,000, meaning that 1 unit on the map represents 5,000 of the same units on the ground); or as a series of graduated marks on a line, each indicating what distance on the ground is represented by the appropriate distance on the map. See also *maps* and *map projections*.

Scandinavia The geographical region comprising Denmark, Norway and Sweden. Often extended to include Finland and, more rarely, Iceland.

scenery The general appearance of the natural features of a landscape, particularly where this is pleasing.

scenic Picturesque or attractive as regards its view.

schedule An alternative name for a timetable.

scheduled carrier A carrier that operates a scheduled service.

scheduled flight *See scheduled service.*

scheduled service A service, generally by air, which is available to all passengers, and which operates at advertised set times between set points, regardless of demand.

Schengen The agreement which in 1995 abolished most frontier controls between participating member countries, which comprises all the current members of the EU except the UK and Ireland, and some associate non-EU members including Norway and Iceland.

schooner 1. A fore-and-aft rigged sailing ship with two or more masts.
2. (US) A tall beer glass.
3. (UK) A large-measure glass, particularly for sherry.

schuss A straight downhill ski-run.

Scotland One of the constituent countries of the United Kingdom of Great Britain and Northern Ireland. > *Great Britain, United Kingdom.*

scrambling grades *See climbing grades.*

scrambling The activity which is a combination of usually rough and strenuous walking and technically easy rock climbing, sometimes requiring use of the hands (or even basic rock climbing equipment) and generally taking place in very exposed situations such as cliff tops or narrow ridges. Generally graded from 1 to 3, with 1 being the easiest.

scree Loose rocks and stones that cover a slope, usually below a cliff.

screw A ship's propeller.

scrub An area of low bushes or stunted forest growth.

scuba Self-contained underwater breathing apparatus. An aqualung.

scupper 1. An opening in the side of a ship that allows any accumulation of water to escape.
2. To sink a vessel deliberately.

scuttle 1. A hole in a ship's deck fitted with a cover.
2. To sink a ship deliberately, usually by letting in water through the sea cocks.

SDMA Scottish Destination Management Association. *See Appendix 5a.*

sea A large body of water, usually salt.

S

Many seas, such as the South China Sea, are contained within oceans.

sea anchor   A device dragged from a ship to control its drift.

sea breeze   A breeze blowing off the sea onto the land.

sea cock   A valve situated below the waterline in a ship to let water in or out.

sea facing   A room in a hotel or similar establishment that faces the sea but may not have a view of it, perhaps due to an abundance of vegetation. > *sea view*.

sea legs   The ability to walk properly on the decks of a ship, even when it is pitching and rolling. It usually takes a day or two for a passenger to acquire their sea legs.

sea travel   Travelling by ship, hovercraft, hydrofoil or other seaborne vessel.

sea view   A room in a hotel or similar establishment that has a view of the sea. Since such rooms are preferred by many guests, a supplement is usually payable. > *sea facing*.

sea wall   A wall or embankment constructed to prevent encroachment by the sea.

seafront   That part of a coastal town or resort that faces onto the shore.

seaplane   An aircraft that can operate from water.

seashore   That part of the land close to the sea.

seasickness   A temporary illness suffered on rough seas when the body's balance is disturbed.

season   1. Any division of the year characterised by clearly identifiable climatic characteristics. The differences between the seasons, particularly as regards temperature and sunlight, become more pronounced as one moves towards the poles.
2. In travel, a particular time of the year during which demand or activity is at a certain and identifiable level.

season ticket   A ticket available for a series of journeys or admissions in a given period.

seasonality   The variation for demand for products and services that is due to different seasons.

seat belt   A retaining device fitted to many vehicles that holds passengers in their seats in the event of accident or violent movement. The use of seat belts in cars and coaches is obligatory in many countries while their use in aircraft is universal.

seat configuration   The arrangement of the seats in a particular aircraft, coach, train, ship or other mode of transport. This will vary from service to service and from carrier to carrier. Aircraft seat configurations may change from time to time, particularly as a result of the controversy surrounding DVT. > *seat pitch, DVT*.

seat pitch   The term used to describe the distance between aircraft seats. Note that the figure does not give the amount of legroom, but the distance occupied by the seat and the legroom combined (in other words, the distance between any position on one seat and the same position on the seat immediately in front of or behind it). Seat pitch varies according to the class of travel, and for many travellers is the main reason for paying a higher fare. Although the CAA's legal minimum is 26 inches, recent policy (particularly in the light of the controversy over DVT) has been for airlines to increase the pitch on economy class services. Typically, the seat pitch in economy class will be around 31 inches; in full-fare economy, around 37 inches; in

S

business class around 48 inches; and in first class around 60 inches. All seat pitches will vary from carrier to carrier and from aircraft to aircraft.

seat plans   Diagrams of an aircraft showing the location of seats, galleys and other services.

seat rotation   A system used on coach tours where passengers change seats at regular intervals so as to ensure that everyone has an opportunity to occupy the better seats.

seating plan   A diagram showing the layout of seats, such as on a vehicle or in a hall.

seatmate   (US) Each of a set of people who share a seat.

seat-only   (UK) A seat on an air charter service for which no associated hotel accommodation is provided.

seaward   Towards the sea.

seaway   An ocean or estuarial traffic lane.

second   1. A sixtieth of a minute of time. 2. A sixtieth of a minute of an angle. > *degree.*

second class   A level of service, accommodation or transport that is less good than first class. It is now rarely employed as an official designation, terms such as 'standard' and 'economy' being preferred.

second floor   1. (UK) The floor of a building two levels above the ground floor. 2. (US) The floor of a building immediately above the ground floor.

second sitting   The later of two meal times on a train or cruise ship.

sector   A complete portion of an itinerary or journey, which can comprise several

legs or segments.

security tax   A charge levied to cover the cost of screening of passengers and their luggage to try to detect acts of terrorism.

sedan   1. An enclosed chair carried by two porters to provide transport. 2. (US) A saloon car.

segment   That portion of a passenger's journey from boarding to disembarking. Since a vehicle may stop several times en route, a segment could comprise several legs. > *leg.*

seiche   A fluctuation in the water level of a lake or other enclosed body of water caused by changes in barometric pressure, rather than by tidal influences.

seif   A long narrow sand dune.

self-catering   Any type of accommodation that allows or expects guests to arrange their own meals.

self-drive   A vehicle driven by the person who has hired it, or their named driver/s, rather than by a chauffeur.

self-righting   A characteristic of a small boat which has been designed to return automatically to its upright position after a capsize.

selling point   A feature or aspect of a holiday or other arrangement that makes it of particular interest or benefit to a prospective customer.

semaphore   1. An early signalling method involving the use of hand-held flags, each position representing a letter. 2. A signal, usually on a railway, that makes use of a moving arm, rather than coloured lights.

semi-basement   A storey in a building that is partly below ground level.

semi-tropical   *See sub-tropical.*

S

senior citizen An elderly or retired person. *See old-age pensioner.*

SEO Society of Event Organisers. *See Appendix 5a.*

sepulchre A tomb cut into rock, or built of stone or rock.

serein Fine rain that occasionally falls from cloudless skies in the tropics.

serial number The number or code on a document that indicates its position in the batch.

series charter A charter based on the use of a vehicle, usually an aircraft, for several journeys between the same points.

service 1. A scheduled transport link provided between one place and another. 2. Public religious worship conducted according to a prescribed form, generally in a place designed or designated for that purpose. 3. The act of waiting at a table, bar or similar, and the manner in which this is done. > *silver service.* 4. An alternative term for service charge. *See service charge.* 5. The set of dinner plates, bowls, cutlery and the like which is used for serving meals. 6. The serving of a meal at any one of a number of separate sittings, often on a train or a ship. 7. A thin cord used as a binding around a rope on a ship to prevent rotting or unravelling. 8. One of the three types of profession (manufacturing and agriculture being the others) into which economic activity is generally divided for statistical purposes. (Generally 'services' in such cases.) 9. The regular checks and overhauls given to a mechanical object, such as a car or a plane.

service area An area by a road, usually for the supply of fuel, refreshments and other services and facilities.

service bus (Australia) A motor coach.

service charge An additional amount added to a bill to cover the cost of service, as opposed to a discretionary tip.

service industry An industry, such as travel, that provides services rather than goods.

service road A road running parallel to a main road giving access to shops or buildings set back from it.

service station An establishment selling fuel and other goods.

serviced accommodation Any accommodation provided by an organisation, such as a hotel, that provides a range of additional services.

set down To offload passengers.

set meal A meal with no choice of dishes.

seven seas The oceans of the world, or the whole world generally. > *ocean.*

sex tourism Tourism that attracts visitors to destinations where they may seek sexual encounters. Although this is frowned on by many, the practice is widespread in some countries.

sextant An instrument that measures angular distance, used in navigation.

SFT Swiss Federation of Travel Agencies. *See Appendix 5c.*

SGTP Society of Government Travel Professionals. *See Appendix 5b.*

shakedown cruise The first cruise operated after a ship has been built or re-fitted. It is intended to identify any flaws before the vessel enters full service.

Shamal A hot dry wind which blows from the north-west in Iraq and the Persian Gulf.

S

Shangri La An imaginary paradise on earth, supposedly located somewhere in Tibet.

shanty A small, crudely built dwelling.

shantytown A residential area made up of shanties, often found on the outskirts of large conurbations, and often occupied by immigrant workers or those originating from the countryside.

shaped ski *See carving skis.*

Sharav *See Khamsin.*

shark billy Short stick with pointed end used for fending off sharks.

Shavuot A festival in the Jewish religious calendar, celebrated seven weeks after Passover (in May or June).

shebeen An unlicensed house that sells alcohol, especially in Ireland and Scotland.

sheikh (or **sheik**) The head of a region, village or family in Muslim countries. The term can also refer to a religious leader. It is also used as a title of respect.

sheikha (or **sheika**) The wife of a sheikh. It is also used as a title of respect.

sheikhdom A country or state ruled by a sheikh.

shingle Small stones or pebbles.

Shinkansen The high-speed train network in Japan, connecting most of the main cities in Honshu and Kyushu. > *Bullet Trains.*

ship 1. A large waterborne vessel, often of many thousands of tons and hundreds of feet in length.
2. (US) An aircraft.

ship canal A canal large enough to take seagoing vessels.

ship density *See passenger space ratio.*

ship of the desert A camel.

shipboard A term that means anything that is used or occurs on board a ship.

shipping lane A busy track across the sea or ocean, such as the Straits of Dover.

shipwreck Any derelict vessel or part thereof abandoned at or on the coast. A shipwreck may be found floating, ashore or on the seabed in either a submerged or partly submerged condition.

shire (UK) A county.

shooting brake (UK) An estate car.

shore The land along the edge of a body of water.

shore excursion A trip taken by passengers whilst a ship is in port.

short break A short duration trip usually taken in addition to a main holiday. Many short breaks are to cities or similar destinations that boast a wide range of attractions.

short haul An inexact term that is applied generally to journeys within one continent.

short takeoff and landing Any aircraft that can operate from a shorter runway than is needed for conventional types.

shoulder season The period between high season and low season.

Shrove Tuesday A festival in the Christian calendar, the day before Ash Wednesday. Also known as Pancake Day.

shuttle service A transport service that simply plies back and forth between two points.

Siberia A vast region of Russia, extending

S

from the Ural Mountains to the Bering Sea and from the Arctic Ocean to Mongolia.

sick flag *See yellow flag.*

sickbay The part of a ship used as a hospital.

sidereal time Time measured by the apparent motion of the stars. A sidereal day is about 20 minutes 23 seconds longer than a solar day.

side-road A road joining or leaving a main road.

sidewalk (US) The area on one or both sides of a road reserved for pedestrians. Referred to as a pavement in the UK.

siding 1. An area of track on a railway used for the marshalling and storage of rolling stock.
2. (US) External cladding material for a building.

sierra A mountain range.

Sierra Madre The continuation of the Rocky Mountains in Mexico, divided into the Orientale (east) and Occidentale (west).

siesta A rest taken in the middle of the afternoon. Once common in hot countries, it is becoming less so with the advent of air conditioning and the demands for full-time working.

sightseeing trip A visit to one or more tourist attractions.

signal box (UK) A building from which the signals and points of a railway are controlled.

signal tower (US) *See signal box.*

Sikhism The religion of the Sikhs. > *religion.*

Silicon Valley An electronics and computer research and manufacturing area in the Santa Clara Valley, California, stretching from Palo Alto in the north to San Jose in the south.

Silk Road 1. A general term for the various ancient trade routes which for many centuries linked China with Europe. 2. A WTO Regional Promotional Project, launched in 1994. It aims to revitalise through tourism the ancient highways used by Marco Polo and the caravan traders who came after him. The Silk Road stretches 12,000 km from Asia to Europe. Sixteen Silk Road countries have joined forces for this project: Japan, Republic of Korea, DPR Korea, China, Kazakstan, Kyrgyzstan, Pakistan, Uzbekistan, Tajikistan, Turkmenistan, Iran, Azerbaijan, Turkey, Georgia, Greece and Egypt. Joint promotional activities include publicity material, familiarisation trips and special events at major tourism trade fairs.

Silver Meteor A rail service running between New York and Miami in the USA.

silver service Restaurant service where the food is brought to the table on large dishes from which it is served in portions to meet the needs of each diner.

Silver Star A rail service running between New York and Miami in the USA.

single 1. A hotel room for one person only. 2. A one-way ticket.

single chair A chair lift designed to carry only one person.

single entry visa A visa valid for one visit only.

Single European Currency *See euro.*

single occupancy rate A special rate charged to a lone guest occupying a multiple bedded room. It would usually be more than the price for a single room, but less than the full rate for the multiple bedded room

single supplement An extra amount payable by a person occupying accommodation for sole use.

single-decker (UK) A bus or coach with only one deck.

Sinic The ancient Chinese civilisation (c.1600BC until AD220).

Sino- Of or relating to China or the Chinese, generally used as a prefix.

Sirocco (or **Scirocco**) A hot dusty wind blowing towards Europe from North Africa. Known as the Ghibli in Libya and Leveche in Spain. Its origins are the same as the Khamsin or Sharav. On the northern Mediterranean coast, particularly in southern Italy, the wind is moist after crossing the Mediterranean.

Site of Special Scientific Interest (SSSI) (UK) An area designated as being of special scientific importance and thus often having restricted access.

six pac See chair lift.

sked (US) See schedule.

Skeena The rail service running between Prince Rupert and Jasper in the Canadian Rockies.

Skeleton Coast The desert coast of Namibia between Walvis Bay and the Angolan border. A national park and part of the Namib Desert, the name comes from the number of ships wrecked on its treacherous rocks or lost in the fogs created by the cold Benguela current.

skerry A Scottish term for a reef or rocky island.

ski area A part of a mountain where ski lifts and ski runs create an area where it is possible to ski or snowboard. All ski resorts have ski areas next or near to

them but may also exist where there is no resort nearby.

ski boot A special boot for skiers, normally with a rigid plastic shell which holds the ankle firm to protect from injury and help the skier control the ski. The boot connects to the ski by means of a binding which is fixed to the ski.

ski évolutif A method of learning to ski where beginners start with special short skis, graduating to longer ones as they improve.

ski kindergarten A facility by which younger children (typically aged four to ten) are offered a mixture of supervised indoor play and meals and well as ski or snowboard lessons in ski resorts. Known as day care in North America and sometimes offered without an outdoor element.

ski lift Any one of a number of types of device to carry skiers up a slope.

ski pass See lift ticket.

ski poles The two metal rods held by a skier to assist propulsion and manoeuvrability.

ski report See snow report.

ski resort A mountain destination developed for the dedicated use of those taking skiing and other winter-sports holidays.

ski run See piste.

ski season The months when ski resorts typically have enough snow on their slopes and operate their ski lifts and prepare their ski runs. In the northern hemisphere this is often from the end of November to mid-April but most tour operators will only run tours from mid-December to late-March to increase the likelihood that there will be adequate snow cover.

S

ski slope   *See piste.*

ski sticks   *See ski poles.*

skiable vertical   The vertical distance that a skier can ski down without having to take a lift up.

ski-bob   A single track vehicle, similar in layout to a bicycle, but with skis instead of wheels.

Skidoo   A brand name for a make of snowmobile, often used as a generic name for all such vehicles.

ski-jump   A man-made slope with a sharp drop from which skiers jump.

ski-plane   An aircraft with skis rather than wheels.

skipper   A colloquial expression for the captain of a ship or aircraft.

skipper charter   A form of charter whereby the vessel is provided with a skipper, but otherwise without supplies or crew.

skirt   The flexible surround that contains the air of a hovercraft or similar vehicle.

ski-run   A slope prepared for skiing.

skis   1. A pair of long narrow devices fitted to the underside of a pair of special boots, that allow rapid travel over snow. Initially made of wood, modern skis are made from increasingly complex compounds of hi-tech materials.
2. The act of using a pair of skis.

skyjack   *See hijack.*

slack water   The time when the tide is turning, especially at low tide.

Slave Coast   The coastal areas of present-day Togo, Benin and western Nigeria. The name comes from the trade in slaves between the 16th and 19th centuries.

Slave Route   A WTO Regional Promotional Project, launched in 1995 as part of the United Nations' International Year of Tolerance. It aims to boost cultural tourism to West African nations. Its immediate goals are to restore monuments, enhance history museums and launch joint promotional campaigns in selected tourism-generating markets, which will motivate foreign visitors to learn about the history of these countries and to discover their roots. The project is expected to be expanded in the future to include other nations in East and Southern and Africa, as well as countries in the Caribbean.

sleeper   1. A railway sleeping car. On UK railways, it is generally a single or two-berth sleeping compartment. UK sleepers have proper beds and bed linen and sexes are segregated.
2. The wooden or concrete transverse supports that hold the metals of a railway track in proper alignment. Known as ties in the USA.

sleeping car   *See sleeper (1).*

sleigh   A sledge, especially one for riding on, often drawn by horses or reindeer.

SLI   *See supplementary liability insurance.*

slip   (US) An artificial slope in a marina or dock where boats can be brought into or out of the water.

slip road   (UK) A road that enters or leaves a motorway or similar.

slipstream   A current of air or water driven back by a moving vehicle.

sloop   A small single-masted vessel with foresail and jib.

slot   An allocated time of departure or arrival at an airport. Slots are at a premium in busy airports.

Slovak Republic   A country in Central

S

Europe, formerly part of Czechoslovakia and sometimes referred to as Slovakia. Not to be confused with Slovenia.

Slovenia A country in the Balkans, formerly part of Yugoslavia. Not to be confused with the Slovak Republic.

SMAL Suomen matkatoimistoalan liitto. *See Appendix 5c.*

small print An informal but widely used expression for the terms, conditions, exclusions, exceptions, definitions and the like that apply to a particular agreement, such as an insurance policy or a package holiday.

smallpox A once deadly, contagious viral disease that has now been eliminated in the wild although strains are still kept in a few laboratories.

SMB *See surface marker buoy.*

smog Fog mixed with smoke.

smokestack *See funnel.*

smuggle To attempt to bring in goods to a country secretly and illegally.

SNAV Syndicat National des Agences de Voyages. *See Appendix 5c.*

snorkel (or **schnorkel**) A J-shaped tube that enables a diver to breathe ordinary air at the surface without having to raise the face out of the water.

snorkelling The act of swimming face down in the water using a snorkel to breathe.

Snow 24 *See Appendix 5a.*

snow blindness A condition, usually temporary and avoided by wearing adequate goggles or sunglasses, caused by looking at the glare of sunlight on snow.

snow cat *See piste groomer.*

snow cover The parts of a ski area that have enough snow on which to ski or snowboard.

snow depth A measurement of the depth of snow given in snow reports, typically at the bottom, middle and top of the mountain.

snow garden A separate and enclosed part of a ski area reserved for younger children. Snow gardens are particularly common in France but similar areas exist under different names at ski resorts in other countries. Snow gardens may contain special lifts and attractions for children and be attached to ski kindergartens.

snow making A process which enables machines to create snow from stored water piped to the slopes. This is particularly common at low-altitude ski areas to ensure snow cover through the season.

snow permanent Snow, usually at high altitudes, which never disappears completely before fresh snow is deposited.

snow report A report produced by a ski resort or an independent agency that advises on the depth of snow and quality and status of ski runs.

snowboard A wide, single ski.

snowboard boot A special boot worn by snowboarders that fixes to their board with a special binding. Snowboard boots are softer, lighter and more comfortable than ski boots.

snow-cap A mountain-top covered with snow.

snowdrift A bank of snow heaped up by the wind.

snowfield A wide expanse of snow, generally present year-round. The term is also colloquially used to describe non-

S

permanent expanses that commonly melt
in the summer.

snowline 1. The height above which snow
never entirely melts.
2. In skiing, the height where the snow
begins and ends on a mountain at a
particular time, according to season and
weather conditions.

snowmobile A powered vehicle fitted with
skis on the front and caterpillar tracks at
the rear, used for moving over snow.

snowplough 1. A device for clearing or
moving snow.
2. The name given to the commonest way
of teaching people to ski. It is derived
from the inverted V-shape made by the
skis in the 'snowplough' position.

snowshoe A tennis-racquet shaped device
that straps over ordinary boots to allow the
wearer to walk on snow without sinking.

soft spikes A type of cleat worn on a
golfer's shoes, using rubber rather than
metal spikes. Some golf courses only
permit soft spikes.

sojourn A temporary stay.

solar Of or relating to the sun.

solar day The length of a day as measured
by the apparent movement of the sun. The
normal measurement of time on earth.

solar eclipse *See eclipse.*

solstice The two days in a year which have
the most and the least hours of daylight.
In the northern hemisphere the summer
solstice is on 21 June and the winter
solstice on 22 December: in the southern
hemisphere the reverse is the case. The
further from the Equator one is, the
greater will be the difference between the
hours of daylight on these two dates.

Somali Current The warm current that
runs off the north-east coast of Africa

flowing north in June, July and August
and south during other times of the year.

sommelier The person in charge of the
wine in a restaurant.

son et lumière From the French 'sound
and light', an entertainment making use
of illuminations and music. Often used at
historic man-made attractions, such as
the Pyramids.

SOS An international distress signal, using
letters in Morse code that were easily
transmitted and recognised.

souk A market place in Muslim countries.

sound 1. A narrow passage of water
connecting two other bodies of water.
2. To test the depth and quality of the
bottom of a body of water.

south One of the four cardinal points of
the compass, 90° clockwise from east and
180° from north; at the foot of maps
where (as is normal) north is at the top.
> *north.*

South America One of the world's
continents. As with most continents,
opinions differ as to its exact composition
and area. > *continent.*

South China Sea The area of the Pacific
Ocean between Indochina, the
Philippines, Borneo and China.

South Equatorial Current Originating
close to the Equator and flowing
westward, this current is diverted
northwards by the Brazilian coast and
feeds the source of the Gulf Stream.

South Pole The southernmost point of
the earth.

South Sea (Also **South Seas**) The
southern Pacific Ocean.

South, the The parts of the USA south of
Pennsylvania and the Ohio river, and in

particular those states south of the Mason-Dixon line that fought on the Confederate side in the American Civil War.

South-East, the   The south-eastern corner of England, including Kent, Sussex, Surrey and London, and sometimes other home counties.

South-East Asia   A general geographic term describing the area comprising Maynmar, Laos, Thailand, Vietnam, Cambodia, Malaysia, Singapore, Brunei and the Philippines. Sometimes also taken to include Indonesia, Taiwan and the southern coastal areas of China including Macau and Hong Kong.

Southern Cone   The region of South America comprising Brazil, Paraguay, Argentina and Uruguay.

Southern Cross   A distinctive cross-shaped constellation visible only in the southern hemisphere.

southern hemisphere   That part of the earth south of the Equator.

southern lights   See *aurora australis*.

Southern Ocean   See *oceans*.

Southwest Chief   The rail service between Chicago and Los Angeles in the USA.

souvenir   A memento bought as a reminder of a journey or visit. Souvenirs are a major earner of foreign exchange in most resorts.

sovereign   A supreme ruler, especially a monarch.

spa   A resort or other establishment which specialises in hydrotherapy treatments.

SPAA   Scottish Passenger Agents Association. See *Appendix 5a*.

space available basis   See *standby*.

Space Coast   An area of coastline east of Orlando, Florida, stretching from New Smyrna Beach in the north to Palm Bay in the south. It encompasses many sites relating to the US space programme, as well as numerous beach resorts and wildlife reserves.

spaghetti junction   (UK) A motorway junction having several levels and complex interchanges. The original is to the east of Birmingham in the UK where the M6, the M42, the A446 and the A452 intersect.

spar   1. A pole used for the mast, yard, boom or other rigid part of the rigging of a ship.
2. The main structural member of an aircraft's wing.

Spartan   The civilisation of ancient Laconia (c.900BC to AD396). The Spartans were reputedly very hardy, and the term now also refers to anything, such as accommodation, that is bare, austere or unadorned.

spear gun   A device for propelling a spear at speed through the water.

special-interest attraction   Any tourist attraction that is designed to appeal to a specific hobby or interest.

special-interest holidays   A holiday arrangement which caters for those following particular interests or hobbies.

special-needs accommodation   Accommodation designed for guests with disabilities.

speedboat   A small, fast boat.

SPF   See *sun protection factor*.

SPH   Skiers per hour. See *uplift capacity*.

Spice Islands   The former name for the

S

Moluccas, or Maluku, Islands, in eastern Indonesia.

spinnaker A large triangular sail.

spit A point of land projecting into a body of water.

split charter An arrangement whereby two or more different companies or individuals hire different parts of the same vehicle.

split season Travelling out and back in different seasons.

split ticketing The issuing of separate tickets for a multi-sector journey to undercut the through fare.

sporting attraction An attraction that capitalises on its ability to offer visitors the chance to participate in or watch a sport.

spot height A specific height marked on a map, for example, the summit of a mountain.

spouse A husband or wife. At one time carriers' special fares for accompanying partners were restricted to spouses. These days such fares are usually available to any partner.

spouse fare *See partner fare.*

spring tide The tide just after the new and the full moon, when there is the greatest difference between high and low water and during which the tidal streams run most strongly.

squall A sudden and violent gust or storm of wind.

square-rigged A form of rigging where the principal sails are arranged at right angles to the length of the ship and extended by horizontal yards attached to the masts.

SRF Svenska Resebyråforeningen. *See Appendix 5c.*

SS When placed in front of a ship's name means steamship.

SSC Sector Skills Council. *See Appendix 5a.*

SSSI *See site of special scientific interest.*

SST *See supersonic transport.*

St Christopher & Nevis The country in the Leeward Islands in the Caribbean now known as St Kitts & Nevis.

St George's The capital of Grenada. Not to be confused with Georgetown, the capital of Guyana, or George Town, the capital of the Cayman Islands.

St Maarten *See St Martin.*

St Martin One of the Leeward Islands in the Caribbean, divided into the French St Martin (administratively part of Guadeloupe) and the Dutch St Maarten (one of the Netherlands Antilles).

stabilisers A mechanism used on cruise ships to provide a smoother journey in rough seas.

stage decompression A specific depth at which the diver must remain before completing the journey to the surface to enable accumulated nitrogen to escape from the body without danger of contracting decompression sickness.

stagecoach Historically, a large, closed horse-drawn coach running to a timetable between various points. Sometimes still used to describe similar motor coach services.

stalactite A deposit of crystallised minerals hanging from the roof of a cave or cavern caused by mineral-laden water seeping through the cavern roof. Most resemble a stone icicle.

S

stalagmite A deposit of crystallised minerals rising from the floor of a cave or cavern caused by drops of mineral-laden water falling from a stalactite.

stall The condition that occurs when the airflow over an aircraft's wings is insufficient to maintain lift.

stamp To endorse a ticket or other items by means of a rubber or metal stamp.

Standard Caribbean Terms Yacht charter terms under which the fee includes the charter of the yacht and all associated costs, including full board for the client, although generally excepting drinks. Other costs, such as cruising taxes and radio telephone and other communication costs, must be paid by the client. These terms may vary.

Standard Eastern Mediterranean Terms Yacht charter terms under which the fee includes the charter of the yacht with all equipment; basic consumables for engine-room, deck and cabins; the crew's wages and food; insurance for the yacht itself, for third party claims and employer's liability insurance for the crew; fuel for up to five hours cruising per day (averaged throughout the charter); berthing dues and other harbour charges (except Corinthian Canal dues); and water or electricity taken from the shore. Other costs, such as fuel for the ski boats, the client's food and drink, berthing and harbour expenses outside the yacht's normal cruising area, laundry and radio telephone and other communication costs, must be paid by the client. These terms may vary.

standby fare A general term for a discounted fare offered to passengers who are prepared to wait until the last minute to obtain a seat.

starboard The right-hand side of a vessel when one is looking towards the forward end. Denoted by a green light.

state 1. An organised political community under one sovereign government.
2. An organised political community forming part of a federal republic. *See Appendix 2 for a list of US states and appendix 4 for a list of Australian states.*

stateless A person who has no nationality or citizenship.

stateroom 1. A state apartment in a palace or hotel.
2. A private room on a ship. Originally the term was reserved for the best cabins, but some shipping lines refer to all their sleeping accommodation as staterooms.
3. (US) A private compartment on a train.

station A stop or terminus for trains or buses.

station wagon (US) An estate car.

status box The space on an air ticket that indicates whether a reservation has been confirmed or not.

statute mile A unit of measurement in the imperial system equal to 1,760 yards or approximately 1.6 kilometres.
> *nautical mile.*

steam engine An engine that produces its power by burning fuel in a boiler to produce steam, which drives a piston or turbine. Steam engines are now used mainly in large static installations such as power plants. However, in transport they can still be found in larger liners and on a few railways.

steamer *See steamship.*

steam-hauled A train pulled by a steam-powered locomotive: usually only found on preserved lines or tourist trains.

steamship A ship powered by steam engines. Usually denoted by the abbreviation SS in front of its name.

steerage Historically the cheapest accommodation on a ship, situated far aft.

S

stem   An alternative name for a ship's bow.

steppe   A level, grassy plain with extreme temperature variations.

sterling   *See pound (2).*

stern   The rear part of a ship.

steward   A male passenger attendant on a ship, aircraft or train.

stewardess   (UK) A female steward.

STF   School Travel Forum. *See Appendix 5a.*

stock   1. The unissued tickets and other documents held pending use.
2. *See rolling stock.*

STOL   *See short take off and landing.*

Stone   (UK) A unit of measurement of weight, equal to 14 pounds, only used for expressing the weight of a person.

stopoff   *See stopover.*

stopover   A deliberate interruption to a journey, agreed in advance, between the origin and destination points. Many discounted fares do not allow stopovers.

storey   A floor of a building.

storm   *See Beaufort scale.*

stowaway   A person who has hidden aboard a vehicle in the hope of obtaining free transport.

STP   *See satellite ticket printer.*

STP location   *See satellite printer location.*

strait   A narrow passage of water joining two seas or other larger areas of water.

stratus   A type of cloud characterised by its generally low, flat base and grey colour.

stream   A small river or similar flowing body of water.

street   A public road in a town or village.

street furniture   The various signs and other artefacts provided in a road or street to assist the public.

streetcar   (US) A tramcar.

strong breeze   *See Beaufort scale.*

strong gale   *See Beaufort scale.*

Stuart   (or **Stewart**) Of or relating to the kings and queens of Scotland between 1371 and 1714 and of England between 1603 and 1714, or to those periods generally.

studio   A one-bedroomed apartment.

sub-aqua   Relating to any underwater activity, especially diving.

sub-continent   A large land mass, smaller than a continent, such as the Indian sub-continent.

subject to load   The situation when a carrier agrees to convey a passenger if space is available. Most discounted tickets are subject to load and the greater the discount the lower the priority of the holder of the subload ticket. Often abbreviated to 'subload' or 'standby'.
> *standby.*

subload   *See subject to load.*

submarine   1. Beneath the sea.
2. A vessel capable of operating beneath water. Submarine excursions are now common in resorts where there are underwater attractions, such as coral reefs.

subsonic   Less than the speed of sound (approximately 1,225 kph or 760 mph at sea level).

S

sub-temperate   The cooler parts of a temperate climatic zone. > *climate zones.*

subterranean   Under ground.

subtropical   A climate zone slightly cooler than tropical. *See climate zones.*

suburban   Often abbreviated to suburb. The area around a city.

subway   1. (UK) An underground passage, often beneath a road.
2. (US) An underground railway. > *metro.*

Subway, the   The urban rail system in New York, and several other cities including Seoul and Tokyo.

Succot   A festival in the Jewish religious calendar, celebrated five days after Yom Kippur.

Suez Canal   The canal that connects the Mediterranean Sea with the Red Sea, running through Egypt.

suite   Accommodation usually with two rooms, including a bedroom and a sitting area.

Sulawesi   *See Celebes.*

sultan   A Muslim sovereign.

sultanate   A state ruled by a sultan.

sultry   Of the weather, hot or oppressive.

Sumerian   The civilisation of ancient Sumeria (c.3500BC to c.1700 BC).

Summer Olympic Games   The world's premier international multi-sport event, which takes place every four years in a different city on each occasion. Accommodation and transport arrangements may need to be made months, and sometimes years, in advance.

summer solstice   *See solstice.*

summit   The highest point of a feature, especially a hill or mountain.

summit   The top of a mountain.

sumptuous   Particularly lavish or costly.

sun deck   The deck of a ship designed for sunbathing.

sun protection factor   The indicator of the effectiveness of sun creams and lotions.

sunbelt   An area receiving more than the average amount of sunshine.

Sunbelt, the   The areas of south and south-west United States (mainly Florida, Arizona and southern California) made popular by holidaymakers and those in retirement.

sunblock   An alternative term for sunscreen, but often referring to the maximum level of sunscreen protection available. > *SPF.*

sunlust   The desire to travel to a sunny destination.

sunscreen   1. A screen providing protection against the sun.
2. A lotion or cream rubbed into the skin to prevent damage from the sun's rays. > *SPF.*

Sunset Ltd   The rail service between Orlando and Los Angeles in the USA.

Sunshine Coast   The resort coast north of Brisbane, Australia, stretching from Bribie Island to Tin Can Bay, less developed than the Gold Coast to the south.

sunstroke   Acute exhaustion or collapse caused by over-exposure to the sun.

suntrap   (UK) A place designed to catch the sun, generally also sheltered from the wind.

S

sunup (US) Sunrise.

superelevation The amount by which the outer edge of a road or railway is above the inner edge.

superhighway 1. (US) A particularly fast main road with multiple carriageways in each direction.
2. An abbreviation of the information superhighway, the means by which information can be transferred rapidly between computers by means of the internet and similar networks.

superior A high class or category of accommodation, usually attracting a supplement.

supersonic Travelling faster than the speed of sound (approximately 1,225 kph or 760 mph at sea level).

superstructure Any structure built onto another structure. Thus the superstructure of a ship will include all the cabins and entertainment facilities built onto the hull.

supplement A fee for an extra, or higher, grade of product or service.

supplementary liability insurance See *vehicle rental insurance*.

supplier Another term for a principal.

surcharge An extra charge on a customer's bill, enforced by a hotelier or tour operator.

surface demand Air supplied to a diver underwater through tubes from a source of air at the surface.

surface lift See *drag lift*.

surface marker buoy A small buoy floating on the surface of the water attached to the end of a long line and pulled by the submerged diver to indicate their presence.

surface tow See *drag lift*.

surface travel A generic term that can denote any form of travel that is not by air, but usually refers to travel over the ground rather than the sea.

surfboard A long narrow buoyant board on which riders are carried over the surf.

surrender Of a ticket or other document, to give it up on demand.

surrey (US) A light four-wheeled horse-drawn carriage often used for sightseeing.

sustainable tourism Tourism that has a minimal or manageable effect on the natural and cultural environment of the area visited.

swallow An area where a river appears to sink into the ground, only to reappear later.

swamp An area of waterlogged land.

sweepback The angle at which an aircraft's wings are set back from the right-angle.

swell The heaving of seas that do not break into waves, often after a storm.

S

Tt

T junction A road junction where one road joins another at right angles without crossing it.

TAANZ Travel Agents Association of New Zealand TAANZ. *See Appendix 5c.*

table d'hôte A menu in a restaurant that is available at a fixed price and which contains relatively few choices.

table top *See terrain park.*

tableland An extensive elevated region.

tables *See decompression tables.*

tachograph A device fitted to vehicles such as coaches that measures the speed, duration of stops and number of hours a driver works.

tack The direction in which a sailing vessel moves as determined by its own direction and that of the wind.

taffrail The rail around a ship's stern.

taiga 1. A stretch of cold, swampy coniferous forest, especially in Siberia.

tail wind A wind blowing in the same direction as a vehicle is travelling.

tailor-made A holiday or other arrangement designed especially for a particular client.

tailplane The smaller horizontal projections from the fuselage of an aircraft, situated towards the rear. These serve to stabilise the machine and provide most of the control.

Taiwan The island off the south-east coast of China (formerly known as Formosa) and the country known variously as Taiwan, Taiwan (ROC) and the Republic of China, > *China, People's Republic of, and ROC.*

take a chance A marketing device used by some cruising companies. By taking a chance on the exact cabin and cruise, prospective passengers can pay a substantially reduced fare. Their accommodation will then be allocated around a month before sailing.

take off The moment when an aircraft leaves the ground and starts to fly.

taking air The act of leaving the snow and jumping into the air, intentionally or not, while skiing or snowboarding. Also known as taking big air.

tall ship A sailing ship with a tall mast or masts.

tannoy A brand name for a type of public address system, but often used in the UK to denote any such system.

tapas Small savoury dishes, often served at a Spanish bar.

taproom A room in which alcoholic drinks, usually beer, are served.

tariff 1. A rate or charge, generally displayed as a list.

T

2. An alternative name for an air fare.

tarmac   A paved surface such as a road or runway.

tarn   A small lake.

Tasman Sea   The area of the Pacific Ocean between Australia and New Zealand.

tavern   An old fashioned name for an inn.

taverna   A Greek name for an eating place or sometimes a small hotel.

taxi   1. A car or similar vehicle licensed to ply for hire.
2. The movement of an aircraft on the ground.

taxi way   Paved tracks on which aircraft move between the parking and loading area and the runway.

taximeter   The device that calculates the distance travelled and the fare payable for a cab journey.

TBA   *See to be advised.*

T-bar   *See drag lift.*

TBN   To be notified. > *to be advised.*

tech stop   *See technical stop.*

technical stop   A planned stop on an air journey that is not scheduled for passenger pick up or drop off. Usually this will be for refuelling or crew change. Passengers may not need to leave the aircraft, but this will depend on local restrictions.

tee-time   The time booked for golfers to begin playing their round. Golfers may wish to know what tee-time has been booked for them in advance of travel, particularly on arrival and departure days. Groups of more than four golfers may be allocated more than one tee-time. It is important for the golfers to know all the tee-times allocated to their group.

télécabine   *See gondola.*

téléférique   Another name for a cable car, commonly used in France and Switzerland.

Telemark skiing   A method of downhill skiing that predates Alpine skiing by approximately 40 years. It was developed in the Telemark region of Norway in the 1860s. The technique has gained popularity worldwide over the past decade following the fragmentation of winter sports holiday options. Telemark skiing uses boots only connected to the ski at the toe.

temperate   A type of climate. *See climate zones.*

temperature-humidity index   A value that gives the measure of discomfort experienced due to the combined effects of the temperature and humidity of the atmosphere.

tempest   A violent, windy storm.

tender   1. A small boat used to transfer passengers from a cruise ship to the land when it is not possible to dock.
2. The putting in of a bid for business. Business travel agents who are often expected to re-tender for a company's travel account at regular intervals.

tent   A portable, temporary dwelling made of canvas or similar. Often the cheapest form of accommodation, although many modern tents are quite luxurious.

terminal   1. A building at an airport, bus station or similar that is used to process arriving and departing passengers.
2. The computer screen and associated equipment in a travel agency that is connected to a GDS or other system.

terminus   (UK) The station at the end of a railway line or bus route.

T

terra firma Solid earth (as opposed to air or sea).

terra incognita An unknown or unexplored area.

terrace 1. A raised, flat area outside a house or similar.
2. A flattened area of hillside, often in progressive steps supported by stone walls, used for cultivation.

terrain The physical features of an area. > *topography.*

terrain park An area of a ski slope, often fenced off from the rest of the ski area, where terrain features are created for snowboarders and increasingly also skiers using the latest short skis. Terrain parks may include a half pipe, rails (a steel rail to slide along above the snow), table top (a flat area of metal or snow) and other features carved from snow.

terrestrial 1. Of or relating to the earth, as opposed to the air. In some cases, its meaning includes all the surface of the earth, including the seas, in others merely to the land.
2. Of or relating to telecommunication systems that do not make use of satellites.

territorial waters The waters under the jurisdiction of a country or state, especially that part of the sea a stated distance from the country's shore.

territory Any piece of land belonging to, or under the jurisdiction of, a state or country.

test pressure The maximum pressure to which a diving cylinder may be safely charged for testing purposes. The process should only be undertaken by a competent testing authority.

tetanus (or **lockjaw**) An acute infectious disease, endemic worldwide, caused by bacterial infection of a wound. > *health precautions.*

Texas Eagle The rail service between Chicago and San Antonio in the USA.

TGV The French high-speed trains (*trains à grande vitesse*) which operate services within France from their Paris hub, and also into Belgium, Switzerland, Germany and Italy. Not all TGV trains run on dedicated high-speed lines. > *LGV.*

Thalys The high-speed train service running between Paris, Brussels, Amsterdam and Cologne.

theatre-style seating plan A common configuration at meetings, conferences or seminars whereby the delegates are seated in rows as in a theatre, usually with a raised stage for the speakers at the front of the hall.

theft protection *See vehicle rental insurance.*

theme cruise A cruise designed to appeal to a certain interest group.

theme park An entertainment centre, usually spread over a large area with a number of separate entertainment facilities, based on a particular special interest.

themed attraction Any tourist attraction that has chosen a particular special subject or topic on which to base its activities and displays.

thermocline The boundary between waters of differing temperature.

third age The period in life of active retirement. Often the time when many people travel extensively.

third class The third-best category of travel or accommodation.

Third World That part of the world that is less advanced or developed.

third-party insurance The cover against

T

claims made by another person, in respect of injury, damage, death or other loss. > *travel insurance.*

thoroughfare A road or path open at both ends for the passage of traffic.

through fare A fare for travel between two points. Usually through fares will allow en route stopovers, unlike point-to-point fares. The publication of a through fare for a journey does not mean that a through service exists.

through service A service that does not require a passenger to change. Through services are not necessarily non-stop services, even by air. In cases where a flight makes an intermediate stop or stops, the entire flight through to the final destination will have the same flight number for every leg of the journey.

throughway 1. A thoroughfare. 2. (US) (often thruway) a motorway.

thrust The force generated by an aircraft engine.

thunder The sound of lightning caused by the rapid heating of air by the electrical discharge. The sound of thunder is generated at the same time as the lightning and the interval between the two is caused by the different speeds at which light and sound travel. Each five-second delay between seeing the lightning and hearing the thunder is equal to about a mile.

thunderbolt A flash of lightning with an almost simultaneous crash of thunder, caused by the nearness of the storm.

thundercloud A tall cumulus cloud, producing thunder and lightning.

thunderstorm A storm producing rain, thunder and lightning.

TIAA Travel Industry Association of America. *See Appendix 5b.*

TIC *See tourist information centre.*

tick-borne encephalitis A viral infection caused by tick bites, generally confined to forested areas of Central Europe and Scandinavia. > *health precautions.*

ticket 1. A document that proves entitlement to travel on a specific journey, subject to the conditions of carriage and the discretion of the airport or airline authorities. It is not the same as a reservation, in that in itself it does not guarantee passage at any particular time. > *reservation.* 2. A document allowing entry to an event or place. 3. A colloquial term for a citation given by a police officer or other authorised person for a motoring offence. In the UK, it generally refers only to a fin for a parking offence.

ticket agent A person or office that sells tickets, such as for entertainment or ground transportation.

ticket collector A person who checks tickets or travel documents, usually on a train or at the barrier of a station.

ticket fraud The defacement, non-purchase, re-sale, forgery or other misuse of a ticket.

ticket inspector A person responsible for checking travel tickets during a journey, usually to detect ticket fraud on trains. They may be in plain clothes, with identification, and may be authorised to levy on-the-spot fines.

ticket office A place where tickets are made available.

ticket on departure A ticket which is collected at the departure point, rather than the purchasing point. > *prepaid ticket advice.*

ticket printer A printer that prints the details on automated tickets.

T

ticket tout A person who obtains tickets, usually for a concert or sporting event, hoping to re-sell them at a profit.

ticketed point mileage (TPM) The published mileage between the origin and destination points of a journey by air. > *MPM.*

ticketed point mileage *See TPM.*

ticket-holder A person who has legitimately obtained and carries a ticket for a journey or facility.

ticketless travel *See electronic ticketing.*

tidal stream The flow of water caused by the tides.

tidal wave A dangerous and destructive wave, usually produced by an earthquake.

tide The regular rise and fall of the surface of seas and oceans that occurs about every 12 hours 25 minutes.

tidetable A table indicating the times of high and low tides.

tideway The channel in which a tide runs, especially the tidal part of a river.

tied house (UK) A pub owned by a brewery and thus usually obliged to sell primarily the brewery's own products. > *free house.*

tiller The horizontal handle fitted to a boat's rudder by which it is turned.

Timbuktu A town in Mali. The term is often used to denote a distant or inaccessible place.

time charter A charter based on the use of a vehicle, usually an aircraft, for an agreed length of time.

time zones The bands into which the earth is divided, within each of which the local time is the same.

Time zones are numerically expressed as variations of hours from the bench-mark of UTC (GMT) time: +3.5, -7 and so on. There are 360 degrees of longitude and 24 hours in a day. 360 divided by 24 is 15; and thus the local time generally advances by one hour for every 15° one moves east, and decreases by one hour for every 15° one moves west. In practice, time zones do not follow this rigid 15° changeover, for some would otherwise cut through the middle of countries, perhaps even of cities. Time zones tend to follow national frontiers. Not counting offshore islands like the Canaries and the Azores, only a handful of countries (including the USA, Canada, Brazil and Australia) span more than one time zone. By contrast, China (despite its size) spans only one. Due to the operation of daylight saving time in some regions, mainly outside the tropics, it is possible that some countries which are in the same time zone may, for about half the year, have different times. Additionally, some countries have time zones in fractions of an hour. Nepal, for example, is five and three-quarter hours ahead of UTC while Newfoundland in Canada is three and a half hours behind. In general, however, the world's time is divided into segments of roughly 15°, each generally corresponding to one hour's difference in local time. There are 36 time zones in all, but the ones which are more than UTC+12 or which contain differences of a fraction of an hour are generally limited to only one country or island group. The local time zones are often given names, such as Central European Time and Pacific Standard Time. > *daylight saving time.*

time-and-mileage A car rental tariff that is calculated on a combination of the period of time for which the vehicle is hired and the distance it is driven.

timeshare The concept where people 'buy' a period of time in a particular accommodation. This time is then reserved for their use year-on-year. Other customers will buy other time slots in the

T

same accommodation and all will share maintenance costs.

timetable   A list of departure and arrival times of a mode of transport or various inter-connecting modes of transport, usually limited to a specified region.

Timor Sea   The area of the Indian Ocean between Indonesia and Australia.

tip   *See gratuity.*

TIPTO   Truly Independent Professional Travel Organisation. *See Appendix 5a.*

TMI   Tourism Management Institute.

to be advised (TBA)   An expression used to express the fact that a particular and generally important item of information for the completion of a travel arrangement is not available at that time but will be supplied later. Commonly used by agents when they are awaiting details about a customer (the passport number, for example). Principals may also use the expression if they are unable to give full details about a booking, such as a timing or accommodation details.

TOC   *See train operating company.*

TOD   *See ticket on departure.*

token   1. A staff or similar object carried by the driver or guard of a train to control access to a section of single track taking two-way traffic.
2. A metal disc, used in some cases instead of a coin, for example in slot machines or on some urban transport systems.

toll   1. A fee charged for the use of a road, bridge or similar.
2. (US) The charge for a long-distance telephone call.

toll booth   The place where a road or bridge toll is collected.

toll free   (US) A telephone call where the charges are paid not by the caller but by the person or (more commonly) the organisation being called.

tonnage   1. A general term referring to the total number of ships in the region, fleet, class or season being considered.
2. A measurement of a ship's capacity with four different meanings: (a) gross registered tonnage or GRT; (b) net registered tonnage or NRT; (c) displacement tonnage, which is the weight of water displaced by a vessel (and thus its actual weight); and (d) dead-weight tonnage is the carrying capacity by weight. Most passenger shipping companies quote GRT in their brochure since this is the most useful measurement when determining a ship's likely comfort. Displacement tonnage is usually quoted for warships (and sometimes for US merchantmen). Dead-weight tonnage is usually quoted for tankers.

topography   That variety or mix of natural or artificial features that make up a landscape.

topside   The side of a ship above the waterline.

tor   A rocky peak or hill, particularly in the west country of England.

tornado   A violent storm, covering a relatively small area and characterised by whirlwinds (revolving, funnel-shaped clouds).

torrent   A rushing stream of water.

torrid   Extremely hot and dry weather.

total eclipse   *See eclipse.*

totalitarian   Of or relating to a centralised and dictatorial form of government.

touch of the sun   A colloquial expression for a feeling of sickness caused by exposure to too much sun. Less severe than sunstroke.

touchdown The moment when an aircraft lands.

tour A trip that visits a number of exhibits, venues, attractions or other locations. Tours are often operated by coach and frequently have a guide. Tours with guides are usually known as escorted tours.

tour conductor *See tour guide.*

tour escort *See tour guide.*

tour guide Someone who escorts a tour. Also known as guide, courier, tour escort, escort, tour conductor or tour leader.

tour leader *See tour guide.*

tour manager A person who manages and supervises a pre-established tour itinerary, using the services of hotels, airlines, local guides and couriers, ensuring that it is carried out according to schedule and to standard.

tour operator An organisation that puts together an inclusive holiday for sale to the public, usually combining transportation, accommodation and ground services. > *organiser.*

tour organiser *See tour operator.*

tourism The all-embracing term for the movement of people to destinations away from their place of residence for pleasure (or – see below – for business), and the many other activities associated with this. Tourism is defined by the WTO as being 'the activities of persons travelling to and staying in places outside their usual environment for not more than one consecutive year for leisure, business and other purposes.' Note the use of the word 'business': the distinction between 'leisure' (or touristic) and 'business' travel is, statistically, very hard to draw on an international level. For a travel organiser, the differences in expectations, carriers, flexibility, accommodation and other details will be obvious; yet, once arrived, the nature and extent of the consumption of goods and services of the two types of traveller will generally be statistically impossible to distinguish, particularly as many travellers will mix business with pleasure. Moreover, many countries or organisations are unable, or unwilling, to separate these reasons for travel in the figures they report; and, even if they do, they do not apply the same criteria in differentiating them. The fact that the WTO, which tends to define 'travel' generally as 'tourism', is the only internationally accepted statistical source of such data, has further confused this distinction. So too has the reduction of border controls within the EU, within which many of the world's most visited countries (for whichever reason) are to be found. For many countries, domestic tourism is also vastly important to the national economy, although statistically very hard to measure. International tourism involves the traveller leaving more 'footprints' which can more easily create statistical records; for obvious reasons, it also tends to involve the expertise of the travel professional to help make the necessary arrangements, particularly in the case of countries such as the UK or the USA where the act of reaching all or some international destinations involve flights or sea crossings. The cost or length of the journey is, however, not always the key factor: a ten-kilometre car ride from France to Belgium, involving no prior arrangements, is an international journey, while a flight of many thousands of miles from New York to Hawaii, crossing five time zones and probably requiring the services of a travel arranger, is a domestic one.

tourism apartheid The situation where discrimination exists against local people in favour of free-spending foreign tourists.

tourist A person who engages in tourism. > *tourism.*

tourist attraction   See *attraction*.

tourist card   A document required by certain countries before travellers will be allowed to enter it. The requirements for obtaining a tourist card are similar to, but usually less onerous than, those required for obtaining a visa.

tourist class   See *economy class*.

tourist enclave   An area of separate tourist accommodation, often provided for security reasons.

tourist generating country   A country from which large numbers of tourists originate.

tourist guide   A person who possesses an area-specific tourist guide qualification recognised by the appropriate public authority in the country concerned. The tourist guide's role is to guide visitors from home or abroad, in languages of their choice, interpreting the natural and cultural heritage of the area.

tourist information centre   (UK) An office, usually run by a tourist board or local authority, which gives information about a destination.

tourist office   An office which exists to promote tourism to a country or region and usually funded by the governments of the countries they promote.

tourist receiving country   A country that large numbers of tourists visit.

tourist region   An area visited by tourists that has a specific name or identity. This will often differ from the name for the region used geographically. For example, the stretch of coast between Valencia and Alicante is officially in the Comunidad de Valenciana, but holidaymakers know it as the Costa Blanca.

tourist trap   A scathing expression for a destination or attraction that is reputedly overcrowded with visitors and offering poor value-for-money.

tow path   A path alongside a canal or navigable river, originally used by draught horses to haul barges.

town   A large urban area with a name and boundaries, not large enough to be classed as a city.

TP   See *theft protection*.

TPI   See *third party insurance*.

TPM   See *ticketed point mileage*.

track   1. A rough path through countryside.
2. A railway line.
3. The course of an aircraft in flight.

track-laying   A vehicle such as a tank that that lays its own tracks as it progresses, often used for haulage where the ground is poor or slippery.

tract   A region or area of indefinite size.

trade body   (Also **trade association**.) An organisation created by or on behalf of the members of a particular industry which generally exists to further the interests of its members, to lobby on their behalf, to provide codes of standards and practice and to organise events where the members may meet socially and professionally. The travel trade has many such organisations, and a selection of these are listed in Appendix 5. The international nature of the industry means that many will have an international membership and, consequently, that many of their conferences and the like will be held in countries other than that in which the trade body is based.

trade discount   A discount given by one business to another, generally in the same industry, for purchasing its products of services.

trade fair   (Also **trade show**) An event set up to meet the interests of people and organisations involved with a particular industry (such as travel) and to provide commercial opportunities. There are many each year throughout the world. Some are international; some national; some regional. Some cater for specialist areas, such as cruising or winter sports; others are industry-wide. Two of the largest are the World Travel Market in London in November, and the ITB in Berlin in March.

trade mission   A tour arranged for business or government representatives to visit a destination with a view to obtaining more business.

trade show   *See trade fair.*

trade winds   The steady winds that blow across the oceans from about 30° north to about 30° south. In the northern hemisphere they blow from north-east to south-west; in the southern, from south-east to north-west. .

traffic   In travel, any movement of people and or vehicles between two points, by any means of transport.

Traffic Area   IATA's division of the world into three areas.
 • TCA 1 is North and South America (sub-divided into North, Mid and South Atlantic)
 • TCA 2 is Europe and Africa (sub-divided into Europe, Middle East, Africa and East Africa)
 • TCA 3 is Asia and Australasia (sub-divided into Asia and South-west Pacific)

traffic calming   The deliberate reduction or slowing of road traffic by the construction of obstacles, such as humps or chicanes, in the roadway or by restricting or charging the vehicles which may access a given area.

Traffic Conference Area   *See Area.*

traffic document   A passenger ticket or similar document. Traffic documents may be issued manually, mechanically or electronically and are generally produced using either the carrier's own forms or those of its handling agents. Such documents include: passenger ticket and baggage check forms; automated ticket/boarding passes; miscellaneous charges orders; multiple-purpose documents; agent's refund vouchers; and on-line tickets supplied by the carrier to accredited agents.

traffic evaporation   The effect by which the closure of a road or an intersection, or the introduction of measures such as congestion charging, have been observed to have the effect of making drivers switch to other forms of transport. This is in contrast to the policy of building more roads to solve congestion, which tends to attract more vehicles and thus creates similar congestion but on a larger scale.

traffic rights   Usually applicable to air travel, but can apply to any form of transport. In a journey between two points, A and B, a carrier may travel via one or more intermediate points, say C and D. The carrier will have the right to carry passengers between A and B, but not necessarily between A and C or C and D. > *freedoms of the air.*

trail   1. A path created for leisure use. 2. (US) A piste. The term is now increasingly widely used in the UK. *See piste.*

trail map   *See piste map.*

trailer   1. An unpowered vehicle drawn by a powered vehicle. 2. (US) A caravan.

train   A collection of vehicles linked together. Generally only used for rail travel, but also to be found for road travel, particularly in Australia. > *road trains.*

train ferry   A ferry designed to carry railway vehicles across water.

T

train operating company   One of the various (currently about 25) private companies operating UK rail services.

tram   1. (or tramcar) (UK) A vehicle that uses a tramway.
2. (US) a cable-car.

tramp steamer   A cargo vessel that travels from point to point on an ad hoc basis, as determined by the demands for cargo.

tramway   1. (UK) A light railway, often running along the roads and penetrating into the very heart of towns.
2. (US) An alternative name for a cable car.

transaction fees   *See management fees.*

transatlantic   Across the Atlantic.

Trans-Caucasus   The region between Russia, Iran, the Black Sea and the Caspian Sea, comprising Azerbaijan, Armenia and Georgia.

transcontinental   Across a continent.

transfer   The transport provided for passengers between their point of arrival and their accommodation.

transferable   Capable of being transferred, such as a ticket or other travel document that can be passed on to another (which is not usual).

transit   1. A stop en route to a final destination at an intermediate airport or port.
2. (Mainly US) Public passenger transport.

transit line   A line joining two fixed objects in order to determine one's position, such as by aligning a church spire in the foreground with another prominent feature in the distance. Used by mariners when offshore.

transit lounge   A room at an airport for transit passengers.

transit passenger   A passenger who has disembarked at an intermediate point, usually to change services, and who will be continuing on a connecting service. In most countries, transit passengers on international flights do not need to undertake immigration and customs clearance provided they stay in a designated transit area.

transit stop   A stop at an intermediate airport or port en route to a final destination.

transit visa   *See visa.*

transliteration   The act of transcribing the letters of a word from one alphabet into another. As there will be often be cases where a particular sound in one alphabet can be rendered in several ways in another, this can give rise to spelling variations, for example of place names, from one publication to another.

Trans-Manchurian Express   An unofficial name for the rail service from Moscow to Beijing via Harbin.

Trans-Mongolian Express   An unofficial name for the rail service from Moscow to Beijing via Ulan Bator.

Trans-Siberian Express   A British-operated luxury train service running on the Trans-Siberian Railway.

Trans-Siberian Railway   The railway from Moscow to Vladivostok via Irkutsk, a distance of some 5,800 miles (9,300 kilometres). The principal train on the route is the Rossiya.

transocean   Across an ocean.

transom   A vertical strong point, forming the rear of a boat, onto which an outboard motor may be attached.

transpacific   Across the Pacific.

transport   The movement of passengers or

goods. Along with accommodation and entertainment, transport is one of the three main elements of travel and tourism. Transport or transportation is usually categorised as surface, sea or air.

transportation order An IATA term for an agent's own order form authorised by a carrier for use by the agent, against which the airline issues its ticket.

trans-ship To transfer from one form of transport to another.

travel agent A broker of travel services, acting as an intermediary between the purchaser and the supplier, traditionally receiving a commission from the supplier but sometimes now receiving a fee from the purchaser.
A travel agent can be a company or an individual. Apart from the term 'travel agent' to describe the person who works in a travel agency, many other titles are used. These include travel clerk, travel counsellor, travel consultant and travel arranger.
Travel agencies can operate from a home or a shop, or be located in vast travel hypermarkets in retail parks. They can also be virtual, with their customer contact being via the internet, a call centre or a television channel. Different countries enforce different levels of professional standards, financial security and regulatory controls. A selection of the major travel agency associations in the UK, the USA and worldwide may be found in Appendix 6, from whom more specific information about that country's industry may be obtained.
At one time, travel agents would undertake bookings for all types of traveller, whether travelling on holiday or for business reasons. Now, it is common to find that many agencies tend to specialise. The two main distinctions are between retail (or leisure) travel, and business travel.
• *Business travel agents* (some of which may located within large companies to conduct their travel arrangements exclusively) usually charge their customers a fee for the maintenance of the travel account. This fee will allow for the provision of large amounts of information on the customer's travel patterns and spend and will also enable the agent to spend time and effort in negotiating preferential travel deals. The business travel agent who charges such a fee is, in effect, acting as an agent for the customer. *See management fee, implant.*
• *Leisure travel agents* will generally sell a wide range of holiday travel products (particularly package tours), but increasingly many are specialising in certain sectors. These include special interest holidays (such as skiing), rail travel and cruising. This drift towards specialisation has been encouraged by the recent revolution in communications and information technology: for, as a result, people no longer expect to visit an agency in person. A specialist can thus service a very wide geographical area. Another emerging trend is for some leisure travel agents to move towards charging a consultancy fee, rather than receiving a commission from suppliers. They then offer their clients discounted prices and a range of other travel-related services (such as visa procurement) and advice (such as on destination information). This is already fairly common in the business-travel sector (see above).

travel agents' commissions *See commission.*

travel bureau Another name for a travel agent, less commonly used nowadays. *See travel agent.*

travel clerk *See travel consultant.*

travel consultant The name usually given to those working in a travel agency and dealing directly with customers over the counter, on-line or by phone.

travel counsellor *See travel consultant.*

T

travel hypermarket   A large outlet for various travel-related products and services on one site, usually in a retail park.

travel industry   The overall global business of travel and tourism, including variously either the organisations directly involved in it (such as airlines, hotels and travel agencies) or also the organisations which are connected to it indirectly (such as fuel companies, electricians and printers). By many reckonings, it is the largest industry in the world.

travel insurance   The various policies which are available to protect the traveller against matters such as theft, delays, illness, injury and third-party claims, and the industry which exists to provide these. All prudent travellers purchase insurance. It is a criminal offence under the terms of the EU Package Travel legislation for travel agents not to advise their customers about this matter.

Most travel insurance policies in the UK are broadly similar, although each will differ in details described in the small print that may be significant for the individual traveller. These include: the precise terms used to describe areas of cover; the amount of cover; the limits (per single article or overall value); the excesses; the exclusions; the special conditions; the age limits of the insured party or parties; and the premiums. Many policies have been designed specifically for certain types of trip, such as winter sports, business, frequent travellers and families. Some are limited to one trip, while others provide cover for a whole year.

The main areas of cover are as follows (not all policies may cover all the examples given below, or may only do so as optional extras):
• *Medical cover*, including medical expenses, personal injury, hospital benefit and repatriation.
• *Personal effects*, including baggage, valuables, personal items, money and travel documents.

• *Cancellation of travel*.
• *Travel delay*, including withdrawal of services, curtailment and missed departures.
• *Personal liability*, including legal expenses and third-party claims.
• *Specialist cover*, including dangerous activities and search and rescue.
Most policies do not cover the financial failure of scheduled airlines or tour operators.

travel publication   A book which has been written with the sole or principal intention of providing information on a country, a region or a travel-related theme, usually with an objective stance. Some travel publications are aimed mainly, but not exclusively, at consumers; other mainly but not exclusively at the travel trade. Particularly of the former kind, there is a vast range available. Most bookshops have a large area devoted to the subject, and a few specialise in nothing else. All budgets and tastes, from backpackers to luxury honeymooners and from birdwatchers to dangerous sports enthusiasts, are catered for, often in exhaustive detail. Increasingly, travellers will supplement information that they receive from a travel agent about a particular destination with what they have themselves researched, which has both advantages and disadvantages for the travel trade professional.

Many of the specialist travel trade titles, such as those dealing with the precise details of accommodation rates or flight timetables, are of little or no interest to those unconnected with the day-to-day running of the industry, except perhaps for a brief glance during discussions about travel arrangements. These have been supplemented by on-line sources of information through which reservations can also be made, such as GDSs.

A list of useful publications, both consumer and trade, can be found in Section 4.2 of the Columbus *Travel Planning Workbook*.

As an addition to both of these categories, the internet looms ever large. Rather than replace the printed page, as many at one time hoped or feared, it has rather opened up new opportunities for direct access to knowledge, particularly when the user is searching for information too whimsical or occasional to merit the purchase of a book, or where up-to-the-minute details are required, such as on health, visas and travel security.

travel sickness   Nausea caused by motion while travelling.

Travel South USA   A US regional marketing organisation covering the south-eastern states of the USA. > *US regional marketing organisations.*

traveller   1. A person who goes from one place to another.
2. A colloquial term to describe those who travel independently, as opposed to 'tourists' who use pre-arranged facilities.

travellers cheques   A form of money that is more secure than cash. The principle of the travellers cheque is that it is purchased for a specific value and then signed by the purchaser. When it is accepted by a vendor of goods or services, the purchaser signs it again and the signature match proves validity. The recent increase in the use and international acceptability of credit and debit cards have made travellers cheques less popular and necessary than previously.

traverse   A horizontal passage across rock, ice or mountains.

travolator   A level or inclined moving walkway, without the steps used on an escalator.

trekking grades   *See climbing grades.*

trekking   A more strenuous form of hill walking which generally takes place at higher altitude and for many days continuously, and may include ascending a high but technically easy mountains

such as Kilimanjaro. > *altitude sickness, acclimatisation.*

tributary   A river or stream flowing into a larger river or a lake.

trike   An abbreviation for tricycle. > *cycle.*

trilingual   1. A person who can speak three languages fluently.
2. Something that is written in, or spoken in, three languages.

trimaran   A three-hulled catamaran.

trip   An informal term for a journey.

triplane   An aeroplane with three pairs of wings. The configuration is no longer used.

triple   A hotel room suitable for sleeping three people.

triple chair   *See chair lift.*

tripper   A person on a trip, usually for pleasure.

triptyque   A term of French origin that describes a customs permit allowing passage of a motor vehicle.

trishaw   A three-wheeled, man-powered rickshaw.

trolley   1. A bus propelled by electricity, drawing its current from an overhead wire.
2. (US) A tramcar.

Tropic of Cancer   The parallel of latitude at 23° 28' N, where the sun appears directly overhead at noon during the northern summer solstice.

Tropic of Capricorn   The parallel of latitude at 23° 28' S, where the sun appears directly overhead at noon during the southern summer solstice.

tropical storm   A severe storm, but not as

T

fierce as a hurricane or cyclone.

tropics   Those areas of the world situated between the tropics of Cancer and Capricorn.

true north   North according to the earth's axis, not as indicated by a magnetic compass. *See poles.*

true south   South according to the earth's axis, not as indicated by a magnetic compass. *See poles.*

TS   The Tourism Society. *See Appendix 5a.*

tsunami   A tidal wave, usually caused by an earthquake.

TTA   Travel Trust Association Ltd. *See Appendix 5a.*

TTENTO   Now part of the SSC. *See Appendix 5a.*

Tube   The name given to the underground railway network in London. > *metro.*

tubing   A reinforced rubber ring used to slide down ski slopes and often provided as an alternative activity by ski resorts. Often special tubing runs are created with bumps and turns to increase the fun.

Tudor   Of or relating to the kings and queens of England between 1485 and 1603, or to that period generally.

tug   1. (Also **tugboat**) A small, powerful boat used to tow ships into and out of their moorings.
2. A small, heavy tractor used to move aircraft around an airport.

tugboat   *See tug (1).*

tuk-tuk   A small three-wheeled scooter taxi, common in India and Thailand. Also called a rickshaw.

tundra   A large, treeless arctic region, usually having a marshy surface with underlying permafrost. > *climate zones.*

turboprop   1. A jet engine designed to drive a propeller rather than rely solely on jet thrust.
2. An aircraft equipped with turbo-prop engines.

turbulence   The violent movement of air. This can cause an aircraft to shake, sometimes violently, which is why airlines recommend that passengers keep their seat belts loosely fastened at all times during a flight.

turnaround   The period when an aircraft or other vehicle, following its arrival, prepares for its next journey.

turnpike   (US) A toll road.

turnstile   A special form of gateway that will admit only one person at a time. Turnstiles allow control of access and exit and can be designed to provide additional functions such as cash collection and usage counts.

Turquoise Coast   Coastal resort region of southern Turkey. The main town is Antalya: other resorts include Alanya and Side.

TURSAB   Turkiye Seyahat Acentalari Birligi. *See Appendix 5c.*

tuxedo   (US) *See dinner jacket.*

twelve-hour clock   The method of determining time whereby each day is divided into two segments of 12 hours each, running from 12 am midnight to 12 pm noon, and from 12 pm noon to 12 am midnight. Although the travel industry throughout most of the world now uses the 24 hour clock, there are still some countries, most importantly the USA, where the 12 hour clock is still used. In such cases, IATA regulations demand that the terms 'am' and 'pm' be written without full stops. > *twenty-four-hour clock.*

T

twenty-four-hour clock The method of determining time whereby each day is regarded as one period of 24 hours, the distinctions of am and pm thus being redundant. With the notable exception of the USA, the travel industry uses the twenty-four hour clock. In this system, times between midnight and noon are counted from 0000 to 1200 (no dots or hyphens should be used) and times thereafter from 1201 to 2359. > *twelve-hour clock.*

twenty-four-hour delegate rate A rate offered by a hotel or similar venue to organisers of conferences and training events. The rate usually includes room hire, refreshments, three meals and overnight accommodation, as well as basic meeting facilities and equipment.

twin A hotel room with two beds.

Twin Cities The two cities of Minneapolis and St Paul situated either side of the Missouri river, USA.

twin double Another name for a double double room.

twin screw A description of a vessel having two propellers, one on each side of its keel.

twin towns An initiative developed in Europe after the Second World War, and now promoted by the EU, by which towns in different countries would establish links to promote social, educational, commercial and cultural exchanges. Some towns may have more than one twin.

twin-set An aqualung with two diving cylinders.

twister (US) A colloquial expression for a tornado.

typhoid An infectious bacterial fever endemic worldwide, usually spread by contaminated food or water. > *health precautions.*

typhoon A violent tropical storm. The Pacific region's equivalent to an Atlantic hurricane.

T

Uu

UAE   The United Arab Emirates, a federation of seven autonomous emirates on the Persian Gulf coast of the Arabian peninsula. Abu Dhabi is the largest: the others – Dubai, Sharjah, Fujairah, Umm al Qaiwain and Ras al-Khaimah – are known collectively as the Northern States.

UATP   *See universal air travel plan.*

UFTTA   Universal Federation of Travel Agents Associations. *See Appendix 5d.*

UK   *See United Kingdom.*

Ulster   The geographical region comprising the six counties of Northern Ireland and the counties of Cavan, Donegal and Monaghan in the Irish Republic. It is often used informally, and technically incorrectly, to describe Northern Ireland as a whole.

ultima thule   A far-away, unknown region.

UM   An airline code used to indicate an unaccompanied minor. > *unaccompanied minor.*

umbra   *See eclipse.*

umiak   An Eskimo open boat made from skins stretched over a wooden frame.

UMTS   *See universal mobile telecommunications system.*

UN   *See United Nations.*

unaccompanied minor   An underage traveller taking a trip on his or her own. All carriers have their own minimum and maximum ages for unaccompanied minors, which can be as low as two years and as high as 15, and each will have its own procedures and regulations regarding their travel arrangements.

uncharted   An area that has not been explored or mapped.

unchecked baggage   *See hand baggage.*

under canvas   A colloquial term for accommodation in tents.

under way   In motion. Often used to refer to a ship moving under its own power.

undercarriage   The wheels and associated landing mechanisms of an aircraft.

undercart   A colloquial term for undercarriage.

underdeveloped   A country or region that has not yet reached its potential level of economic development.

Underground   The name given to the underground railway networks in London (also known as the Tube) and Glasgow. > *metro.*

underground railway   A railway that has a significant part of its route below ground. Commonly used in large towns and cities. > *metro.*

underpass   A road or railway that passes under another by means of a short tunnel.

undertow   When the current below the surface of a stretch of water flows in an opposite direction from that on the surface. This is especially dangerous to swimmers from a beach when the direction of the undertow is away from the land.

UNESCO   The United Nations Educational, Scientific and Cultural organisation, a specialised agency of the UN. Its purpose is to contribute to peace and security by promoting collaboration amongst nations by education, science and culture. UNESCO also selects, promotes and helps to safeguard natural and cultural heritage sites world-wide. > *UNESCO World Heritage Sites.*

UNESCO World Heritage Sites   A register of world sites considered to be of global importance either because of their natural heritage or their significant man-made contribution to world culture. Countries which are signatories to the World Heritage Convention can submit potential sites to UNESCO, which considers each proposal under strict criteria and lists each site where one or more natural or cultural criteria have been met. > *UNESCO.*

ungroomed   The condition of a piste or trail where the snow has not been compacted but left in a more-or-less virgin condition.

UNICEF   United Nations Children's Fund.

unicycle   A cycle with only one wheel.

Union flag   The United Kingdom's national flag, often referred to as the Union Jack (technically, the latter term is only correct when the flag is flying from a jackstaff).

Union Jack   *See Union flag.*

unique selling point   A selling point that is unequalled by other providers or products.

United Arab Emirates   *See UAE.*

United Kingdom   The country comprising England, Scotland, Wales and Northern Ireland. The full title is United Kingdom of Great Britain and Northern Ireland. The Channel Islands and the Isle of Man are not part of the United Kingdom although they retain very close links with it. Some organisations, such as travel insurance companies, may use a slightly different definition of the term 'United Kingdom'. > *Great Britain.*

United Nations   An international body established in the aftermath of the Secomd World War in 1945 to promote world-wide peace and security.. It is based in New York and has many specialist agencies. Every independent state in the world is a member except for Switzerland and Taiwan. > *UNESCO.*

United States of America   The country comprising the 50 states and the District of Colombia. The USA also has very close ties of various natures with Puerto Rico, the US Virgin Islands, Guam and certain other Pacific Islands.

universal air travel plan (UATP)   The credit card scheme operated by IATA.

universal mobile telecommunications system   A proposed new high-capacity system that will allow the genuinely universal use of portable telephones.

Universal Time Coordinate   *See UTC.*

unlade   To unload a ship, generally of its cargo.

unladen   A vehicle without passengers or cargo.

unlimited mileage   A car rental tariff whereby the hirer has paid a set amount to cover a duration of hire and where no extra amount is payable whatever the distance travelled.

U

unmapped *See uncharted.*

UNO United Nations Organisation. *See United Nations.*

unpressurised An aircraft without a pressurised cabin. Usually only found on smaller aircraft that fly at relatively low altitudes or in less developed countries where older aircraft are still in service.

UNPROFOR United Nations Protection Force.

unpublished fare A fare that is not advertised in tariffs. Often an air fare made available through a consolidator.

UNRWA United Nations Relief and Works Agency.

unscheduled Not in the advertised schedule. Often used to describe a stop on a journey that has become necessary through abnormal operational circumstances.

unsurfaced A road without a suitable all-weather surface suitable for vehicles.

up-anchor *See weigh anchor.*

up-country Toward the interior of a country.

upgrade The switching of a passenger or guest to accommodation in a higher class than that originally paid for.
> *complimentary upgrade.*

uplift capacity The number of skiers a lift, or the total numbers of lifts in a resort, can carry up a slope in one hour.

upmarket Of a holiday or other travel arrangement, towards or relating to the more expensive.

upper works That part of a ship that is above water when it is fully laden.

upscale (US) *See upmarket.*

uptown (US) The residential or more sophisticated part of a town or city, particularly where this forms a distinct area.

Ural Mountains The main mountain range in Russia, running roughly north-south to the north of the Aral Sea, and forming what is often regarded as the geographic frontier between the European and Asiatic parts of the country.

urban Living in, situated in or relating to a city. *See city.*

urban agglomeration A contiguous area inhabited at an urban density of population, but ignoring any administrative boundaries. The urban agglomeration of New York thus includes Jersey City, Newark, Patterson and Yonkers. According to UN estimates, in 2000 there were worldwide exactly 100 urban agglomerations with a population in excess of 3 million, the largest of which, at over 28 million, was Tokyo. In 1900, there were three (London, New York and Paris).

urban tourism Tourism concentrated in urban areas.

US 1. An abbreviation for United States (of America), particularly when used as an adjective.
2. (UK) Unserviceable.

US external territories Scattered throughout the world, mainly in the Pacific, are various US possessions which enjoy varying degrees of autonomy. For more information, please consult the Columbus *World Travel Guide.*

US regional marketing organisations One of currently eight bodies which exist to co-ordinate regional tourism issues in the USA. Participation by each state is voluntary. A state may be represented in more than one region, or none, and

U

membership is subject to change.

US Virgin Islands   *See Virgin Islands.*

USA   *See United States of America.*

useful load   The load that can be carried by a vehicle in addition to its own weight.

user-friendly   Any system or procedure that is designed to be easy to understand and use.

U-shape seating plan   A common configuration at meetings, conferences or seminars whereby the delegates are seated around tables arranged together in the shape of a U.

USP   *See unique selling point.*

USSR   Union of Soviet Socialist Republics, the former state (also known as the Soviet Union) dominated by the Russian Republic. It has now fragmented into 15 independent states. *> former Soviet Union.*

USTI   United States Tourism Industries. *See Appendix 5b.*

UT   *See UTC.*

UTC   Universal Time Co-ordinate. Formerly known as Greenwich Mean Time (GMT), a term which is still widely used and understood. UTC is the time on the Greenwich meridian and in the time zone associated with it. Other time zones are expressed as their variation behind or in advance of this. UTC is used throughout the world for airline and marine navigation. It is sometimes known as 'Zulu'. *> time zones, Greenwich meridian, British Summer Time, Daylight Saving Time, International Date Line.*

Utopia   An imaginary perfect place or situation.

UV   Ultra-violet.

U

vacancy The availability of space or accommodation.

vacate To leave accommodation.

vacation (US) A holiday.

vaccination The process of introducing a vaccine into a person's body. > *health precautions.*

vaccine A protective substance made from the organisms that cause a particular disease. It will stimulate the production of antibodies in humans and thus afford them protection from that disease. > *health precautions.*

validation The act of making a ticket good for travel, usually by stamping or imprinting. A validation stamp will contain, at least, the name of the issuing office and the date of issue of the document.

validator A machine for endorsing an agency's name and other details when validating documents.

validity The condition of a document being good for use. The most common use of the term refers to the period of validity – the dates or times between which it can be used. London Tube tickets, for example, are only valid for use on their day of purchase, and many airline tickets are only valid for a particular flight.

valley A long and often narrow depression in the land, usually between two ranges of hills or mountains. Many valleys have a river running along the bottom.

Valley of the Kings A region of great archaeological significance near Luxor in Egypt, about 500km south of Cairo.

Valley of the Olifants *See Blue Train.*

Valley of the Queens A region of great archaeological significance near Luxor in Egypt, about 500km south of Cairo.

Valley of the Sun The valley in which Phoenix, Arizona is situated, together with most of its major suburbs including Mesa and Scottsdale. One of the fastest-growing parts of the Sunbelt.

Valois Of or relating to the kings of France between 1328 and 1589, and to that period of French history generally.

Valsalva manoeuvre The term for a method for equalising the pressure inside the ear-drum with that on the outside. It is achieved by holding the nose firmly closed and then trying to breathe out through it, until the ears are felt to gently 'pop' The technique is typically used by divers but some find it useful when travelling by air, especially during descent.

valuables Items of high worth, such as jewellery, computer equipment and cameras. Most insurance policies can offer cover in the event that valuables are lost, damaged or stolen. The conditions under which such a claim can be made will be set out in the small print and will vary from policy to policy. Insurance for

V

valuables often includes a limit on the repayment per single article, and on the overall value of all such items claimed for. > *travel insurance*.

van 1. An enclosed vehicle designed for the conveyance of goods. 2. (UK) The railway carriage provided for the use of the guard and the conveyance of luggage.

vaporetto A small motor boat, especially one used on the canals of Venice.

vapour trail *See contrail.*

VDU Visual Display Unit. A monitor or similar used to display computer data.

vegan A person who abstains from eating any food of animal origin, including fish, eggs and dairy products.

vegetarian A person who abstains from eating meat, but who will eat eggs and dairy products, and possibly also fish.

vehicle Any machine designed for the transport of passengers or goods.

vehicle hire *See vehicle rental.*

vehicle rental The act of hiring a car for a specified period of time, and the industry which exists to provide this. The term generally refers to self-drive vehicles, but also can include those hired with a chauffeur. > *vehicle rental insurance*.

vehicle rental insurance The various insurance policies that are available for anyone renting a vehicle. There are many different types of cover: the terms used to describe them, and the conditions that apply to each, will vary from agency to agency and from country to country. Many of these, such as third-party cover, will be obligatory, although in some cases it may be possible for the renter to show that cover is already in place under existing insurance policies.
• *Damage to the car* is covered by what is normally termed collision (or loss) damage waiver (CDW/LDW), which will cover the cost of repair or replacement in the event of an accident, less an excess which will have to be paid by the renter. The excess, although fixed, will sometimes be quite high, but can sometimes be reduced or eliminated on payment of a further premium.
• *Third-party insurance* covers claims made by someone else against the renter. In some countries, particularly the USA, it is advisable to top up this insurance with some form of additional cover: supplementary liability insurance, extended protection and liability insurance supplement are some of the terms used for this kind of additional protection.
• *Injury to the driver and passengers* will be covered by a personal accident insurance policy. Some renters may have this as part of general travel insurance that might be in place.
• *The theft or attempted theft of the vehicle* is covered by a theft protection cover, on which an excess might apply.
• *The theft of personal possessions from the vehicle* can, in some cases, be covered by a personal effects cover. This may also cover time spent in accommodation en route. Some renters may already have this as part of general travel insurance that might be in place.
Non-compliance with the terms of the rental agreement (such as leaving the car unlocked or driving dangerously) may result in the cover being invalidated. It is also worth remembering that almost all rental agreements require the renter to pay the full cost of any damage caused by the vehicle striking overhead or overhanging objects, such as bridges.

veld (or **veldt**) A South African term for open country or grassland.

Venice of... A term used to market a town or city anywhere in the world by virtue of the number or splendour of its canals.

Venice-Simplon Orient Express The luxury rail service which has operated

V

since 1982 between London and Venice via Paris. Occasional journeys also run to Prague, Rome or Istanbul.

veranda (or **verandah**) A raised platform, sometimes roofed, along the side of a house.

verify To check the accuracy of something.

vernal equinox *See equinox.*

vertical drop The difference in height between the top of the highest lift in a resort and the bottom of the lowest lift. This is one of the most important indicators as to how much skiing is likely to be available in an area.

vertical integration The term used to describe the ownership, by one organisation, of both the means of production and the means of distribution of a commodity. In travel, for example, the same organisation could own an airline, a tour operator and a travel agency.

vertical take off and landing Of an aircraft that can take off vertically, for example, a helicopter

vessel A waterborne vehicle.

vestibule 1. A hall or ante-chamber. 2. (US) An enclosed entrance to a railway carriage.

vexillology The study of flags.

VFR *See visiting friends and relatives.*

via By way of.

via ferrata Literally 'the iron roads', these are long scrambling routes equipped with ladders, metal spikes and safety rails to enable passage over sections that would otherwise require technical rock climbing. The routes exist mainly in Italy France and Spain, but require more specialised equipment than

that needed for regular scrambles. See also *scrambling*.

viaduct A bridge, often constructed of a number of short spans, that conveys a road or railway across a valley.

vicinity The local area.

victoria A low, light four-wheeled horse-drawn carriage with a collapsible top.

Victorian Of or relating to the period of English history during the reign of Queen Victoria (1837 to 1901).

view That which can be seen from a particular point, usually with the implication that it is attractive.

viewdata Any computerised information and booking service, generally using on-line communication: In the UK, Prestel was the first widely available system, but it has long-since been replaced by far more sophisticated networks such as the various GDSs.

Viking The Scandinavian seafaring pirates, and later settlers and traders, who were active in Northern Europe between the 8th and 11th centuries.

villa Self catering accommodation, usually in a private, detached house or bungalow. The name originally applied to prestigious houses privately owned and rented to selected guests. Now however, a villa may be in a specially built complex containing many similar properties

village A group of houses and other buildings, larger than a hamlet and smaller than a town.

violent storm *See Beaufort scale.*

VIP Very Important Person. The designation is usually reserved for public figures who might appreciate, require or expect special treatment and additional security. > *CIP.*

V

Virgin Islands A group of islands in the Leeward Islands in the Caribbean, to the east of Puerto Rico. They are divided into the US Virgin Islands (an Unincorporated Territory of the USA) and the British Virgin Islands (a British Overseas Territory).

visa The physical evidence of the granting of permission for travel to or via or out of a country. This generally takes the form of a stamp in a passport, although in some cases (particularly where evidence of travel to or from that country might cause the traveller problems when later trying to enter another country) it is recorded on a piece of paper which can removed from the passport after use. Charges are often made for issuing visas, and the procedure can take a long time. Visas are generally of three types:
• *Entry visa*. This gives the traveller the right to travel to the country, although the right to enter it will be at the discretion of the immigration officials. Entry visas will generally be valid for use within a specified period from the date of issue, and valid for a specified length of visit, or number of visits, from the first date of entry. In some cases there may be restrictions as to the part/s of the country that can be visited or the activities that can be engaged in. Different types of visas may be required depending on the purpose of travel: business travellers, for example, often need to undergo different formalities. The definition of what exactly is meant by business travel will vary from country to country.
• *Transit visa*. This gives the traveller the right to pass through the country for a specified period of time, generally because of the need to change planes. Transit visas generally do not permit the traveller to leave a designated area in the airport.
• *Exit visa*. In rare cases, countries may require travellers to obtain an exit visa before departure, although this is generally applied to nationals of the country in question where travel restrictions apply.

visibility The greatest distance at which an object can be seen against its background.

Visigoth A member of the branch of the Goths who settled in France and Spain during the 5th century, ruling Spain until the early 8th century.

visit 1. To go to a place for a short period. 2. (US) A chat.

Visit Scotland *See Appendix 5a.*

visiting friends and relatives (VFR) A term used to describe travellers whose main purpose for their journey is to visit friends or relatives who live abroad.

visitor One who is undertaking a visit.

visitor attraction *See attraction.*

visitor's book A register in which visitors to a hotel, an attraction or similar record their names and comments.

vista A long narrow view, especially between trees.

void An endorsement on a ticket that shows that the particular section is not to be used.

volcano A mountain formed through the expulsion of lava from the earth's interior. Volcanoes can be active, that is, still likely to erupt, dormant (inactive) and therefore unlikely to erupt, or extinct and very unlikely to erupt.

voltage The pressure of an electrical supply. In most of Europe the mains supply is delivered at between 220 and 250 volts. In most of the Americas it is delivered at 110 volts. Travellers must take care when using appliances in other countries since poor operation or damage can arise if suitable adjustment or adaptation is not made.

voluntary changes Changes to an

V

itinerary that are made at a passenger's own request.

voucher A document that may be exchanged for services such as meals or accommodation, in the same way that a ticket may be exchanged for travel. The terms 'voucher' and 'ticket' are often used interchangeably.

voyage A journey, especially one by sea.

voyager A person on a voyage.

V-shape seating plan *See herringbone seating plan.*

VTOL *See Vertical Take Off and Landing.*

V

Ww

W pattern   A pattern of aircraft operation designed to maximise fare-paying usage and to avoid ferry mileage. For example, an aircraft may take passengers from Gatwick to Palma, pick up passengers there and take them to Cardiff, pick up more passengers there and take them to Palma then pick up a further load and take them back to Gatwick. This type of intensive utilisation is generally more common with short-haul charter operations than it is with long-haul or scheduled services.

WEF   (UK) With effect from.

WP   *See working pressure.*

wadi   A rocky watercourse, usually in Arabia, that is dry for most of the year.

Wagon-Lit   A European sleeping car. They are more comfortable than a couchette and usually more expensive.

wait list   (or **waiting-list**) A record of potential travellers or customers for a particular service or product that is currently fully booked. Once the waiting list reaches such a length that it is unlikely that all those on it will be accommodated, the principal will refuse to add further names and the waiting list is said to be closed.

waiter   1. (UK) A man employed to serve customers in a restaurant or similar establishment with food, drinks or other requirements.
2. (US) A person of either sex providing waiting services as described above.

waiting room   A room provided, especially at a railway or bus station, for passengers waiting for the arrival of their service.

waiting-list   *See wait-list.*

waitress   (UK) A woman employed to perform the same job as a waiter.

waive   To refrain from insisting on or making use of a right or claim. The term is usually used in connection with a legally binding document.

waiver   A clause in a contract or agreement by which one or more parties agrees to waive their right to make a specific claim, usually in exchange for some compensation in cash or kind. If, for example, a damage waiver is paid to a car rental company, the company will waive its right to charge if the car suffers damage. > *vehicle rental insurance.*

wake   The waves caused by the motion of a ship through water.

Wales   One of the constituent countries of the United Kingdom of Great Britain and Northern Ireland. > *Great Britain, United Kingdom.*

walk-in   1. A guest who arrives without having made a reservation.
2. A service not requiring a prior appointment or reservation.
3. A wardrobe or other storage space large enough for a person to enter.

walking tour   A holiday on foot, usually of several days.

W

walk-on (UK) A traveller who purchases a ticket just prior to departure.

walk-out (US) A passage, doorway or other exit that provides outdoor access.

walk-through A building or room that can be entered from either end.

walk-up 1. (US) A floor of a building that can only be reached by stairs, rather than a lift.
2. (US) A traveller who purchases a ticket just prior to departure.

walkway A passage or path, often a raised passageway connecting parts of a building or similar.

wall bed A bed designed to be folded away against the wall when not in use.

Wallace's line A hypothetical boundary between Asia and Oceania, following zoogeographical rather than political divisions. It runs between the Indonesian islands of Bali and Lombock, through the Macassar Strait (between Sulawesi and Borneo) and to the south-east of the Philippines.

wanderlust The desire to travel or explore.

warrant A document, often issued by the military or a government department, that can be exchanged for tickets or other travel documents.

Warsaw Convention An international agreement, ratified in 1928, which limits the liability of airlines for loss or damage to international passengers and their baggage. It has been considerably modified over the years, but most of its terms and conditions still apply.

wash-out A breach in a road or railway track caused by flooding.

washroom (US) A room with washing and lavatory facilities.

wat A Buddhist temple.

WATA World Association Of Travel Agents. *See Appendix 5d.*

watch A period of duty for a seaman, usually four hours.

water bus A boat carrying passengers on a regular service on a river, lake or canal. Usually the journeys will be fairly short.

water closet A lavatory with a means for flushing. Usually abbreviated to WC.

water park A recreational area where the facilities are mainly based on activities involving water.

water taxi A small boat, usually motor-driven, taking passengers on a casual basis. Commonly used in cities such as Venice.

watercourse A stream or artificial channel.

waterfall A stream or river flowing over a precipice. Waterfalls are often spectacular and are therefore significant tourist attractions.

waterfront The area adjacent to water, often a dock or harbour.

watering hole 1. A place at which animals regularly drink. Often a focal point for visitors to game reserves.
2. A colloquial term for a bar or pub.

waterline The point on a ship's hull up to which the water reaches.

waterman A boatman plying for hire.

water-ski A sport whose participants are towed across a stretch of water, usually by a speedboat, with special skis attached to their feet.

waterspout An up-welling of water caused by a tornado.

watertight doors Heavy doors that, when closed, divide a ship into a series of separate compartments. This minimises the risk of sinking following damage to the hull.

waterway Any route used for travel by water, but usually applied to rivers and canals.

watt A measurement of power. In an electrical appliance it will be shown on the data plate. Dividing the power rating of the appliance by the voltage at which it is being operated will give an indication of the current that will be drawn.

wave The undulations in the sea, caused by wind and tides. The distance between the crests of waves will vary according to the weather conditions and the body of water.

wave machine A device for producing waves in a swimming pool.

Way of St James *See Camino de Compostela.*

way station (US) A minor railway station.

waybill A list of passengers or goods on a vehicle.

wayside The edge of a road or other land route.

WC A universal term for a lavatory or toilet.

weather The day to day variations of temperature, rainfall, humidity and other indicators. Unlike climate, which indicates the overall situation of a region, weather can be variable and unpredictable. The UK is an example of a region with a mild and temperate climate but with very unpredictable weather. > *climate.*

weddings abroad These have become increasingly popular in recent years. Several companies now specialise in organising such events, and many hotels, resorts and cruise lines worldwide are actively promoting themselves as wedding venues. The formalities required will vary from country to country and these will require attention before departure. The Columbus *World Travel Guide* contains a dedicated section on this subject, including details of necessary documentation and procedures for a selection of popular wedding destinations.

week Officially a period of seven days, nowadays generally regarded to run from midnight at the end of the traditional day of rest: thus in Christian countries, most would agree that the week runs from Monday to Sunday. In travel it usually means a period of seven days from the start of a provided facility. In airline timetables, the days are generally given numeric codes: 1 (Monday) through to 7 (Sunday). 'Dly' indicates that the service operates daily, while an X preceding a number or numbers indicates that it does *not* operate on those days: thus X35 means that the service operates every day except Wednesday and Friday.

weekday A day other than at the weekend.

weekend The days at the end of the normal working week when many businesses are shut. In most of Europe and the USA it falls on Saturday and Sunday:. Moslems observe Fridays, and Jews Saturdays.

weigh anchor To raise the anchor of a ship prior to sailing.

weir A small dam built across a river to raise its level or regulate its flow.

well-appointed Accommodation having fixtures and fittings to a good and suitable standard.

W

well-travelled A person who has travelled a great deal and who is, by implication, knowledgeable about travel procedures and terminology.

west One of the four cardinal points of the compass, 90° clockwise from south and 180° from east; on the left of maps where (as is normal) north is at the top. > *north*.

west country The western part of any country, and particularly the area including the counties of Cornwall, Devon and Somerset (and sometimes others) in England.

West Highland Line A spectacular railway journey in Scotland between Glasgow and Mallaig.

West Indies The islands enclosing the Caribbean Sea including the Bahama Islands and the Greater and Lesser Antilles. Also known as The Caribbean.

West, the Generally used to refer to Europe and North America.

Westerlies The winds that blow from mainly west to east, between latitudes 30° and 70°. In the northern hemisphere their prevailing direction is from the south-west; in the southern hemisphere it is from the north-west.

western hemisphere The half of the earth to the west of 0° longitude and to the east of 180° longitude.

Western Mediterranean Terms Yacht charter terms under which the fee includes the charter of the yacht with all equipment; basic consumables for engine-room, deck and cabins; the crew's wages and food; and insurance for the yacht itself, for third party claims and employer's liability insurance for the crew. Other costs, such as fuel, the client's food and drink, berthing charges, laundry and radio telephone and other communication costs, must be paid by the client. These terms may vary.

Western Standard Time One of the time zones used in Australia, eight hours ahead of UTC.

Western States Tourism Policy Council An informal US regional marketing organisation covering many of the western states of the USA. > *US regional marketing organisations*.

wet bar (US) A small area in a hotel room or similar where drinks can be mixed and served.

wet bike *See jet ski*.

wet lease To hire a vehicle, usually a ship, boat or aircraft, with all its crew and supplies.

wet suit A protective rubber suit worn by divers that allows water to enter the suit before being largely retained in place. The layer of water thus formed provides an extra layer of insulation.

wetland A marsh, bog or similar area.

wharf A structure projecting into water to which vessels can be moored.

wherry 1. A light rowing boat. 2. (UK) A large, light barge.

whirlpool A powerful circular eddy in water.

whirlwind A tornado.

whirlybird A colloquial term for a helicopter.

whistle-stop 1. (US) A small, unimportant railway station. 2. A very fast tour or journey with few and brief stops.

Whit Sunday A festival in the Christian religious calendar, celebrated seven weeks after Easter.

W

white ensign   The flag of the British Royal Navy and the Royal Yacht Squadron.

white night   A night in extremely high latitudes when it never gets properly dark.

white tie   A name given to the very formal mode of evening dress for men that involves the wearing of a tail coat and white bow tie.

white-out   A condition, often caused by blizzard conditions, where it is impossible to see anything except white snow in the air and on the ground.

white-water rafting   An extreme sport involving taking a raft or similar vessel through a stretch of very rough water such as rapids on a river.

wholesaler   An organisation that buys in bulk from a manufacturer to sell to retailers. In travel, this is usually a tour operator.

wide-bodied aircraft   An large passenger aircraft with two or more aisles. The Boeing 747 is probably the best known example.

Wild Coast   The scenic coastal area between East London and Port Shepstone in South Africa.

Wild West   The western USA during its historical period of lawlessness.

wilderness   A wild or undeveloped region.

wildlife attraction   Any attraction, such as a wildlife park, where animals, birds or other fauna are on view to visitors.

wildlife park   A place where exotic animals are kept in a semi-wild state in conditions that allow them to be viewed by visitors, often at close quarters. Sometimes known as a safari park.

WIN   Worldwide Independent Travel Network. *See Appendix 5a.*

wind chill   The extent to which the speed of the wind reduces the perceived temperature of the air.

wind force   The force of the wind as measured by the Beaufort scale. *See Beaufort Scale.*

wind shear   A sudden downward rush of air, often experienced in storm conditions. Wind shear has caused several aircraft accidents.

windbound   When a sailing vessel is unable to operate because of contrary winds.

windjammer   A merchant sailing vessel.

windward   On the side from which the wind is blowing.

Windward Islands   The group of Caribbean islands including Grenada, Martinique, St Lucia and St Vincent and the Grenadines.

wine bar   A bar or small restaurant serving drink and food.

wine waiter   A waiter in larger restaurants whose sole responsibility is the provision of the wine and other drinks.

wing   1. One of the projections from the fuselage of an aircraft that create the lift that support it during flight.
2. (UK) The side panels of a car.
3. Any protruding part of a hotel or other large building.

wingspan   The measurement across the wings or an aircraft.

Winter Olympic Games   The world's premier international winter-sports event, which takes place every four years in a different city on each occasion.

W

Accommodation and transport arrangements may need to be made months, and sometimes years, in advance.

winter solstice *See solstice.*

winter sports Sports performed on snow and ice, such as skating, sledging and skiing.

wipe out 1. A colloquial term given by winter sports enthusiasts to a crash or fall from a snowboard or skis. 2. A similar accident from a surfboard.

withdrawal of services insurance A 'loss of enjoyment' insurance cover paid when a pre-arranged service or facility was not provided, regardless of any financial loss. > *travel insurance.*

workday (US) A day on which work is usually done.

working pressure The maximum pressure to which a diving cylinder should be normally charged for everyday use.

World Athletics Championships A major international athletics event, which takes place every four years in a different city on each occasion. Accommodation and transport arrangements may need to be made months, and sometimes years, in advance.

world cup Any of the regular international competitions for national teams in a particular sport, taking place at regular intervals in a different country or countries on each occasion. Many sports now organise a world cup; the three most important are cricket (generally every four years since 1975), rugby union (every four years since 1987) and, largest of all, football (1930, 1934, 1938 and every four years since 1950). Accommodation and transport arrangements may need to be made months, and sometimes years, in advance.

World Heritage Site *See UNESCO World Heritage Site.*

World Travel Market One of the most important travel exhibitions in the world, held in London, in November each year. Attendance is generally restricted to persons connected with the travel industry.

Worldspan A GDS sponsored by Delta and other airlines.

Worldwide Fund for Nature One of the world's largest private nature conservation organisations. Its aim is to conserve the natural environment by preserving species and ecosystem diversity. Formerly known as the World Wildlife Fund.

WP Word processor.

wreck *See shipwreck.*

write out To issue a document manually.

WTB Wales Tourist Board. *See Appendix 5a.*

WTM *See World Travel Market.*

WTO World Tourism Organisation. The WTO describes itself as: 'the leading international body in the field of travel and tourism. It serves as a global forum for tourism policy issues and a practical source of tourism know-how and statistics. Its membership includes 139 countries, seven territories and some 350 Affiliate Members representing regional and local promotion boards, tourism trade associations, educational institutions and private sector companies, including airlines, hotel groups and tour operators. With its headquarters in Madrid and an international staff of 90 tourism specialists, WTO is an intergovernmental body vested by the United Nations with a central and decisive role in promoting the development of responsible, sustainable

W

and universally accessible tourism.
Through tourism, WTO aims to stimulate
economic growth and job creation,
provide incentives for protecting the
environment and cultural heritage, and
promote peace, prosperity and respect for
human rights.' The WTO is the source of
the most comprehensive and
authoritative statistics on global travel
and tourism. *See Appendix 5d.*

WTO Regional Promotional Projects
Specialised initiatives organised by the
WTO to promote tourism to a group of
member countries. The Silk Road and the
Slave Route are currently two of these.

WTO   World Tourism Organisation. *See
Appendix 5d.*

WWF   *See Worldwide Fund for Nature.*

W

x   Conventionally used to indicate an unknown quantity, price, time or other numeric variable.

x axis   The horizontal axis of a chart or graph.

Xanadu   A place of unattainable splendour and luxury.

xebec   A small, three-masted Mediterranean sailing vessel.

xenophile   A person who likes foreign things or people.

xenophillia   The state of liking foreign things or people.

xenophobe   A person who fears or distrusts foreign things or people.

xenophobia   The fear or distrust of foreign things or people.

xeric   Characterised by dry climate.

Xmas   A commonly used abbreviation for Christmas.

x-rays   Short-wave radiation that can pass through many solid materials. X-rays are sometimes used for baggage screening at airports and other sensitive places. Since they can affect photographic film, travellers should ask for their baggage to be hand-searched if they are concerned as to the impact of the screening equipment.

X

Yy

y axis The vertical axis of a chart or graph.

yacht 1. A small sailing vessel used for pleasure.
2. A large and generally luxurious motor vessel.

yard 1. A unit of measurement in the imperial system equal to three feet (0.9144m).
2. A spar slung across a mast to hold a sail.
3. (UK) Any piece of uncultivated land around a commercial or domestic property.
4. (US) Any piece of land around a commercial or domestic property, regardless of whether it is cultivated or not.

yaw The failure of a ship or aircraft to hold a straight course; veering from side to side.

yawl A two-masted sailing vessel.

yellow fever A tropical disease caused by a virus, and difficult to cure. Travellers should ensure that they are vaccinated before visiting endemic zones (Central Africa and the northern part of South America). Certificates of vaccination may be required when travelling to or from countries in these areas. > *health precautions.*

yellow flag A flag displayed by a vessel in quarantine.

Yellow Sea The area of the Pacific Ocean between China and Korea.

Yemen A country in the Arabian peninsula, officially the Republic of Yemen. Between 1970 and 1990, it was divided between the Republic of Yemen (North Yemen) and the People's Democratic Republic of Yemen (South Yemen).

Yeti A large, ape-like creature reputedly living in the Himalayas.

yield A term covering various ways of expressing the financial gain from specified activities, including the percentage return on a total amount invested, the profit derived per item sold, or the income resulting from the allocation of seats and accommodation to different market sectors. Different organisations will often have different ways of calculating this. Airlines, for example, may refer to yield in terms of operating revenue per kilometre , a figure which will vary depending on measurable factors such as the revenue from the ticket sales, operating costs and distance flown.

yield management The control of the way in which space is used on aircraft and other means of transport. Typically a carrier will adjust the ratio of accommodation available at various rates so as to maximise the load factor and revenue of a service.

Yom Kippur A festival in the Jewish religious calendar, celebrated ten days after Rosh Hashanah.

youth A young person, generally aged between the early teens and early twenties.

Y

youth fare   A fare offered to people up to the age of approximately 25 years.

youth hostel   An inexpensive form of accommodation originally restricted to young people. Most youth hostels will now accept travellers of any age.

Yugoslavia   The name by which two former Balkan states were commonly known. The first of these, the Federal People's Republic of Yugoslavia, was established after the Second World War and dissolved in the early 1990s and comprised the modern-day states of Bosnia-Herzegovina, Croatia, Slovenia, Macedonia, Serbia and Montenegro. Subsequently the Federal Republic of Yugoslavia, comprising Serbia and Montenegro, was briefly established. This country changed its name to the Republic of Serbia & Montenegro in March 2003.

Y

Zz

Zaire The former name for the African country now called the Democratic Republic of Congo.

zawn (UK) A deep and narrow fold or inlet in a sea cliff.

zebra crossing (UK) A pedestrian crossing, marked on the road with black and white stripes and often on the kerb with flashing orange lights. Once on the crossing, the pedestrian has right of way. Crossings in other countries that look similar to this will not necessarily give the pedestrian right of way, but rather indicate that this is a place where they are permitted to cross the road.

zenith The highest point, often used to describe a period of prosperity.

zephyr A soft, gentle breeze.

Zeppelin A German manufacturer of airships, whose name is still sometimes used as a generic term for this type of aircraft.

zero emission vehicle A vehicle that produces no emissions at the point of operation. Presently the only successful ZEVs are electrically or cable operated.

ZEV *See zero emission vehicle.*

zip code (US) The mail sorting code appearing at the end of the address.

zócalo A Mexican term for the main square and focal point of a town.

zone An area or region having particular properties that make it special or identifiable.

zoo (or **zoological garden, zoological park**) A place where visitors can see animals in captivity, often as well as other attractions. Many zoos are now finding a new role in the conservation and preservation of endangered species.

zoogeographical Of or relating to the study of animals according to their geographical distribution.

zorbing An extreme sport invented in New Zealand in 1996 that involves being strapped into a large plastic ball that is then rolled down a steep hill.

Z

Appendix 1
Countries

The chart below gives a selection of information for every country in the world.

The matter of deciding what is and what is not a country is by no means clear-cut, but no political or other subjective stance has been adopted. Some of the places listed below are not truly independent, but have been included separately because they are generally regarded as being separate travel destinations. In general, figures for places that are fully integrated into another state – such as Hawaii (USA), the Balearic and Canary Islands (Spain) and the Azores and Madeira (Portugal) – have been included in those for the main country. For more information on countries worldwide, consult the most recent editions of the Columbus *World Travel Guide* or *World Travel Atlas*. The latter title provides a more detailed version of this chart, and includes a range of economic indicators and travel statistics as well as world rankings for each category.

The **country** names are rarely the full official title. Some have been shortened for reasons of space. The **region** for each entry does not follow any official divisions, but is merely a guide for locating the country on a map. For a few countries, the matter of what is the **capital** causes some confusion: these will be referred to in the notes below the chart. **Area** figures ('000 sq km) relate to land area and disregard major lakes. **Population** figures ('000) have been taken from a range of sources, generally dating from between 1998 and 2001. **Population density (P.D.)** is population divided by area, and is rounded to the nearest whole number for figures above 10, and to the nearest decimal point for figures under 9.5. Under **nationality** the chart lists the term that is most commonly used to describe the country or its citizens. In many cases this can be used as an adjective ('a French resort') and as a noun ('the French'). Only one such word as been listed per country. In many cases, others also exist: these include spelling variations, local expressions, slang, feminine and plural forms, and separate terms for the place and for the people. A few terms describing the smaller parts of federal countries have been provided in the footnotes. Where no term is given, this is because research has failed to discover a commonly accepted one. Finally, the **main language/s** spoken have been listed. In addition to these, many countries have many other widely-spoken languages and dialects; sometimes over a hundred.

Country	Region	Capital	Area	Pop.	P.D.	Nationality	Main language/s
Afghanistan	Asia W	Kabul	652.1	25,869	40	Afghan	Dari, Pashtó
Albania	Europe E	Tirana	28.7	3,375	118	Albanian	Albanian, Greek
Algeria	Africa N	Algiers	2,381.70	29,950	13	Algerian	Arabic, French
American Samoa	Pacific E	Pago Pago	0.2	64	320	Samoan	Samoan, English
Andorra	Europe W	Andorra la Vella	0.45	66	147	Andorran	Catalan, French, Spanish

Country	Region	Capital	Area	Pop.	P.D.	Nationality	Main language/s
Angola	Africa S	Luanda	1,246.70	12,357	9.9	Angolan	Portuguese
Anguilla	Caribbean	The Valley	0.16	11	69	Anguillan	English
Antigua & Barbuda	Caribbean	St John's	0.44	67	152	Antiguan (12)	English
Argentina	America S	Buenos Aires	2,780.40	36,580	13	Argentine	Spanish
Armenia	Asia W	Yerevan	29.8	3,809	128	Armenian	Armenian, Russian
Aruba	Caribbean	Oranjestad	0.18	98	544	Aruban	Dutch, Papiamento, English, Spanish
Australia	Australasia	Canberra	7,682.30	18,967	2.5	Australian	English
Austria	Europe W	Vienna	83.9	8,092	96	Austrian	German
Azerbaijan	Asia W	Baku	86.6	7,983	92	Azerbajani	Azerbajani, Russian
Bahamas	Caribbean	Nassau	13.9	298	21	Bahamanian	English
Bahrain	Asia W	Manama	0.71	666	938	Bahraini	Arabic, English
Bangladesh	Asia S	Dhaka	148.4	127,669	860	Bangladeshi	Bengali
Barbados	Caribbean	Bridgetown	0.43	267	621	Barbadian	English
Belarus	Europe E	Minsk	207.6	10,032	48	Belorussian	Russian, Belorussian
Belgium	Europe W	Brussels	30.5	10,226	335	Belgian	Flemish, French
Belize	America C	Belmopan	23	247	11	Belizian	English, Spanish
Benin	Africa W	Porto Novo	112.6	6,114	54	Beninese	French
Bermuda	Atlantic N	Hamilton	0.05	64	1,280	Bermudan	English
Bhutan	Asia S	Thimphu	46.5	782	17	Bhutanese	Dzongkha
Bolivia	America S	(1)	1,098.60	8,138	7.4	Bolivian	Spanish
Bosnia-Herzegovina	Europe E	Sarajevo	51.1	3,881	76	Bosnian	Serbo-Croat and Croato-Serb
Botswana	Africa S	Gaborone	581.7	1,588	2.7	Tswana	English, Setswana
Brazil	America S	Brasília	8,547.40	167,967	20	Brazilian	Portuguese
British Virgin Is.	Caribbean	Road Town	0.13	19	146	Virgin Islander	English
Brunei	Asia SE	Bandar Seri Begawan	5.8	322	56	Bruneian	Malay, English
Bulgaria	Europe E	Sofia	111	8,208	74	Bulgarian	Bulgarian
Burkina	Africa W	Ouagadougou	274.1	10,996	40	Burkinese	French, Moré, Dioula, Peulh
Burundi	Africa E	Bujumbura	27.8	6,678	240	Burundian	Kirundi, French
Cambodia	Asia SE	Phnom Penh	181	11,757	65	Cambodian	Khmer, Chinese, Vietnamese

Country	Region	Capital	Area	Pop.	P.D.	Nationality	Main language/s
Cameroon	Africa W	Yaoundé	475.4	14,691	31	Cameroonian	French, English
Canada	America N	Ottawa	9,970.60	30,491	3.1	Canadian	English, French, Inuktitut
Cape Verde	Atlantic E	Praia	4	428	107	Cape Verdean	Portuguese, Creole, English
Cayman Is.	Caribbean	George Town	0.26	39	150	Cayman Islander	English
Central African Rep.	Africa C	Bangui	622.4	3,540	5.7		French, Sangho
Chad	Africa C	Ndjaména	1,284.00	7,486	5.8	Chadian	Arabic, French, Sara
Channel Is.	Europe W	(2)	0.2	149	745	Channel Islander	English, Norman-French dialect
Chile	America S	Santiago	736.9	15,018	20	Chilean	Spanish
China	Asia E	Beijing	9,536.70	1,253,595	131	Chinese	Mandarin, Cantonese
China: Hong Kong	Asia E	-	1.1	6,721	6,110		Cantonese, English
China: Macau	Asia E	-	0.02	434	21,700	Macanese	Cantonese, Portuguese
Colombia	America S	Bogotá	1,141.70	41,539	36	Colombian	Spanish
Comoros	Indian Ocean	Moroni	1.9	544	286	Comoran	French, Arabic
Congo, Rep.	Africa W	Brazzaville	341.8	2,859	8.4	Congolese	French, Lingala, Kilcongo
Congo, Dem. Rep.	Africa C	Kinshasa	2,344.90	49,776	21	Congolese	French, Lingala, Kilcongo
Cook Is.	Pacific E	Avarua	0.23	20	87	Cook Islander	Cook Islands Maori, English
Costa Rica	America C	San José	51.1	3,589	70	Costa Rican	Spanish
Côte d'Ivoire	Africa W	(3)	320.8	15,545	48	Ivorian	French
Croatia	Europe E	Zagreb	56.5	4,464	79	Croatian	Croatian (Croato-Serb)
Cuba	Caribbean	Havana	110.9	11,178	101	Cuban	Spanish
Cyprus	Europe E	Nicosia	9.3	760	82	Cypriot	Greek, Turkish, English
Czech Rep.	Europe E	Prague	78.9	10,278	130	Czech	Czech
Denmark	Europe N	Copenhagen	43.1	5,326	124	Dane	Danish, English
Djibouti	Africa E	Djibouti	23.2	648	28	Djiboutian	Arabic, French, Afar, Somali
Dominica	Caribbean	Roseau	0.75	73	97	Dominican	English, Creole
Dominican Rep.	Caribbean	Santo Domingo	48.4	8,404	174	Dominican	Spanish
East Timor	Asia SE	Dili	14.6	750	51	Timorese	Tetum, Portuguese, English
Ecuador	America S	Quito	275.8	12,412	45	Ecuadorian	Spanish
Egypt	Africa N	Cairo	997.7	62,655	63	Egyptian	Arabic, English, French

Country	Region	Capital	Area	Pop.	P.D.	Nationality	Main language/s
El Salvador	America C	San Salvador	21	6,154	293	Salvadorean	Spanish
Equatorial Guinea	Africa W	Malabo	28.1	443	16	Guinean	Spanish, Fang, Bubi
Eritrea	Africa E	Asmara	93.7	3,991	43	Eritrean	Arabic, Tigrinya, Italian
Estonia	Europe E	Tallinn	45.2	1,442	32	Estonian	Estonian, Russian, English
Ethiopia	Africa E	Addis Ababa	1,104.30	62,782	57	Ethiopean	Amharic, English
Falkland Is.	Atlantic S	Stanley	12.2	3	0.2	Falkland Islander	English
Faroe Is.	Europe N	Tórshavn	1.4	44	31	Faroese	Danish
Fiji Is.	Pacific W	Suva	18.3	801	44	Fijian	Fijian, Hindi
Finland	Europe N	Helsinki	338.1	5,166	15	Finn	Finish, English
France	Europe W	Paris	549.1	58,620	107	French	French
French Guiana	America S	Cayenne	85.5	173	2	Guianese	French, Creole
French Polynesia	Pacific E	Papeete	4.2	231	55	Tahitian	Tahitian, French
Gabon	Africa W	Libreville	267.7	1,208	4.5	Gabonese	French, Fang
Gambia, The	Africa W	Banjul	10.7	1,251	117	Gambian	English
Georgia	Asia W	Tbilisi	69.7	5,452	78	Georgian	Georgian, Russian
Germany	Europe W	Berlin	357	82,100	230	German	German
Ghana	Africa W	Accra	238.5	18,785	79	Ghanaian	English
Gibraltar	Europe W	Gibraltar	0.006	27	4,500	Gibraltarian	English, Spanish
Greece	Europe E	Athens	132	10,538	80	Greek	Greek
Greenland	Atlantic N	Nuuk	2,166.10	56	0.03	Greenlander	Greenlandic, Inuit, Danish
Grenada	Caribbean	St George's	0.34	97	285	Grenadian	English
Guadeloupe	Caribbean	(4)	1.7	425	250	Guadeloupian	French, Creole
Guam	Pacific W	Agaña	0.54	152	281	Guamanian	English, Chamorro
Guatemala	America C	Guatemala City	108.9	11,088	102	Guatemalan	Spanish
Guinea	Africa W	Conakry	245.9	7,251	29	Guinean	French, Susu, Malinké, Fula
Guinea-Bissau	Africa W	Bissau	36.1	1,185	33	Guinean	Portuguese, Guinean Creole
Guyana	America S	Georgetown	215	856	4	Guyanese	English
Haiti	Caribbean	Port-au-Prince	27.8	7,803	281	Haitian	French, Creole
Honduras	America C	Tegucigalpa	112.1	6,318	56	Honduran	Spanish, English

Country	Region	Capital	Area	Pop.	P.D.	Nationality	Main language/s
Hungary	Europe E	Budapest	93	10,068	108	Hungarian	Hungarian
Iceland	Europe N	Reykjavik	103	278	2.7	Icelander	Icelandic, Danish, English
India	Asia S	New Delhi	3,065.00	997,507	325	Indian	English plus 14 other official languages
Indonesia	Asia SE	Jakarta	1,919.40	207,022	108	Indonesian	Bahasa Indonesian (Malay)
Iran	Asia W	Tehran	1,648.00	62,977	38	Iranian	Persian (Farsi), Arabic
Iraq	Asia W	Baghdad	438.3	22,797	52	Iraqi	Arabic, Kurdish
Ireland	Europe W	Dublin	70.3	3,752	53	Irish	English, Gaelic
Israel	Asia W	Jerusalem	21.9	6,105	279	Israeli	Hebrew, Arabic, English
Italy	Europe W	Rome	301.3	57,646	191	Italian	Italian
Jamaica	Caribbean	Kingston	11.4	2,598	228	Jamaican	English
Japan	Asia E	Tokyo	377.8	126,570	335	Japanese	Japanese
Jordan	Asia W	Amman	91.9	4,740	52	Jordanian	Arabic, English
Kazakstan	Asia C	(5)	2,717.30	14,927	5.5	Kazakh	Kazakh
Kenya	Africa E	Nairobi	582.6	29,410	50	Kenyan	Kiswahili, English
Kiribati	Pacific E	Bairiki	0.72	88	122	Kiriwinian	Kiribati, English
Korea, DPR (North)	Asia E	Pyongyang	122.8	23,414	191	Korean	Korean
Korea, Rep. (South)	Asia E	Seoul	99.4	46,858	471	Korean	Korean
Kuwait	Asia W	Kuwait City	17.8	1,924	108	Kuwaiti	Arabic, English
Kyrgyzstan	Asia C	Bishkek	199.9	4,865	24	Kyrgyz	Kyrgyz, Russian
Laos	Asia SE	Vientiane	236.8	5,097	22	Laotian	Lao, French, Vietnamese
Latvia	Europe E	Riga	64.6	2,431	38	Latvian	Latvian, Russian
Lebanon	Asia W	Beirut	10.5	4,271	407	Lebanese	Arabic, French, English
Lesotho	Africa S	Maseru	30.4	2,105	69	Mosotho	Sesotho, English
Liberia	Africa W	Monrovia	99.1	3,044	31	Liberian	English, Bassa, Kpelle, Kru
Libya	Africa N	Tripoli	1,775.50	5,419	3.1	Libyan	Arabic
Liechtenstein	Europe W	Vaduz	0.16	33	206	Liechtensteiner	German, Alemmanish
Lithuania	Europe E	Vilnius	65.3	3,699	57	Lithuanian	Lithuanian, Russian
Luxembourg	Europe W	Luxembourg	2.6	432	166	Luxemburger	French, German, Letzeburgesch
Macedonia, FYR	Europe E	Skopje	25.7	2,021	79	Macedonian	Macedonian

Country	Region	Capital	Area	Pop.	P.D.	Nationality	Main language/s
Madagascar	Indian Ocean	Antananarivo	587	15,051	26	Madagascan	Malagasy, French
Malawi	Africa S	Lilongwe	118.5	10,788	91	Malawian	English, Chichewa
Malaysia	Asia SE	Kuala Lumpur	329.8	22,710	69	Malaysian	Bahasa Malay
Maldives	Indian Ocean	Malé	0.3	269	897	Maldivian	Dhiveli
Mali	Africa W	Bamako	1,248.60	10,584	8.5	Malian	French
Malta	Europe W	Valletta	0.32	379	1,184	Maltese	Maltese, English
Marshall Is.	Pacific W	Majuro	0.18	51	283	Marshall Islander	English
Martinique	Caribbean	Fort-de-France	1.1	384	349	Martiniquan	French, Creole
Mauritania	Africa W	Nouakchott	1,030.70	2,598	2.5	Mauritanian	Arabic, French
Mauritius	Indian Ocean	Port Louis	2	1,174	587	Mauritian	English, Creole, Hindi, Bojpuri
Mayotte	Indian Ocean	Dzaoudzi	0.37	140	378		French
Mexico	America N	Mexico City	1,967.20	96,586	49	Mexican	Spanish, English
Micronesia, Fed. States	Pacific W	Palikir	0.7	116	166	Micronesian	English, Micronesian languages
Moldova	Europe E	Chisinău	33.7	4,281	127	Moldavian	Moldavian (Romanian), Russian
Monaco	Europe W	Monaco-Ville	0.002	32	16,000	Monégasque	French, Monégasque
Mongolia	Asia E	Ulan Bator	1,565.00	2,378	1.5	Mongolian	Mongolian Khalkha
Montserrat	Caribbean	Plymouth (6)	0.1	5	50	Montserratian	English
Morocco	Africa N	Rabat	458.7	27,985	61	Moroccan	Arabic, Berber, French
Mozambique	Africa S	Maputo	799.4	17,299	22	Mozambican	Portuguese
Myanmar	Asia SE	Yangon (7)	676.6	45,029	67	Burmese	Burmese
Namibia	Africa S	Windhoek	824.3	1,701	2.1	Namibian	English
Nauru	Pacific W	Yaren District	0.02	11	550	Nauruan	Nauruan, English
Nepal	Asia S	Kathmandu	140.8	23,384	166	Nepalese	Nepali, Maithir, Bhojpuri
Netherlands	Europe W	Amsterdam (8)	41.5	15,805	381	Dutch	Dutch
Netherlands Antilles	Caribbean	Willemstad	0.8	215	269		Dutch, Papiamento
New Caledonia	Pacific W	Nouméa	18.6	209	11	New Caledonian	French, Polynesian, Melanesian
New Zealand	Australasia	Wellington	270.5	3,811	14	New Zealander	English, Maori
Nicaragua	America C	Managua	130.7	4,919	38	Nicaraguan	Spanish
Niger	Africa C	Niamey	1,186.40	10,496	8.8	Nigerian	French, Hausa

Country	Region	Capital	Area	Pop.	P.D.	Nationality	Main language/s
Nigeria	Africa W	Abuja (9)	923.8	123,897	134	Nigerian	English
Niue	Pacific E	Alofi	0.26	2	7.7	Niuean	Niuean, English
Northern Mariana Is.	Pacific W	Saipan	0.46	69	150		English, Chamorro, Carolinian, Japanese
Norway	Europe N	Oslo	323.8	4,460	14	Norwegian	Norwegian, Lappish
Oman	Asia W	Muscat	309.5	2,348	7.6	Omani	Arabic, English
Pakistan	Asia S	Islamabad	796.1	130,580	164	Pakistani	Urdu, English
Palau	Pacific W	Koror	0.51	19	37	Palauan	Palauan, English
Palestine NAR	Asia W	Jerusalem (9)	6.2	2,839	458	Palestinian	Arabic
Panama	America C	Panama City	75.5	2,811	37	Panamanian	Spanish, English
Papua New Guinea	Australasia	Port Moresby	462.8	4,705	10	Papuan	English, Pidgin English, Hiri Motu
Paraguay	America S	Asunción	406.8	5,359	13	Paraguayan	Spanish, Guaraní
Peru	America S	Lima	1,285.20	25,230	20	Peruvian	Spanish, Quechua
Philippines	Asia SE	Manila	300	74,259	248	Filipino	Filipino (Tagalog), English
Poland	Europe E	Warsaw	312.7	38,654	124	Pole	Polish
Portugal	Europe W	Lisbon	91.9	9,989	109	Portuguese	Portuguese
Puerto Rico	Caribbean	San Juan	8.9	3,890	437	Puerto Rican	Spanish, English
Qatar	Asia W	Doha	11.4	565	50	Qatari	Arabic
Réunion	Indian Ocean	Saint-Denis	2.5	707	283		French, Creole
Romania	Europe E	Bucharest	236.4	22,458	95	Romanian	Romanian
Russian Federation	Europe E	Moscow	17,075.40	146,200	8.6	Russian	Russian
Rwanda	Africa S	Kigali	26.3	8,310	316	Rwandan	Kinyardwanda, French, Kiswahili
St Kitts & Nevis	Caribbean	Basseterre	0.26	41	158	Kittitian (13)	English
St Lucia	Caribbean	Castries	0.62	154	248	St. Lucian	English, French patois
St Pierre et Miquelon	America N	St Pierre	0.24	7	29		French, English
St Vincent & the Gren.	Caribbean	Kingstown	0.39	114	292	Vincentian	English
Samoa	Pacific E	Apia	2.8	169	60	Samoan	Samoan, English
San Marino	Europe W	San Marino	0.06	26	433	San Marinese	Italian
São Tomé e Príncipe	Atlantic E	São Tomé	1	145	145	São Tomean	Portuguese, Fórro, Agolares
Saudi Arabia	Asia W	Riyadh	2,200.00	20,198	9.2	Saudi	Arabic

Country	Region	Capital	Area	Pop.	P.D.	Nationality	Main language/s
Senegal	Africa W	Dakar	196.2	9,285	47	Senegalese	French, Wolof
Serbia & Montenegro	Europe E	Belgrade	102.2	10,616	104	Serbian (14)	Serbo-Croat
Seychelles	Indian Ocean	Victoria	0.46	80	174	Seychellois	Creole, English, French
Sierra Leone	Africa W	Freetown	73.3	4,949	68	Sierra Leonean	French, Krio
Singapore	Asia SE	Singapore	0.65	3,952	6,080	Singaporean	Mandarin, English, Malay, Tamil
Slovak Rep.	Europe E	Bratislava	49	5,396	110	Slovakian	Slovak
Slovenia	Europe E	Ljubljana	20.3	1,986	98	Slovenian	Slovene
Solomon Is.	Pacific W	Honiara	28.4	429	15	Solomon Islander	English, Pidgin English
Somalia	Africa E	Mogadishu	637.7	9,388	15	Somali	Somali, Arabic
South Africa	Africa S	(10)	1,224.70	42,106	34	South African	English, Afrikaans
Spain	Europe W	Madrid	504.8	39,410	78	Spaniard	Spanish, Catalan, Galician, Basque
Sri Lanka	Asia S	(11)	65.6	18,985	289	Sri Lankan	Sinhala, Tamil, English
St Helena	Atlantic S	Jamestown	0.12	7	58	St Helenian	English
Sudan	Africa N	Khartoum	2,505.80	28,993	12	Sudanese	Arabic
Surinam	America S	Paramaribo	163.8	413	2.5	Surinamese	Dutch, Sranan Tongo (Creole)
Swaziland	Africa S	Mbabane	17.4	1,019	59	Swazi	English, Siswati
Sweden	Europe N	Stockholm	450	8,857	20	Swede	Swedish, Lapp, English
Switzerland	Europe W	Bern	41.1	7,136	174	Swiss	German, French, Italian
Syria	Asia W	Damascus	185.2	15,711	85	Syrian	Arabic, French, English
Taiwan	Asia E	Taipei	36.2	21,740	601	Taiwanese	Mandarin
Tajikistan	Asia C	Dushanbe	143.1	6,237	44	Tajik	Tajik, Russian
Tanzania	Africa S	Dodoma	945	32,923	35	Tanzanian	Swahili, English
Thailand	Asia SE	Bangkok	513.1	60,246	117	Thai	Thai, English, Malay, Chinese (Tachew)
Togo	Africa W	Lomé	56.8	4,567	80	Togolese	French, Ewe, Watchi, Kabiyé
Tonga	Pacific W	Nuku'alofa	0.75	100	133	Tongan	Tongan, English
Trinidad & Tobago	Caribbean	Port of Spain	5.1	1,293	254	Trinidadian (15)	English
Tunisia	Africa N	Tunis	154.5	9,457	61	Tunisian	Arabic, French
Turkey	Asia W	Ankara	779.5	64,385	83	Turk	Turkish
Turkmenistan	Asia C	Ashgabat	488.1	4,779	9.8	Turkoman	Turkmen

Country	Region	Capital	Area	Pop.	P.D.	Nationality	Main language/s
Turks & Caicos Is.	Caribbean	Cockburn Town	0.5	17	34	Turks & Caicos Islander	English
Tuvalu	Pacific W	Funafuti	0.02	11	550	Tuvaluan	Tuvaluan, English
Uganda	Africa E	Kampala	241	21,479	89	Ugandan	English, Luganda, Kiswahili
Ukraine	Europe E	Kyyiv (Kiev)	603.7	49,950	83	Ukrainian	Ukrainian
United Arab Emirates	Asia W	Abu Dhabi	83.7	2,815	34		Arabic
United Kingdom	Europe W	London	243.5	59,501	244	British	English
United States	America N	Washington DC	9,372.60	278,230	30	American	English, Spanish
Uruguay	America S	Montevideo	176.2	3,313	19	Uruguayan	Spanish
US Virgin Is.	Caribbean	Charlotte Amalie	0.35	120	343	Virgin Islander	English, Spanish, Creole
Uzbekistan	Asia C	Tashkent	447.4	24,406	55	Uzbek	Uzbek
Vanuatu	Pacific W	Port Vila	12.2	193	16	Vanuatuan	Bislama (Pidgin English)
Venezuela	America S	Caracas	916.5	23,707	26	Venezuelan	Spanish
Vietnam	Asia SE	Hanoi	331.7	77,515	234	Vietnamese	Vietnamese, English, French
Wallis & Futuna	Pacific W	Matu Utu	0.24	15	63		French
Western Sahara	Africa N	al-Aioun	252.1	253	1	Sahrawi	Arabic
Yemen	Asia W	San'a	555	17,048	31	Yemeni	Arabic
Zambia	Africa S	Lusaka	752.6	9,881	13	Zambian	English
Zimbabwe	Africa S	Harare	390.7	11,904	30	Zimbabwean	English, Shona, Ndebele

Notes

1 *Bolivia* – La Paz (seat of government); Sucre (judicial).
2 *Channel Islands* – St Peter Port (Guernsey); St Helier (Jersey).
3 *Côte d'Ivoire* – Yamassoukro (official); Abidjan (administrative & commercial).
4 *Guadeloupe* – Basse-Terre (administrative); Pointe-à-Pitre (commercial).
5 *Kazakstan* – Astana (Almaty until December 1998).
6 *Montserrat* – Plymouth was largely destroyed in 1997 by volcanic eruption. A temporary administrative centre has been established at Brades.
7 *Myanmar* – Formerly called Rangoon.
8 *Netherlands* – Amsterdam (capital); The Hague (seat of government).
9 *Palestine NAR* – Jerusalem, as declared by Palestinian Authority.
10 *South Africa* – Pretoria (administrative); Cape Town (legislative), Bloemfontein (judicial). This arrangement is currently under review.
11 *Sri Lanka* – Colombo (administrative & commercial); Sri Jayewardenepura Kotte (legislative).
12 *Barbuda* – Barbudan.
13 *Nevis* – Nevissian.
14 *Montenegro* – Montenegrin.
15 *Tobago* – Tobagan.

Appendix 2
US States

ISO* Abbr.	State	Nickname	Date of admission to the Union	State Capital
AL	Alabama	Heart of Dixie	14th Dec 1819	Montgomery
AK	Alaska	The Last Frontier	3rd Jan 1959	Juneau
AZ	Arizona	Grand Canyon State	14th Feb 1912	Phoenix
AR	Arkansas	The Natural State	15th June 1836	Little Rock
CA	California	Golden State	9th Sept 1850	Sacramento
CO	Colorado	Centennial State	1st Aug 1876	Denver
CT	Connecticut	Constitution State	9th Jan 1788 †	Hartford
DE	Delaware	First State / Diamond State	7th Dec 1787 †	Dover
DC	District of Columbia – Federal District, coextensive with the city of Washington			
FL	Florida	Sunshine State	3rd Mar 1845	Tallahassee
GA	Georgia	Empire State of the South/Peach State	2nd Jan 1788 †	Atlanta
HI	Hawaii	Aloha State	21st Aug 1959	Honolulu
ID	Idaho	Gem State	3rd July 1890	Boise
IL	Illinois	Land of Lincoln	3rd Dec 1818	Springfield
IN	Indiana	Hoosier State	11th Dec 1816	Indianapolis
IA	Iowa	Hawkeye State	28th Dec 1846	Des Moines
KS	Kansas	Sunflower State	29th Jan 1861	Topeka
KY	Kentucky	Bluegrass State	1st June 1792	Frankfort
LA	Louisiana	Pelican State	30th Apr 1812	Baton Rouge
ME	Maine	Pine Tree State	15th Mar 1820	Augusta
MD	Maryland	Old Line State	28th Apr 1788 †	Annapolis
MA	Massachusetts	Bay State	6th Feb 1788 †	Boston
MI	Michigan	Great Lakes State	26th Jan 1837	Lansing
MN	Minnesota	Gopher State/North Star State	11th May 1858	St Paul
MS	Mississippi	Magnolia State	10th Dec 1817	Jackson
MO	Missouri	Show Me State	10th Aug 1821	Jefferson City
MT	Montana	Treasure State	8th Nov 1889	Helena
NE	Nebraska	Cornhusker State	1st Mar 1867	Lincoln
NV	Nevada	Silver State	31st Oct 1864	Carson City
NH	New Hampshire	Granite State	21st June 1788 †	Concord
NJ	New Jersey	Garden State	18th Dec 1787 †	Trenton
NM	New Mexico	Land of Enchantment	6th Jan 1912	Santa Fe
NY	New York	Empire State	26th July 1788 †	Albany
NC	North Carolina	Tar Heel State	21st Nov 1789 †	Raleigh
ND	North Dakota	Flickertail State/Peace Garden State	2nd Nov 1889	Bismarck
OH	Ohio	Buckeye State	1st Mar 1803	Columbus
OK	Oklahoma	Sooner State	16th Nov 1907	Oklahoma City
OR	Oregon	Beaver State	14th Feb 1859	Salem
PA	Pennsylvania	Keystone State	12th Dec 1787 †	Harrisburg
RI	Rhode Island	Ocean State	29th May 1790 †	Providence
SC	South Carolina	Palmetto State	23rd May 1788 †	Columbia
SD	South Dakota	Mount Rushmore State	2nd Nov 1889	Pierre
TN	Tennessee	Volunteer State	1st June 1796	Nashville
TX	Texas	Lone Star State	29th Dec 1845	Austin
UT	Utah	Beehive State	4th Jan 1896	Salt Lake City
VT	Vermont	Green Mountain State	4th Mar 1791	Montpelier
VA	Virginia	Old Dominion State	25th June 1788 †	Richmond
WA	Washington	Evergreen State	11th Nov 1889	Olympia
WV	West Virginia	Mountain State	20th June 1863	Charleston
WI	Wisconsin	Badger State	29th May 1848	Madison
WY	Wyoming	Cowboy State/Equality State	10th July 1890	Cheyenne

* International Organisation for Standardisation.
† Original 13 states: date of ratification of the Constitution.

Appendix 3
Canadian Provinces and Territories

ISO Abbr.	State	Language*	Date of admission to the Dominion	State Capital
AL	Alberta	English	1st Sept 1905	Edmonton
BC	British Columbia	English	20th July 1871	Victoria
MN	Manitoba	English	15th July 1870	Winnipeg
NB	New Brunswick	English †	1st July 1867	Fredericton
NF	Newfoundland & Labrador	English	31st March 1949	St John's
NT	Northwest Territories	English	15th July 1870	Yellowknife
NS	Nova Scotia	English	1st July 1867	Halifax
NU	Nunavut *(Territory)*	Inuktitut	1st April 1999	Iqaluit
OT	Ontario	English	1st July 1867	Toronto
PE	Prince Edward Island	English	1st July 1873	Charlottetown
QU	Québec	French	1st July 1867	Québec
SA	Saskatchewan	English	1st Sept 1905	Regina
YT	Yukon Territory	English	13th June 1898	Whitehorse

* Although Canada is officially bilingual (English & French), this column indicates the most commonly-spoken language in each region.
† Approx. 35% of the population are French-speaking.

Appendix 4
Australian States and Territories

ISO Abbr.	State	Nickname	Date of granting of responsible government	State Capital
AC	Australian Capital Territory	Nation's Capital	1911	Canberra *
CL	Coral Sea Territory (External Territory bordering the Queensland coast and the Great Barrier Reef)			
NS	New South Wales	Premier State	1788 †	Sydney
NT	Northern Territory	Outback Australia	1911 **	Darwin
QL	Queensland	Sunshine State	1859	Brisbane
SA	South Australia	Festival State	1856	Adelaide
TS	Tasmania	Holiday Isle	1856	Hobart
VI	Victoria	Garden State	1855	Melbourne
WA	Western Australia	State of Excitement	1890	Perth

* Canberra became the seat of the Australian government on 9th May 1927.
† Date of first settlement: New South Wales originally covered the whole island with the exception of Western Australia.
** Transferred to Commonwealth from South Australia in 1911, self-government within the Commonwealth granted 1978.

Appendix 5a
Travel Associations: UK

This section provides details of a selection of travel trade associations in the UK. The descriptive text was supplied by, or with the approval of, the organisation concerned.

AA
Automobile Association
AA Travel
Fanum House
Basingstoke
Hampshire RG21 4EA
Tel: 0870 5500 600
Web: www.theaa.com
  Provides an information, support and breakdown service for motorists.

AAC
Association of ATOL Companies
Beaumont House
Lambton Road
London SW20 0LW
Tel: 020 8288 1430
  Keeps members abreast of current legislation as it affects their business, and provides a platform for members to voice their views to opinion formers.

ABPCO
Association of British Professional Conference Organisers
Charles House
148-9 Great Charles Street
Birmingham B3 3HT
Tel: 0121 212 1400

Email: tony@abpco.org
Web: www. abpco.org
  A trade association offering advice and services to professional conference organisers.

ABTA
Association of British Travel Agents
68-71 Newman Street
London W1T 3AH
Tel: 020 7637 2444
Fax: 020 7637 0713
Email: abta@abta.co.uk
Web: www.abta.com
  Promotes and regulates the activities of its members, and protects the interests of consumers.

ABTOF
Association of British Tour Operators to France
PO Box 54
Ross-on-Wye HR9 5YQ
Tel: 01989 769140
Fax: 01989 769066
Email: abtof@aol.com
  Promotes travel to France and represents the interests of its member companies.

ABTOT
Association of Bonded Travel Organisers Trust Ltd
86 Jermyn Street
London SW1Y 6JD
Tel: 020 7930 2388

Fax: 020 7930 7718
Email: tgic.mail@travel-general.com
Web: www.travel-general.com
A simple, economical and fully DTI-approved bonding scheme, enabling travel organisers to provide financial protection for their non-licensable arrangements.

ACE
Association for Conferences and Events
Riverside House
High Street
Huntingdon
Camb PE29 3SG
Tel: 01480 457595
Fax: 01480 412863
Email: ace@martex.co.uk
Provides a service to, and forum for, its members who are involved in various aspects of the conference and meetings industry.

AEO
Association of Exhibition Organisers
113 High Street
Berkhamstead
Herts HP4 2DJ
Tel: 01442 873331
Fax: 01442 875551
Email: info@aeo.org.uk
Works to increase the significance of exhibitions within the marketing mix, and to satisfy an increasing number of visitors.

AITO
Association of Independent Tour Operators
133a St Margaret's Road
Twickenham TW1 1RG
Tel: 020 8744 9280
Fax: 020 8744 3187
Email: aito@martex.co.uk
Represents the specialist tour operator to the trade and the public through joint marketing and promotional activities.

ANTOR
Association of National Tourist Office Representatives
37 Peter Avenue
London NW10 2DD
Tel: 0208 459 4052
Email: antor@ukonline.co.uk
Web: www.tourist-offices.org.uk
Promotes travel and tourism worldwide, to the trade and to the public, and represents its member tourist organizations.

AOA
Airport Operators Association
3 Birdcage Walk
London SW1H 9JJ
Tel: 020 7222 2249
Fax: 020 7976 7405
Email: enquiries@aoa.org.uk
Trade association for British airports representing views on legislative and regulatory matters.

APTG
Association of Professional Tourist Guides
40 Bermondsey Street
London SE1 3UD
Tel: 020 7403 2962
Fax: 020 7403 2963
Email: aptg@aptg.org.uk
Web: www.aptg.org.uk
The professional body of London's 'Blue Badge' guides. It seeks to promote the highest possible standards in tourism in general and guiding in particular.

ASVA
Association of Scottish Visitor Attractions
Argylls Lodgings

Castle Wynd
Stirling FK8 1EG
Tel: 01786 475152
Fax: 01786 474288
Email: info@asva.co.uk
Improves the quality and viability of
visitor attractions in Scotland, and
assists with tour development by
identifying appropriate places to visit.

ATII
**Association of Travel Insurance
Intermediaries**
Renown House
33-34 Bury Street
London EC3A 5AR
Tel: 020 7621 2608
Fax: 020 7451 1408
Email: info@atii.co.uk
Web: www.atii.co.uk
An association of travel insurance
intermediaries committed high
standards in travel insurance.
Amongst its members are Lloyds
Brokers, regulated insurance brokers
and intermediaries.

ATOC
**Association of Train Operating
Companies**
40 Bernard Street
London WC1N 1BY
Tel: 020 7904 3033
Email: Anthony.ewers@atoc.org
Web: www.atoc.org
Represents the interests of the train
operating companies to government
and key opinion-formers, as well as
managing a range of network
services, products and responsibilities
on their behalf.

AUC
Air Transport Users Council
CAA House K2
45-59 Kingsway
London WC2B 6TE

Tel: 020 7240 6061
Fax: 020 7240 7071
As the Civil Aviation Authority's
official consumer watchdog, protects
the interests of users of aviation
services.

AWTE
**Association of Women Travel
Executives**
co Pauline Young
G&O Publications
Coppice Lane
Reigate
Surrey RH2 9JG
Tel: 01737 247033
Fax: 01737 225305
Email: paulinegopr@ic24.net
Provides a social forum for female
executives employed in the travel
industry.

BAA
British Airports Authority
130 Wilton Road
London, SW1V 1LQ
Tel: 020 7834 9449
Fax: 020 7932 6699
Email: caroline_corfield@baa.com
Manages airport facilities at various
airports in the UK and overseas.

BACD
**British Association of Conference
Destinations**
Charles House
148-149 Great Charles Street
Queensway
Birmingham, B3 3HT
Tel: 0121 616 1400212 1400
Fax: 0121 616 1364 212 3131
Email: info@bacd.org.uk
Represents and promotes all the
major British conference
destinations, providing information,
venue finding and related services in
respect of 3,000 venues countrywide.

BAHA
British Activity Holiday Association Ltd
22 Green Lane
Hersham
Walton-on-Thames KT12 5HD
Tel: 01932 252994
Fax: 01932 252994
Email: les@baha119.fsnet.com
Web: www.baha.org.uk
Works towards improving quality and safety in the activity holiday industry.

BAHREP
British Association of Hotel Representatives
127 New House Park
St Albans AL1 1UT
Tel: 01727 862327
Fax: 01727 862327
Promotes sales through marketing and representation companies for member hotels.

BALPA
British Airline Pilots Association
81 New Road
Harlington UB3 5BG
Tel: 020 8476 4000
Fax: 020 8476 4077
Email: balpa@balpa.org.uk
The professional union representing pilots and flight engineers in the UK

BAR UK Ltd
Board of Airline Representatives in the UK
5 Hobart Place
London SW1W 0HU
Tel: 020 7393 1261
Fax: 020 7393 1206
Email: office@bar-uk.org
Web: www.bar-uk.org
Trade association representing full-service scheduled airlines doing business in the UK.

BATA
British Air Transport Association
Artillery House
11-19 Artillery Row
London SW1P 1RT
Tel: 020 7222 9494
Fax: 0171 321 0970 020 7222 9595
Email: admin@bata.uk.com
Encourages the safe, healthy and economic development of UK civil aviation.

BCH
Bonded Coach Holiday Group
Imperial House
15-19 Kingsway
London WC2B 6UN
Tel: 020 7240 3131
Fax: 020 7240 6565
Email: bch@cpt-uk.org
Provides a government-approved bonding scheme for the operators of coach holidays.

BH&HPA
British Holiday & Home Parks Association Ltd
6 Pullman Court
Great Western Road
Gloucester GL1 3ND
Tel: 01452 526911
Fax: 01452 508508
Email: enquiries@bhhpa.org.uk
Represents the parks industry including caravans, chalets, tents and self-catering accommodation.

BHA
British Hospitality Association
Queens House
55-56 Lincoln's Inn Fields
London WC2A 3BH
Tel: 020 7404 7744
Fax: 020 7404 7799
Email: bha@bha.org.uk
Website: www.bha_online.org.uk
Protects and develops the interests of

its members in the British hospitality industry.

BIBA
British Insurance Brokers' Association
BIBA House
14 Bevis Marks
London EC3A 7NT
Tel: 020 7623 9043
Fax: 020 7626 9676
Email: enquiries@biba.org.uk
Trade association for insurance brokers, mainly on the commercial side.

BITOA
British Incoming Tour Operators Association
Vigilant House
120 Wilton Road
London SW1V 1JZ
Tel: 020 7931 0601
Fax: 020 7828 0531
Email: info@bitoa.co.uk
Web: www.biota.co.uk
Represents members of the inbound tourism industry and provides them with services such as research, lobbying and training.

BMC
British Mountaineering Council
177-179 Burton Road
Manchester
M20 2BB
Tel: 0870 010 4878
Fax: 0161 445 4500
Email: office@thebmc.co.uk
Web: www.thebmc.co.uk
Represents and promotes the interests of climbers, hill walkers and mountaineers in England and Wales, encourages sustainable development and conservation, promotes good practice and training, supports events and specialist programmes and

provides information and services for members.

BPA
British Ports Association
Africa House
64-78 Kingsway
London WC2B 6AH
Tel: 020 7242 1200
Fax: 020 7430 7474
Email: info@britishports.org.uk
Lobbies the government on behalf of ports and harbours in the UK.

BRA
British Resorts Association
Crown Building
Eastbank Street
Southport
Merseyside PR8 1DL
Tel: 0151 934 2286
Fax: 0151 934 2287
Email: bresorts@sefton.u-net.com
A national organisation promoting the mutual interests of all member resorts (inland and coastal) and tourist regions.

BTA
British Tourist Authority
Thames Tower
Blacks Road
London W6 9EL
Tel: 020 8846 9000
Fax: 020 8563 0302
Web: www.visitbritain.com
Promotes tourism to Britain, and ensures that the national and regional tourist boards respond effectively to the needs of government, the industry and the public. (The English Tourism Council has now merged with the BTA.)

BVRLA
British Vehicle Rental & Leasing Association
River Lodge
Badminton Court
Amersham HP7 0DD
Tel: 01494 434 747
Fax: 01494 434 499
Email: info@bvrla.co.uk
Represents the short- and long-term vehicle rental and contract hire industry, and presents their views to government.

BW
British Waterways
Willow Grange
Church Road
Watford, WD1 3QA
Tel: 01923 226422
Fax: 01923 201400
Email: enquiries@britishwaterways.co.uk
Cares for over 2,000 miles of Britain's canals and rivers.

CAA
Civil Aviation Authority
CAA House
45-59 Kingsway
London WC2B 6TE
Tel: 020 7379 7311
Fax: 020 7240 1153
Email: tom.hamilton@srg.caa.co.uk
Provides air navigation services, regulates the civil aviation industry including the licensing of air travel organisers, and advises government on civil aviation.

CIMTIG
Chartered Institute of Marketing Travel Industry Group
Home Cottage
Old Lane
Tatsfield
Westerham TN16 2LN
Tel: 01959 577469
Fax: 01959 577469
Email: ugo@cimtig.com
Improves the success and profitability of its members and their organisations by understanding and applying modern marketing techniques, and offering networking opportunities.

CPT
Confederation of Passenger Transport UK
Imperial House
15-19 Kingsway
London WC2B 6UN
Tel: 020 7240 3131
Fax: 020 7240 6565
Email: admin@cpt-uk.org
Represents the views of bus, coach and light rail operators to government, the European Union and the media and protects the commercial environment of the industry.

CRAC
Continental Rail Agents Consortium
co Gerry Harris
Ultima Travel
424 Chester Road
Little Sutton
South Wirral CH66 3RB
Tel: 0151 339 6171
Fax: 0151 339 9199
Represents the interests of those selling European rail travel and provides a forum for discussion with European rail principals

CTC
Coach Tourism Council
Berkeley House
18 Elmfield Road
Bromley
BR1 1LR

Tel: 020 8461 8325
Fax: 020 8461 8326
Email:
info@coachtourismcouncil.co.uk
Promotes travel and tourism by
coach.

CTO
Caribbean Tourism Organisation
42 Westminster Palace Gardens
Artillery Row
London SW1P 1RR
Tel: 020 7222 4335
Fax: 020 7222 4325
Email: cto@carib-tourism.com
Represents its members from the
travel and tourism industry, and
promotes travel to and within the
Caribbean region.

CTT
Council for Travel & Tourism
LGM House
Mill Green Road
Hayward's Heath
Sussex RH16 1XL
Tel: 01444 452277
Fax: 01444 452244
Email: info@ctt-online.co.uk
Provides a forum for member
organisations to exchange
information, news and views on
current developments, and lobbies
government on issues of concern to
the travel and tourism industries.

EBTA
**European Business Travel
Association**
34 Chester Road
Macclesfield
Cheshire SK11 8DG
Tel: 01625 410710
Fax: 01625 439183
Email: info@ibta.com
A federation of business travel
organisations around Europe,

providing a forum for its members to
network with travel managers and
suppliers.

ESITO
**Events Sector Industry Training
Organisation**
Riverside House
High Street
Huntingdon PE29 3SG
Tel: 01480 457595
Fax: 01480 412863
Email: ace@martex.co.uk
Acts as the forum for training and
development in the events industry,
and to pursue issues with
government, education and other
bodies.

ETC
English Tourism Council
See British Tourist Authority.

ETOA
**European Tour Operators
Association**
6 Weighhouse Street
London W1K 5LT
Tel: 020 7499 4412
Fax: 020 7499 4413
Email: info@etoa.org
Web: www@etoa.org
A trade association representing the
interests of its members – mostly
tour operators, but also including
other sectors of the travel industry.

FHA
Family Holiday Association
16 Mortimer Street
London W1T3JL
Tel: 020 7436 3304
Fax: 020 7436 3302
Email: info@fhaonline.org.uk
A charity providing holidays for
families in need.

FTO
Federation of Tour Operators
170 High Street
Lewes BN7 1YE
Tel: 01273 477722
Fax: 01273 483746
Email fto@ifto.demon.co.uk
Works with tour operators to bring about change and improvement in all areas affecting customers' holidays on the journey and in resort.

GBCO
Guild of British Coach Operators
272 Shoebury Road
Southend-on-Sea
Essex SS1 3TT
Retford, DN22 0LP
Tel: 01702 588590
Fax: 0870 1399469
Email: admin@coach-tours.co.uk
Web: www.coach-tours.co.uk
A consortium of independently owned and quality-driven coach operators.

GBTA
Guild of Business Travel Agents
Artillery House
Artillery Row
London SW1P 1RT
Tel: 020 7222 2744
Fax: 020 7976 7094
Email: info@gbta-guild.com
Provides a forum for business and corporate travel agencies, and seeks the highest standards for its members and their clients.

GRTG
The Guild of Registered Tourist Guides
Guild House
52d Borough High Street
London SE1 1XN
Tel: 020 7403 1115
Fax: 020 7378 1705
Email: guild@blue-badge.org.uk

Acts as the national professional association of registered guides in the UK.

GTOA
Group Travel Organisers Association
28a Rectory Close
Carlton
Bedford MK43 7JY
Tel: 01234 720784
Fax: 01234 720784
Email: yvonne@hodsony.freeserve.co.uk
Enhances the status and professionalism of group travel organisers and represents their interests in dealing with industry suppliers and official bodies.

GTT
The Guild of Travel and Tourism
Suite 193
Temple Chambers
3-7 Temple Ave
London EC4Y 0DB
Tel: 020 7583 6333
Fax: 01895 834028
Email: Nigel.bishop@traveltourismguild.com
Web: www. traveltourismguild.com
Acts as a forum for anyone in the travel, tourism or transport sectors, to provide benefits for its members, and to lobby for industry issues of concern.

HBAA
Hotel Booking Agents Association
Association House
South Park Road
Macclesfield SK11 6SH
Tel: 01625 267887
Fax: 01625 267879
Email: secretariat@hbaa.org

A leading professional and ethical body representing the hotel and conference agency community for the benefit of its members, hotels, venues and corporate buyers.

HC
Holiday Care
Sunley House
4 Bedford Park
Croydon CR0 2AP
Tel: 0845 124 9971
Fax: 0845 124 9972
Minicom: 0845 124 9976
Email: holiday.care@virgin.net
Web: www.holidaycare.org.uk
A registered charity and the UK's central source of holiday information for people with disabilities.

HCA
Holiday Centres Association
Pillars
Eastacombe Lane
Heanton Punchardon
Barnstaple EX31 4DG
Tel: 01271 816696
Fax: 01271 817411
Email: holidaycentres@aol.com
Web: www.holidaycentres.com
Represents all of the major and independent holiday centres in the UK that provide inclusive accommodation, entertainment, sporting and leisure activities packages.

HMA
Hotel Marketing Association
The Old Mill
High Street
Selbourne
Alton GU34 3LG
Tel: 0845 758 5435
Fax: 0845 758 5435
Email: alyryan@aol.com
Promotes a good marketing practice in the hotel industry, through educational events, industry-wide research studies and recognition of hotel marketing excellence.

IAGTO
International Association of Golf Tour Operators
1 Trafalgar House
Grenville Place
London, NW7 3SA
Tel: 020 8906 3377
Fax: 020 8906 8181
Email: info@iagto.com
Web: www.iagto.com
The global trade association of the golf tourism industry with over 700 member companies and organisations in more than 60 countries, including 140 golf tour operators in 28 countries.

IATM
International Association of Tour Managers
397 Walworth Road
London SE17 2AW
Tel: 020 7703 9154
Fax: 020 7703 0358
Email: iatm@iatm.co.uk
Web:www.iatm.co.uk
Recognises, represent and promote tour managers in the UK and internationally.

IFTO
International Federation of Tour Operators
170 High Street
Lewes BN7 1YE
Tel: 01273 477722
Fax: 01273 483746
Email: fto@ifto.demon.co.uk
Enables tour operators throughout Europe to cooperate in order to solve the major problems which confront package holiday makers.

ILAM
Institute of Leisure and Amenity Management
ILAM House
Lower Basildon
Reading RG8 9NE
Tel: 01491 874800
Fax: 01491 874801
Email: info@ilam.co.uk
The professional body for the leisure industry.

ITM
Institute of Travel Management
34 Chester Road
Macclesfield
Cheshire SK11 8DG
Tel: 01625 430472
Fax: 01625 439183
Email: secretariat@itm.org.uk
Provides networking opportunities for members, comprising travel managers within corporations and suppliers.

ITMA
Incentive Travel & Meetings Association Ltd
2628 Station Road
Redhill
Sussex RH1 1PD
Tel: 01737 779928
Fax: 01737 779749
Email: itma@martex.co.uk
Represents the UK event-management industry.

ITOA
Irish Incoming Tour Operators Association
19 Kerrymount Rise
Dublin, 18
Tel: 00 353 1-289 9366
Fax: 00 353 1-289 9369
Email: info@itoa-ireland.com
Represents over 30 incoming operators which provide professional services for overseas travel trade.

ITT
Institute of Travel & Tourism
Mill Studio
Crane Mead, Ware
Herts SG12 9PY
Tel: 0870 7707960
Fax: 0870 7707961
Email: admin@itt.co.uk
Develops the professionalism of its members within the industry.

LCA
Leading Cruise Agents of the UK
14 Findhorn Place
Troon KA10 7DJ
Tel: 01292 316820
Fax: 01292 311953
Email: lca.info@virgin.net
Represents a group of over 50 travel agents who concentrate on the sale of cruises, each achieving cruise sales in excess of £250,000 per year.

MCS
Mountaineering Council of Scotland
The Old Granary
West Mill Street
Perth
PH1 5QP
Tel: 01738 638 227
Fax: 01738 442 095
Email: admin@mountaineering-scotland.org.uk
Web: www.the mcofsorg.uk
Represents and promotes the interests of climbers, hill walkers and mountaineers in Scotland, encourages sustainable development and conservation, promotes good practice and training, supports events and specialist programmes and provides information and services for members.

MIA
Meetings Industry Association
34 High Street
Broadway, WR12 7DT
Tel: 01386 858572
Fax: 01386 858986
Email: mia@meetings.org
  Leading professional trade association
  for the meetings and conference
  industries in the UK and Ireland.

NAITA
National Association of
Independent Travel Agents
Kenilworth House
79-80 Margaret Street
London W1W 8TA
Tel: 020 7323 3408
Fax: 0171 323 5189
Email: naita@advantage4travel.com
  Enables independent agents to
  compete with the 'multiples' without
  losing their personal service and
  independent management.

NEA
National Exhibitors Association
29a Market Square
Biggleswade SG18 8AQ
Tel: 01767 316255
Fax: 01767 316430
Web: www.seoevent.co.uk
  A national organisation of exhibiting
  companies, offering information and
  seminars on all aspects of exhibiting.

NITB
Northern Ireland Tourist Board
St Anne's Court
59 North Street
Belfast BT1 1NB
Tel: 028 9023 1221
Fax: 028 9024 0960
Email: info@nitb.com
Web: www.discovernorthnireland.com
  Promotes tourism to and within
  Northern Ireland.

NT
National Trust
36 Queen Anne's Gate
London SW1H 9AS
Tel: 0171 222 9251
Fax: 0171 447 6701 222 5097
Email: traveltrade@ntrust.org.uk
  Promotes the permanent
  preservation, for the benefit of the
  nation, of lands and buildings of
  beauty or historic interest.

NTS
National Trust for Scotland
28 Charlotte Square
Edinburgh EH2 4ET
Tel: 0131 243 9300
Fax: 0131 243 9301
Email: information@nts.org.uk
Web: www.nts.org.uk
  The conservation charity that
  protects and promotes Scotland's
  natural and cultural heritage for
  present and future generations to
  enjoy.

PSA
Passenger Shipping Association
Ltd
Walmar House
288-292 Regent Street
London W1R 5HE
Tel: 020 7436 2449
Fax: 020 7636 9206
Email: h.tapping@psa-pasara.org
Web: www.psa-psara.org
  Represents member organisations
  from the cruising and ferry
  industries.

PSARA
Passenger Shipping Association
Retail Agents Scheme
Walmar House
288-292 Regent Street
London,W1R 5HE
Tel: 020 7436 2449

Fax: 020 7636 9206
Email: admin@psa-psara.org
Web: www.psa-psara.org
The training arm of the PSA (see above).

RAC
Royal Automobile Club
RAC Motoring Services
Great Park Road
Bradley Stoke
Bristol BS32 4QN
Tel: 0800 029 029
Web: www.rac.co.uk
Provides information, support and breakdown services for motorists.

SATH
Society for the Advancement of Travel for the Handicapped
Whiteridge
Chalkpit Lane
Marlow SL7 2JE
Tel: 01628 487494
Fax: 01628 487494
Creates a forum for the exchange and development of information within the travel industry and to promote barrier-free access to travel for those with disabilities.

SDMA
Scottish Destination Management Association
14 Learmonth Terrace
Edinburgh EH4 1PG
Tel: 0131 343 3770
Fax: 0131 343 1368
Email:
scot.dest.man@btinternet.com
Official body that represents incoming tour operators and destination management companies in Scotland.

SEO
Society of Event Organisers
29a Market Square
Biggleswade SG18 8AQ
Tel: 01767 316255
Fax: 01767 316430
Website: www.seoevent.co.uk
A membership group of organisations involved in event organising , offering advice, publications and seminars.

Snow 24
21 Camault Muir
Kiltarlity
Inverness IV4 7JH
Tel: 01463 741809
Fax: 01463 741802
Email: in@snow24.com
Web: www.snow24.com
An information service providing up-to-date details on virtually every winter sport resorts throughout the world.

SPAA
Scottish Passenger Agents Association
22 Dunveran Avenue
Gourock
PA19 1AE
Tel: 01475 639924
Fax: 01475 635408
Email: alistairt@aol.com
A trade association representing the interests of retail travel agents in Scotland.

SSC
Sector Skills Council
International House
High Street
London W5 5DB
Tel: 020 8579 2400
Fax: 020 8840 6217
Email: info@htf.org.uk
Web: www.htf.org.uk

The result of a merger between TTENTO and HTF to form a new employer-led organisation that will take responsibility for driving up levels of skills, productivity and employability across the hospitality, leisure, travel and tourism sector.

STF
School Travel Forum
PO Box 54
Ross-on-Wye
HR9 5YQ
Tel: 01989 566617
Fax: 01989 769066
Provides a forum for businesses within the school travel industry, and a focus for members to explore and act on industry issues.

TIPTO
Truly Independent Professional Travel Organisation
Lockwood House
Lockwood Park
Brewery Drive
Huddersfield
Tel: 01484 345028
Fax: 01484 345030
Email: tipto@thenetwork-uk.com
A marketing organisation of independent tour operators and travel-service providers which is able to offer independent travel agents an unrivalled choice of holiday options under one banner.

TMI
Tourism Management Institute
18 Cuninghill Avenue
Inverurie
Aberdeenshire AB51 3TZ
Tel: 01467 620 769
Email: cathguth@aol.com
Web: www.tmi.org.uk
The professional body for tourism destination management in the

United Kingdom, aiming to advance the profession and its standing, and to be an independent voice for its members.

TS
The Tourism Society
1 Queen Victoria Terrace
Sovereign Court
London E1W 3HA
Tel: 020 7488 2789
Fax: 020 7488 9148
Email: tour.soc@btinternet.com
A leading tourism membership body promoting professionalism in travel and tourism.

TTA
Travel Trust Association Ltd
Albion House
High Street
Woking
Surrey
GU21 6BD
Tel: 0870 889 0577
Fax: 01483 730746
Email: info@traveltrust.co.uk
www.traveltrust.co.uk
Trade association that licenses travel agents and tour operators to trade within the industry, providing financial protection for their customers.

Visit Scotland
23 Ravelston Terrace
Edinburgh EH4 3TP
Tel: 0131 332 2433
Fax: 0131 343 1513
Email: info@visitscotland.com
Web: www.visitscotland.com
Promotes tourism to and within Scotland.

WIN
Worldwide Independent Travel Network
Co Advantage Travel Centre
Kenilworth House
79/80 Margaret Street
London W1W 8TA
Tel: 020 7323 3408
Fax: 020 7323 5189
Email: neil.armorgie@win-travel.org
 An international commercial and marketing organisation for over 7,000 independent travel agents around the world.

WTB
Wales Tourist Board
Brunel House, 2 Fitzalan Road
Cardiff CF2 1UY
Tel: 02920 499909
Fax: 02920 485031
Email: info@visitwales.com
Web: www.wtbonline.gov.uk
 Promotes tourism to and within Wales.

Appendix 5b
Travel Associations: USA

This section provides details of a selection of travel trade associations in the USA. The descriptive text was supplied by, or with the approval of, the organisation concerned.

AH&LA
American Hotel & Lodging Association
1201 New York Avenue N.W.
Suite 600
Washington DC 20005
Tel: 202 289 3100
Fax: 202 289 3199
Email: info@ahla.com
Web site: www.ahla.com
A federation of state lodging associations which provides operational, technical, educational, marketing and communications services, plus governmental-affairs representation to the lodging industry.

ARTA
Association of Retail Travel Agents
3161 Custer Drive, Suite 8
Lexington KY 40517-4067
Tel: 859.269.9739
Fax: 859.266.9396
Email: artalexhdq@aol.com
Web site: www.artaonline.com
The largest non-profit travel-trade association in North America that represents travel agents exclusively.

ASIRT
The Association for Safe International Road Travel
11769 Gainsborough Road
Potomac MD 20854
Tel: 301 983 5252
Fax: 301 983 3663
Email: asirt@erols.com
Web: www.asirt.org
An international, non-profit organisation that promotes road safety through education and advocacy. Alerts individuals and corporations to road conditions in 150 countries.

ASTA
American Society of Travel Agents
1101 King Street
Alexandria VA 22314
Tel: 703 739 2782
Fax: 703 684 8319
Email: asta@astahq.com
Web: www.astanet.com
Enhances the professionalism and profitability of members worldwide through effective representation in industry and government affairs, education and training, and by identifying and meeting the needs of the travelling public.

ATA
Air Transport Association
1301 Pennsylvania Avenue,
Suite 1100
Washington DC 20004-1707

Tel: 202 626 4000
Fax: 202 626 4181
Email: prata@airlines.org
Web: www.airlines.org
Advocates and supports measures to enhance air transport safety, ensures efficiency, fosters growth and promotes economic health of the travel industry.

CLIA
Cruise Lines International Association
500 5th Avenue
Suite 1407
New York NY 10016
Tel: 212 921 0066
Fax: 212 921 0549
Email: CLIA@cruising.org
Web: cruising.org
Represents the North American cruise industry, and works to expand and promote cruise holidays.

HEDNA
Hotel Electronic Distribution Network Association
333 John Carlyle Street
Suite 600
Alexandria VA 22314
Tel: 703 837 6181
Fax: 412 781 2871 703 548 5738
Email: info@hedna.org
Web site: www.HEDNA.org
Promotes the use of electronic distribution in the booking of hotel rooms.

IATAN
International Airlines Travel Agent Network
300 Garden City Plaza, Suite 342
Garden City NY 11530
Tel: 516 747 4716
Fax: 516 747 4462
Email: no general address
Web site: www.iatan.org

Promotes professionalism, administers business standards, and provides a vital link between the supplier community and the US travel distribution network.

IFTTA
International Forum of Travel and Tourism Advocates
2107 van Ness Avenue, Suite 200
San Francisco CA 94109
Tel: 415 673 3333
Fax: 415 673 3548
Email: anolik@travellaw.com
Web site: www.tay.ac.uk/iftta or www.travellaw.com
Travel law attorneys, professors and industry personnel dealing with legal issues from 40 countries worldwide.

NACOA
National Association of Cruise Oriented Agencies
7600 Red Road
Suite 128
Miami FL 33143
Tel: 305 663 5626
Fax: 305 663 5625
Email: nacoafl@aol.com
Web site: www.nacoa.com
Non-profit trade association dedicated to the cruise product and the cruise professionals who sell it.

NACTA
National Association of Commissioned Travel Agents
1101 King Street
Suite 300
Alexandria VA 22314
Tel: 703 739 6826
Fax: 703 739 6861
Email: nacta@aol.com
Web: www.nacta.com
National association of travel agents whose members include independent contractors, outside sales agents,

cruise- and tour-orientated agents and their host agency partners.

SATH
The Society for the Advancement of Travel for the Handicapped
347 5th Avenue, Ste 610
New York NY 10016
Tel: 212 447 7284
Fax: 212 725 8253
Email: sathtravel@aol.com
Web: www.sath.org
   A non-profit organisation which assists and advises on travel arrangements of all kinds for people with disabilities.

SGTP
Society of Government Travel Professionals
6935 Wisconsin Avenue,
Bethesda MD 20815-6109
Tel: 301 654 8595
Fax: 301 654 6663
Email: govtvlmkt@aol.com
Web: www.government-travel.org
   National association focusing on research, education, buyer/seller opportunities, networking, mentoring and advocacy.

TIA
Travel Industry Association of America
1100 New York Avenue NW
Suite 450 West
Washington DC 20005
Tel: 202 408 8422
Fax: 202 408 1255
Web: www.tia.org
   The national, non-profit organisation representing all components of the US travel industry which promotes and facilitates increased travel to and within the US.

USTI
United States Tourism Industries
Office of Travel and Tourism Industries
14th & Constitution Avenue NW
Suite 7025
Washington DC 20230
Tel: 202-482-0140
Fax: 202-482-2887
web: www.tinet.ita.doc.gov
   The National Tourism Office for the United States of America, providing research, technical assistance and policy guidance on the international travel market to and from the USA.

Appendix 5c
Travel Agency Associations: Global

This section provides details of the travel agency associations for a selection of countries of major importance for travel and tourism.

Australia
AFTA
(Australian Federation of Travel Agents)
309 Pitt Street
3rd floor
Sydney
NSW 2000
Australia
Tel: 00 61 29 2643299
Fax: 00 61 - 29 2641085
Email: afta@afta.com.au
Web: www.afta.com.au

Austria
ÖRV
(Österreichischer Reisebüro- und Reiseveranstalter Verband)
Wiener Kongreßzentrum Hofburg
Heldentplatz - Postfach Box 113
A - 1014 WIEN
Tel: 00 43 1 587 36 66-24
Fax.: 00 43 1 532 26 91
Email: office@oerv.at
Web: www.oerv.at

Belgium
FIT/FTI
(Fédération de l'Industrie du Tourisme – Federatie van de Toeristische Industrie)
Avenue de la Métrologie, 8
B - 1130 Bruxelles
Tel: 00 32 2 240 16 69
Fax.: 00 32 2 245 20 50
Email: piet.vintevogel@fti-fit.be
Web: www.fti-fit.be

Canada
ACTA
(Association of Canadian Travel Agents)
130 Albert Street
Suite 1705
Ottawa
K1P 5G4
Canada
Tel: 00 1 - 613 237 3657
Fax: 00 1 - 613 237 7052
Email: actacan@acta.ca

China
CTA
(China Tourism Association)
9A Jianguo-Mennei Dajie
Beijing 100740
China
Tel: 00 86 10 6512 2907
Fax: 00 86 10 6513 5383
Email: cta@cnta.gov.cn
Web: www.cnta.gov.cn

China – Hong Kong
HATA
(Hong Kong Association of Travel Agents)
Room 1003
Tung Ming Building 40
Des Voeux Road

Central
Hong Kong
Tel: 00 852 2869 8624
Fax: 00 852 2869 8632
Email: gloriadr@att.net.hk
Web: www.hata.org

Czech Republic
ACCKA
(Association of Czech Travel Agencies)
Vinohradska 46
Prague 2
Tel: 00 42 02 2158 0256
Email: secretariat@accka.cz

Denmark
DRF
(Danmarks Rejsebureau Forening)
Falkoner Allé 58 b
DK - 2000 Frederiksberg
Tel: 00 45 31 3566 11
Fax.: 00 45 31 3588 59
Email: drf@travelassoc.dk
Web: www.drf-dk.dk

Finland
SMAL
(Suomen matkatoimistoalan liitto)
Vilhonkatu, 4B
FIN – 00100 Helsinki
Tel: 00 358 9 4133 3500
Fax.: 00 358 9 4133 3555
Email: smal@smal.fi
Web: www.smal.fi

France
SNAV
(Syndicat National des Agences de Voyages)
15, Place du Général Catroux
F – 75017 Paris
Tel: 00 33 1 44 0199 90
Fax.: 00 33 1 440199 99
Email: contact@snav.org
Web: www.snav.org

Germany
DRV
(Deutscher Reisebüro- und Reiseveranstalter Verband e.V.)
Albrechtstrasse 10
D - 10177 Berlin
Tel: 00 49 30 284 060
Fax: 00 49 30 284 0630
Email: info@drv.de
Web: www.drv.de
ASR
(Bundesverband mittelstndischer Reiseunternehmen)
Mainzer Landstrae 82-84
60327 Frankfurt/Main
Tel: 00 49 69 756 0540
Fax: 00 49 69 756 05420
Email: geschaeftsstelle@asr-online.de
Web: www.asr-online.de

Greece
HATTA
(Hellenic Association of Travel and Tourist Agencies)
11 losif Rogon Street
GR – 11743 Athens
Tel: 00 30 1 9223522
Fax.: 00 30 1 9233307
Email: hatta@hatta.gr
Web: www.hatta.gr

Hungary
MUISZ
(Association of Hungarian Travel Agencies)
PO Box 267
1364 Budapest
HUNGARY
Tel: 00 36 1 318 4977
Fax: 00 36 1 318 4977
Email: muisz@mail.selectrade.hu

Ireland
ITAA
(Irish Travel Agents Association)

32, South William Street
IE – Dublin 2
Tel: 00 353 1 679 40 89
Fax.: 00 353 1 671 98 97
Email: info@itaa.ie
Web: www.itaa.ie

Italy
FIAVET
(Federazione Italiana Associazioni Imprese Viaggi e Turismo)
Via Ravenna 8
I– 00161 Roma
Tel: 00 39 6 44 02 552
Fax.: 00 39 6 44 02 205
Email: fiavet.nazionale@fiavet.it
Web: www.fiavet.it

Japan
JATA
(Japan Association of Travel Agents)
Zen-Nittu Kasumigaseki Bldg. 3-3
Kasumegaseki 3
Chome Chiyoda-ku
Tokyo 100
Japan
Tel: 00 81 3 35921271
Fax: 00 81 3 35921268
Email: jata@jata-net.or.jp
Web: www.jata-net.or.jp

Luxembourg
GAVL
(Groupement des Agences de Voyages du Grand-Duché du Luxembourg)
31, Boulevard Konrad Adenauer,
Kirchberg BP 482
L – 2014 Luxembourg
Tel: 00 352 43 94 44
Fax.: 00 352 43 94 50
Email: info@clc.lu
Web: www.clc.lu

Mexico
AMAV
(Asociacion Mexicana de Agencias de Viajes)
Calle Guanajuato 128
Colonia Roma Sur
Mexico DF O6700
Mexico
Tel: 00 52 5 5849300
Fax: 00 52 5 5849933
Email: amav_nacional@uole.com

Netherlands
ANVR
(Algemeen Nederlands Verbond van Reisondernemingen)
Rijnzathe 8d
NL - 3454 ZH De Meern
Tel: 00 31 30 669 7033
Fax: 00 31 30 669 7034
Email: info@anvr.nl
Web: www.anvr.nl

New Zealand
TAANZ
(Travel Agents Association of New Zealand)
Level 5
79 Boulcott Street
1888
Wellington
DX SX 10033
New Zealand
Tel: 00 64 4 4990104
Fax: 00 64 4 499 0786
Email: info@taanz.org.nz
Web: www.taanz.org.nz

Portugal
APAVT
(Associação Portuguesa das Agências de Viagens e Turismo)
Rua Sousa Martins n° 21, 5 audor
P – 1050-217 Lisboa
Tel: 00 351 21 355 30 10
Fax.: 00 351 21 314 50 80

Email: apavt@apavtnet.pt
Web: www.apavtnet.pt

South Africa
ASATA
(Association of South African Travel Agents)
11 Wellington Road
Parktown
2193 Johannesburg
South Africa
Tel: 00 27 11 484 05 80
Fax: 00 27 11 484 08 28
Email: general@asata.co.za
Web: www.asata.co.za

Spain
AEDAVE
(Associación Empresarial de Agencias de Viajes Españolas)
Plaza de Castilla, 3-9° A
E – 28046 Madrid
Tel: 00 34 91 314 18 30
Fax.: 00 34 91 31418 77
Email: aedave@aedave.es
Web: www.aedave.es
ACAV
(Associació Catalana d'Agencies de Viatges)
Avda. Roma 13-15, entres 2A
E - 08029 Barcelona
Tel: 00 34 93 321 97 29
Fax.: 00 34 93 322 12 04
Email: acav@acav.net
Web: www.acav.net

Sweden
SRF
(Svenska Resebyråforeningen)
Kammakargatan 39
P.O. Box 1375
S–111 93 Stockholm
Tel: 00 46 8 762 74 60
Fax.: 00 46 8 212 555
Email: kansli@srf-travelagent.se
Web:: www.srf-travelagent.se

Switzerland
SFT
(Swiss Federation of Travel Agencies)
Secretariat
Etzelstrasse 42
CH-8038 Zurich
Switzerland
Tel: 00 411 487 330 0
Fax: 00 41 1 480 09 45
E.mail: mail@srv.ch
Web: www.srv.ch

Turkey
TURSAB
(Turkiye Seyahat Acentalari Birligi)
Dikilitas
Asik Kerem Sokak 48-50
Besiktas
Istanbul - 80690
Turkey
Tel: 00 90 212 2598404
Fax: 00 90 212 2590656 & 2363978
Email: tursab@sim.net.tr
Web: www.tursab.org.tr

UK
ABTA
(Association of British Travel Agents)
68-71 Newman Street
London W1T 3AH
Tel: 020 7637 2444
Fax: 020 7637 0713
Email: abta@abta.co.uk
Web: www.abta.com

USA
ASTA
(American Society of Travel Agents)
1101 King Street
Alexandria VA 22314
Tel: 703 739 2782
Fax: 703 684 8319
Email: asta@astahq.com
Web: www.astanet.com

Appendix 5d
Travel Associations: Global

This section provides details of a selection of regional or international travel trade associations.

AEA
Association of European Airlines,
350 Avenue Louise,
Postfach 4,
B-1050 Brussels
Belgium
Tel: 00 32 2 639 8989
Fax: 00 32 2 639 8999
Email: aea.secretariat@aea.be
Web: www.aea.be

ECTAA
**Group of National Travel Agents'
and Tour Operators' Associations
within the EU,**
Rue Dautzenberg 36,
Box 6,
B-1050 Brussels
Belgium
Tel: 00 32 2 6443450
Fax: 00 32 2 6442421
Email: ectaa@skynet.be
Web: www.ecta.org

ERA
**European Regional Airlines
Association,**
The Baker Suite,
Fairoaks Airport,
Chobham,
Surrey GU24 8HX

UK
Tel: 00 44 1276 856495
Fax: 00 44 1276 857038
Email: info@eraa.org
Web: www.erea.org

ETC
European Travel Commission,
61, rue du Marche aux Herbes,
B-1000 Brussels
Belgium
Tel: 00 32 2 504 0303
Fax: 00 32 2 514 1843
Email: etc@planetinternet.be
Web: www.etc-europe-travel.org

GBTAI
**Guild of Business Travel Agents
Ireland**
12 South Leinster Street,
Dublin 2
Ireland
Tel : 00 353 1 607 9944
Fax : 00 353 1 676 7830
Email: gillian.neenan@neenantrav.ie

GEBTA
**Guild of European Business Travel
Agents**
Rue Dautzenberg 36/38,
Boite 6,
Brussels, B-1050
Tel: 00 32 2 6442187
Fax: 00 32 2 6442421
Email: gebta@gebta.org

ICCA
International Congress and
Conference Association,
Entrada 121,
NL-1096
EB Amsterdam,
The Netherlands
Tel: 00 31 20 398 1919
Fax: 00 31 20 699 0781
Email: icca@icca.nl
Web: www.icca.nl

IATA
International Air Transport
Association,
800 Place Victoria
PO Box 113
Montréal
Québec H42 1M1
Canada
Tel: 00 1 514 0202
Fax: 00 1 514 874 9632
Web: www.iata.org

PATA
Pacific and Asian Travel Agents
Association,
Unit B1
Siam Tower
989 Rama I Road
Pathumwan
Bangkok 10330
Thailand
Tel: 00 66 2 658 2000
Fax: 00 66 2 658 2010
Email: patabkk@pata.th.com
Web: www.pata.org

WATA
World Association Of Travel
Agents,
11 Ch. Riant-Coteau
1196 Gland
Switzerland
Tel: 00 41 22 995 1545
Fax: 00 41 22 995 1546
Email: wata@wata.net
Web: www.wata.net

WTO
World Tourism Organisation
Capitán Haya 42
28020 Madrid
Spain
Tel: 00 34 91 567 81 00
Fax: 00 34 91 571 37 33
Email: omt@world-tourism.org
Web: www.world-tourism.org

UFTAA
Universal Federation of Travel
Agents Associations
1, avenue des Castelans
MC98000
Monaco
Tél. : 00 377 92 05 28 29
Fax : 00 377 92 05 29 87
Email : uftaa@uftaa.org
Web: www. uftaa.org

Appendix 6
British & American English

The English language has evolved in different ways in the various parts of the world where it has taken root. Probably the most important variations, and those that concern this section, are between the forms of English used in the UK and in the USA. While important differences in meaning, style, spelling and pronunciation do exist, these are often overstated. Indeed, considering how long the two countries have been politically separated, and the distance between them, and the lack (until recently) of regular mass communication across the pond (whether digitally or by air), it is perhaps surprising that the two forms of the language are as similar as they are. Since the Second World War, a shared popular culture and increased trans-Atlantic travel have helped bridge a linguistic gulf that in the mid-20th century seemed to growing at an alarming rate. It is probably true to say that the two variations of English are now more mutually understandable than ever before.

None the less, important areas of confusion remain, and this section has tried to address those that are of particular relevance to the travel industry. The interpretations are shown both from UK to US English and vice versa although some terms will appear in only one interpretation. The presence of an interpretation does not necessarily mean that the original term is quite unknown in the other country: 'soccer', for example, is universally understood in the UK, but 'football' is the official and generally preferred term.

In general, words which are substantially the same in both but are spelled differently (ax/axe, color/colour, for example) have not been included, as only a few of the spelling variations affect the respective meanings. As a general rule, where spelling variations exist, the American word tends to be the shorter.

The main differences are as follows:

- Words ending *–ise* (such as enterprise) in UK English are generally spelled *–ize* in America. In UK English either ending is acceptable for most constructions. However, words ending *–yse* (such as analyse and paralyse) will be spelt analyze and paralyze in US English; this usage is not acceptable in UK English.

- In UK English the ending *–ise* usually denotes a verb (to license), and the ending *–ice* a noun (a licence). This distinction does not usually apply in US English where the *–ise* ending is commonly used for both. There are exceptions, most notably practise and practice, which in US English form the opposite parts of speech from their UK English equivalents.

- Words ending *–our* (such as colour or flavour) are generally spelt *–or* (color or flavor) in US English.

- The French-derived ending using a double consonant followed by 'e' (such as cigarette or programme), common in UK English, is not normally used in US English. The usual US ending is a single consonant (cigaret, program). It should be noted, though, that the US spellings are now accepted in cases where the word is applied to a US-originating term. An example is the word program, spelled the US way in both countries when used to describe a computer program but spelled programme in the UK when used to describe a sequence of events or the document that lists them.

- In UK English, the letter 'l' in a word is usually doubled if it follows a single vowel, such as in labelled or travelled. In US English this does not occur and labeled or traveled would be used.

- The UK English ending *–re* is usually replaced by *–er* in US English. Thus, centre becomes center and theatre becomes theater.

The alphabets are the same in both forms of the language, except for Z. This is pronounced zed in the UK, and zee in the USA.

Numbers are the same in both forms. Americans prefer using the word 'zero': the British tend to say 'oh', 'nought' and 'zero' more indiscrimately, but this is generally clearly understood in the USA. The American billion (a thousand million) has ousted the British billion (a million million), and is now universally used. Fractions are now very rarely used in British documents but are more common in American ones: this can sometimes cause problems when a text has been emailed from the USA and needs to be printed out in the UK.

Americans usually show dates in the form month/day/year, not day/month/year as is the case in the rest of the world. See the entry for *date order* in the main listing for more information on this point.

The metric system is not widely used or understood in the USA, and weights and measures are expressed in a form of what is known in Britain as the imperial system (which, apart from pints and miles, has been phased out of official life in the UK: in general, the younger a British person is, the less likely they will be to use or understand it). In addition, there are some important differences between the British and the American usages. A US pint is about 20% smaller than a British one, which has a knock-on effect on the respective sizes of quarts and gallons. Americans always express personal weights in pounds; the UK stone of 14 pounds is not used. Thus a 14-stone man would be referred to in the USA as being 196 pounds. For weightier matters, the UK ton is 240 pounds heavier than the US one.

Weights and measures thus reflect the UK/US English differences as a whole: two languages superficially similar and with most terms identical, but with some that are unique and often mutually incomprehensible, and others that seem familiar but which in fact mean something quite different. Language changes fast – English more than most – and any suggestions as to how this section can be updated, refined or expanded for future editions will be gratefully received.

British to American

A

accommodation	accommodations
aerial	antenna
afters	dessert
air hostess	flight attendant (female)
aluminium	aluminum
American muffin	muffin
anorak	parka
antenatal	prenatal
anticlockwise	counterclockwise
articulated lorry	tractor-trailer
aubergine	eggplant
autumn	fall

B

baby's dummy	pacifier
baggage reclaim	baggage claim
bank holiday	public holiday
banknote	bill
bap	hamburger bun
barrister	trial lawyer, attorney
bath	bathtub, tub
beetroot	beet
big dipper	roller coaster
bill (in restaurant)	check
bin liner	trash bag
biscuit (savoury)	cracker
biscuit (sweet)	cookie
Black Maria	paddy wagon
blancmange	vanilla pudding
blind (roller)	shade
boiler suit	overalls, coveralls
bonnet (car)	hood
boot (car)	trunk
braces	suspenders
bubble and squeak	cabbage and potato
bumbag	fanny pack
busker	street performer

C

cake shop	bakery, pastry shop
candy floss	cotton candy
car park	parking lot
car silencer	muffler
caravan	motorhome, trailer, campervan, RV
carriageway	highway
carry on	continue, drive on
cashpoint	ATM (Automated Teller Machine)
casualty unit	hospital emergency room
cat's eyes (on road)	reflectors
central reservation (of a highway)	median strip
chemist's shop	pharmacy, drugstore
cheque	check
chest of drawers	dresser
chips (potato)	French fries
cinema (building)	moviehouse, movie theater
cinema (in general)	movies
cloakroom	check room
coach (railway)	car (railroad)
coach	bus
collection (car rental)	pickup
condom	rubber
confectionery	candy
conserves, jams	jams, jellies, preserves
constable	police officer
cooker	oven
corn	grain
cot	crib
courgette	zucchini
crèche	nursery
crisps	chips
crossroads	intersection, crossroads
crumpet	unknown in the USA
cul-de-sac	dead end
cupboard (in a kitchen)	cupboard
cupboard (such as for clothes)	closet
current account	checking account
cuttings (newspaper)	clippings

British	American
D	
demister	defroster
deposit account	savings account
dialling code	area code
dialling tone	dial tone
dinner jacket	tuxedo
dipped headlights	low beam
diversion	detour
double glazing	storm windows
draught	draft
drawing pin	thumb tack
dressing gown	bathrobe
driving licence	driver's license
dual carriageway	divided highway, two-lane highway
dummy (for child)	pacifier
dustbin	trashcan, garbage can
duvet	comforter
E	
eiderdown	comforter, quilt
elastic band	rubber band
elastoplast	band aid
electric fire	electric heater
electrical socket	outlet
encircle	circle
engaged	busy, occupied
ensuite (bathroom)	private (bathroom)
entitle	title
entrecôte steak	rib steak, prime rib
estate agent	realtor, real estate agent
F	
filling station	gas station
film (noun)	movie
fire brigade	fire department
fire station	fire house
first floor	second floor
fishmonger	fish market
flat (dwelling)	apartment
flyover	overpass
football	soccer
fortnight	two weeks
front stalls	orchestra seats

British	American
full headlights	high beams, brights
full stop (punctuation)	period
funfair	amusement park
G	
gammon	ham, hamsteak
gas fire	gas heater
gear lever	gearshift
gearbox	transmission
gents	men's room
greaseproof paper	wax paper
grilled (meat)	broiled
ground floor	first floor
guard (on a vehicle)	conductor
guard's van	caboose
H	
hand luggage	carry-on bags, carry-on luggage
handbag	purse, pocket book
headmaster, head teacher	principal
high street	main street
hoarding (advertising)	billboard
hockey	field hockey
holiday	vacation (but 'holiday' for public or religious holidays)
holidaymaker	vacationer
hood (of a convertible car)	top
horse riding	horseback riding
housing estate	housing development housing project
I	
ice lolly	popsicle
indicator (vehicle)	turn signal
J	
jam (clear)	jelly
jam (with fruit)	jam

British	American	British	American
jelly	jello	motorway	highway, expressway, freeway, interstate, turnpike
jumper	pullover, sweater		
K		mudguard	fender
kerb	curb	muesli	granola
kipper	smoked herring	muffin	English muffin
knickers	panties		
L		**N**	
ladies'	women's restroom	nappy	diaper
laundrette	laundromat	near-side lane	the lane furthest from the center of the road
lavatory	bathroom		
lay on	provide, arrange for		
lay-by	pull-off, rest stop	neat (drink)	straight
left-luggage office	baggage room, storage	newsagent	news stand
		nil	nothing, zero
letterbox	mailbox (or letterbox)	note (banknote)	bill
		number plate	license plate
level crossing	train crossing, grade crossing	**O**	
lift (for freight)	lift	off-licence	liquor store
lift (for people)	elevator	off-side lane	the lane nearest the center of the road
limited (company)	incorporated		
liqueur	after-dinner drink (or liqueur)	on offer	for sale, offered
		on show	on display, displayed
lobster tail and steak	surf-and-turf	on stream	on line
loo	bathroom, rest room	one-off	one-of-a-kind (or one-off)
lorry	truck	open day	open house
lost property	lost-and-found	orbital road	beltway
luggage trolley	baggage cart	out-of-hours	after-hours
M		overtaking	passing
mackintosh	raincoat	**P**	
main course	entrée	pack of cards	deck of cards
maize	corn	paddle steamer	side wheeler
mange-tout	snow pea	paddle-steamer with rear propulsion	sternwheeler
marrow	squash		
metalled (road)	paved	page (in a hotel)	bell-hop, bell boy
meter (electricity meter)	meter	pants	underwear, jockey shorts
metre (unit of measurement)	meter	paracetamol	acetaminophen
mileometer	odometer	paraffin, aviation fuel	kerosene
mince	ground meat		
minibus	minivan		

British	American
pardon?	excuse me?, pardon me?
pavement	sidewalk
pelican crossing	pedestrian crossing
penknife	pocket knife
petrol station	gas station
petrol	gasoline, gas
phone box	pay-phone
pickle	relish
pillar box	mailbox
plimsolls	deck shoes
plus-fours	knickers
porridge	oatmeal
porter (in a building)	superintendent, super
porter	janitor
post	mail
post box	mailbox
postcode	zip code
postman	mailman
practice (noun)	practise
practise (verb)	practice
pram	baby carriage
prawn	shrimp
prom	a walkway, or kind of musical concert
proper	standard
pub	bar
public school	private school
pull down (demolish)	tear down
pulses	legumes
puncture	blowout, flat
purpose built	built to order, specially designed
purse	coin purse, wallet
put paid to	finish, put an end to

Q

British	American
queue (verb)	stand in line
queue	line

R

British	American
railway goods wagon	boxcar
railway station	train station

British	American
railway	railroad
rasher	slice
rates (domestic)	local property taxes
read (for a degree)	study
rear lights	tail lights
reception	front desk
recovery vehicle	tow truck
redundant	laid off
return ticket	round trip ticket)
reverse-charge telephone call	collect call
ring (to telephone)	call
ring road	beltway
rise (in salary)	raise
roadside embankment	berm
roadworks	construction
roast beef, entrecôte steak	prime rib
roundabout	traffic circle
rowing boat	rowboat
rubber (pencil)	eraser
rubbish bin	garbage can
rucksack	backpack

S

British	American
sack (dismiss from a job)	fire
sailing boat	sailboat
saloon (car)	sedan
self-catering	efficiency apartment, efficiency
sellotape	scotch tape
semi-detached	duplex
shorts	short pants
sideboard	buffet
sign-posted	marked, well-marked
silencer (car)	muffler
single ticket	one-way ticket
situated, situation	located, location
sledge	sled
sleeper (railway)	railroad tie
sleeping car	pullman, sleeper
sleeping policeman	speed bump
smoked salmon	lox

British	American	British	American
socket (electrical)	outlet	traffic jam	backup
soft drink	soda	traffic lights	stop lights
solicitor	lawyer, attorney	train driver	engineer
spanner	wrench	trainers (footwear)	sneakers
speciality	specialty	tram	trolley, streetcar
spirits (drinks)	liquor	transport	transportation
squash (drink)	juice concentrate	treacle	molasses, syrup
stalls (theatre)	orchestra seats	trolley	baggage cart
starter	appetizer	trousers	pants, slacks
steam train driver	engineer	tyre	tire
steward (aircraft)	flight attendant		
stewardess	flight attendant	**U**	
sticking plaster	adhesive tape, band-aid	underground	subway
stone (weight, of people only)	14 pounds	unsurfaced road	dirt road, unpaved road
stop lights	traffic lights (or traffic lights)	**V**	
stopover	layover	van	minibus (or more likely van)
subway (pedestrian)	underground(or pedestrian) passageway	venue	arena (or venue
surname, family name	last name	vest	undershirt
suspenders	garter belt	**W**	
sweet (confectionery)	candy	waistcoat	vest
		washing	laundry
T		WC	toilet, restroom
take-away (meal)	take-out	Wellington boots	gumboots
tap (noun)	faucet	white coffee	light coffee
tariff	rate-sheet	windscreen	windshield
taxi rank	taxi stand	wing (car)	fender
tea towel	dish towel	wing mirror	rear-view mirror
teat (baby's bottle)	nipple	woman's handbag	purse
telephone box	telephone booth, pay-phone	**Y**	
term (academic year)	semester	yard	an uncultivated area around a property.
terminus	terminal	Y-fronts	one kind of men's underpants
tights	panty-hose		
till	cash register	**Z**	
tinned	canned	Z (zed)	Z (zee)
toilet	restroom	zebra crossing	pedestrian crossing
toll road	turnpike	zip fastener	zipper
torch	flashlight		
tower block	high rise		

American to British

A

accommodations	accommodation
acetaminophen	paracetamol
affordable	value for money
after-dinner drink or liquer	liqueur
aluminum	aluminium
amusement park	funfair
annex	annexe
antenna	aerial
apartment	flat
appetizer	starter
area code	dialling code
ATM (Automated Teller Machine)	cash dispenser
attorney	solicitor, lawyer

B

baby carriage	pram
backpack	rucksack
baggage cart	luggage trolley
baggage cart	trolley
baggage claim	baggage reclaim
baggage room, storage	left-luggage office
bakery, pastry shop	cake shop
band-aid	elastoplast, sticking plaster
bar	pub
bathrobe	dressing gown
bathroom, toilet, rest rooms	lavatory, toilet, WC
bathtub, tub	bath
beet	beetroot
bell-boy, bell hop	page (in hotel)
bell-captain	head porter
beltway	ring road, orbital road
bid (for a contract)	tender
bill ($10 bill)	banknote
billboard (advertising)	hoarding
block (city block)	area bounded by streets on four sides, distance between two streets
blowout	puncture
boondocks, boonies	remote location, backwoods
boxcar	railway goods wagon
broiled (meat)	grilled
brownie	small rich chocolate biscuit
bus	coach
busy (phone)	engaged

C

cabbage and potato	bubble and squeak
caboose	last wagon on goods train, guard's van
call (on the phone)	ring
call collect	reverse the charges
candy	sweets, confectionery
canned	tinned
car (railroad)	coach (railway)
carbonated	fizzy
carry-on bags	hand luggage
carryout, take-out (meal)	take-away
check (banking)	cheque
check (in restaurant)	bill
check room	cloakroom
checking account	current account
circle (verb)	encircle
clippings (newspaper)	cuttings
closet	cupboard
coffee with milk, or cream	white coffee
collect call	reverse charge telephone call
comforter	duvet, eiderdown
conductor (on a vehicle)	guard
continue, drive on	carry on
cookie	biscuit (sweet)
corn	corn on the cob, maize

American	British	American	British
cotton candy	candy floss	expressway	dual-carriageway, generally in and around cities
counter clockwise	anticlockwise		
cracker	biscuit (savoury)		
crazy bone	funny bone		
crib	cot	**F**	
curb	kerb	fall	autumn
czar	tsar	fanny pack	bumbag
		faucet	tap
D		fender (car)	wing
dead end	cul-de-sac	field hockey	hockey
deck of cards	pack of cards	fire (dismiss	
deck shoe	plimsoll	from a job)	sack
defroster	demister	fire department	fire brigade
dessert	afters, sweet, pudding	firehouse	fire station
		first floor	ground floor
detour	diversion, bypass	fishstore	fishmonger
dial tone	dialling tone	flashlight	torch
diaper	nappy	flat (tire)	puncture
dirt road	unmade, unsurfaced road	flight attendant (female)	stewardess, air hostess
dishtowel	tea towel		
divided highway	dual carriageway	flight attendant (male)	steward
divider (of a highway)	central reservation	football	American football
		for sale	on offer
draft (wind under a door)	draught	formula	liquid baby-food
		four lane road	dual carriageway
dresser	chest of drawers	fourteen pounds (weight)	one stone (only for weights of people)
driver's license	driving licence		
drugstore	chemist's shop, pharmacy	freeway	dual-carriageway, generally in and around cities
duplex	semi-detached		
		French fries	chips
E		front desk	reception
efficiency	self-catering apartment, room with kitchenette		
		G	
eggplant	aubergine	garbage can	rubbish bin
electric heater	electric fire	garden	flower garden
elevator	lift (for people)	garters	suspenders
emergency room	casualty unit	gas heater	gas fire
engineer	train driver	gas station	filling station, petrol station
English muffin	muffin		
enter	join (a highway)	gas, gasoline	petrol
entrée	main course	gearshift	gear stick, gear lever
eraser	rubber (pencil)	grade crossing	level crossing
excuse me? pardon me?	pardon?	granola	muesli

American	British
ground meat, ground beef	mince
gumboots	wellingtons

H

American	British
half-and-half	half cream/half milk mixture for coffee
ham, hamsteak	gammon
high beams, brights	full headlights
high rise	tower block
highway construction	roadworks
highway	road, carriageway
hockey	ice hockey
hood (car)	bonnet
horseback riding	horse riding
huddle	planning or tactics meeting or conference

I

American	British
incorporated (company)	limited
insure	ensure
intersection	crossroads
interstate highway	motorway

J

American	British
jam	jam (with fruit)
janitor	caretaker
jello	jelly
jelly	jam (clear)
john (the john)	toilet, lavatory
juice concentrate	squash

K

American	British
kerosene	paraffin, aviation fuel
knickers	plus-fours

L

American	British
laundromat	laundrette
laundry	washing
layover	stopover
legumes	pulses

American	British
license plate	number plate
light coffee	white coffee
line (of people)	queue
liquor store	off-licence
liquor	alcoholic spirits
lobby	foyer
longshoreman	dock worker
low beams	dipped headlights
lox	smoked salmon

M

American	British
mail	post
mailbox	letterbox, pillar box, post box
mailman	postman
main street	high street
median strip (of a highway)	central reservation
men's room	gents, gent's toilet
meter (electricity meter)	meter
meter (unit of measurement)	metre
minibus	van
minivan	minibus
mobile home	motorhome, trailer, caravan
motorhome, trailer	caravan
movie theater	cinema
muffin	American muffin
muffler (car)	silencer

N

American	British
nature preserve	nature reserve
night crawler	worm used by fishermen
nipple (on a baby's bottle)	teat

O

American	British
oatmeal	porridge
odometer	milometer
off-hours	out-of-hours
on display	on show
one-way ticket	single ticket
open house	open day

American	British
orchestra seats	front stalls
outlet (electrical)	socket
outlet (factory)	discount store
outlet	electrical socket
oven	cooker
overpass	flyover

P

American	British
pacifier	baby's dummy
paddy wagon	Black Maria
pantiehose	tights
pants	trousers
parka	anorak
parking lot	car park
passing	overtaking
paved (road)	metalled
pavement	tarmaced road
pay-phone	phone box
Ped Xing	pedestrian crossing, zebra crossing
period (punctuation)	full stop
pharmacy	chemist's shop
pickup (car rental)	collection
pocket book	handbag
pop	soft drink
popsicle	ice lolly
potato chips	crisps
power train	transmission
practice (verb)	practise
practise (noun)	practice
prenatal	antenatal
preserves	conserves, jams
prime rib	roast beef, entrecôte steak
principal (school)	head teacher
private (bathroom)	en suite
private school	public school
program	programme
prom	a school or university formal ball or dance
provide, arrange	lay on
public address system	tannoy
pullman	sleeping car
pull-off	lay-by
purse	handbag

American	British

R

American	British
railroad tie	sleeper
railroad	railway
raincheck	postponement
raise (in salary)	rise
rate-sheet	tariff
real estate	land, or the property on it
realtor	estate agent
reflectors (embedded in road)	cat's eyes
regular coffee	coffee with milk and sugar
relish	pickle
rent	hire
reservation	booking
rest stop	lay-by
restrooms	toilets
roller coaster	big dipper
roundtrip ticket	return ticket
rubber	condom
RV (recreational vehicle)	motor home, caravan

S

American	British
savings account	deposit account
scallion	spring onion
scotch tape	sellotape
second floor	first floor
sedan	saloon car
semester (academic year)	term
shade (on a window)	blind
shellac	high-gloss varnish
short pants	shorts
shorts (underwear)	pants
shrimp	prawn
side wheeler	paddle-steamer
sidewalk	pavement
sled	sledge
sleeper	sleeping car
sneakers	trainers
snow pea	mange-tout
soccer	football
soda	soft drink
specialty	speciality

American	British	American	British
speed bump	sleeping policeman	tuxedo	dinner jacket
sports utility vehicle (SUV)	people carrier, generally with off-road capability	**U**	
		underpants (men's)	pants
squash (vegetable)	a sort of marrow	underpants (women's)	knickers
stand in line	queue	underpass	subway
standard or regular	proper (of coffee, white)	undershirt	vest
sternwheeler	paddle-steamer with rear propulsion	unpaved road	dirt road
stick shift (car)	manual transmission	**V**	
stop lights	traffic lights	vacation	holiday
storm windows	double glazing	vacationer	holidaymaker
street musician	busker	van	van (if carrying goods), minibus or people carrier (if carrying people)
subway (train)	underground railway		
superintendent, super	porter (in a building)	vanilla pudding	blancmange
suspenders	braces	vest	waistcoat
		vet	ex-serviceman, veteran
T		**W**	
tail lights	rear lights	wax paper	greaseproof paper
taxi stand	taxi rank	whole wheat	wholemeal
tear down (demolish)	pull down	windshield	windscreen
tenement	housing estate	wrench	spanner
thumbtack	drawing pin	**Y**	
tire (on a car)	tyre	yard	any piece of land around a property, regardless of whether or not it is cultivated
tire (to exhaust)	tire		
title	entitle		
tow truck	recovery vehicle		
tractor-trailer	articulated lorry		
traffic circle	roundabout		
traffic jam	hold up, backup	**Z**	
train crossing	level crossing		
transmission	gearbox	Z (zee)	Z (zed)
transportation	transport	zip code	postcode
trash bag	bin liner	zipper	zip fastener, zip
trashcan	dustbin	zucchini	courgette
trial lawyer, attorney	barrister		
truck (road)	lorry		
trunk	boot (car)		
turn signals	indicators		
turnpike	toll road		

Appendix 7
Phonetic Alphabets

Although English is effectively the international language of travel, and although many communications within the industry are in writing and so can, if necessary, be translated at leisure, there are times when phone conversations need to take place with someone who does not speak English. This section has been designed to enable names, dates and the like to be spelled out in French, German, Spanish and Italian, using one of two methods: the Alpha-Bravo-Charlie-style phonetic alphabet; and a pronunciation guide to the A-B-C and the numbers from 0 to 9.

For the English Alpha-Bravo-Charlie-style phonetic alphabet, please see under *phonetic alphabet* in the main listing.

Many languages have more than one phonetic alphabet and there is no one 'official' one for all purposes. Some languages have separate phonetic terms for certain diagraphs (such as sch in German and ch in Spanish) and for accented letters (such as ü in German), but for reasons of simplicity these have not been included here.

The pronunciation guides are approximate, as in some cases there is no exact sound in English that corresponds with that used to pronounce certain letters in other languages. It must be stressed that these only represent how the letters are pronounced in a recital of each language's alphabet, and not how they are pronounced when forming words. Where the guide consists of a single letter in capitals, the pronunciation of that letter is similar to how a British person would pronounce that letter in English: the few occasions where an example word has been used also assumes the British pronunciation. It can be seen that many letters, including most of the vowels, are often pronounced in quite different ways from one language to another. In some languages, certain diagraphs (such as ch in Spanish) and accented letters (such as é in French) are, in a recital of the alphabet, sometimes regarded as if they were letters in their own right. As these will only very rarely affect the sense of what is being communicated, they have not been included here.

The pronunciation guides for the numbers generally bear little similarity to how they are actually spelled. Numbers from 10 and above can either be concocted from these basic integers, or learned in the appropriate language, or spoken in English; space does not permit listing them here.

Any suggestions as to how this section can be updated, refined or expanded for future editions will be gratefully received.

French

A	Anatole	a (as in bat)
B	Berthe	bay
C	Célestin	say
D	Désiré	day
E	Eugène	uh
F	François	F
G	Gaston	gea (as in orangeade)
H	Henri	arsh
I	Irma	ee
J	Joseph	gee (as in orangey)
K	Kléber	car
L	Louis	L
M	Marcel	M
N	Nicolas	N
O	Oscar	o (as in dot)
P	Pierre	pay
Q	Quintal	coo
R	Raoul	air
S	Suzanne	S
T	Thérèse	tay
U	Ursule	oo
V	Victor	vay
W	William	doob-ler-vay
X	Xavier	eeks
Y	Yvonne	ee-grek
Z	Zoé	Z

0	zair-oh
1	urn
2	dur
3	twah
4	katre
5	sank
6	cease
7	set
8	wheat
9	nurf

German

A	Anton	a (as in bat)
B	Berta	bay
C	Cäsar	tzee
D	Dora	day
E	Emil	ay
F	Friedrich	F
G	Gustav	geh (as in get)
H	Heinrich	ha
I	Ida	ee
J	Julius	yott
K	Kaufmann	car
L	Ludwig	L
M	Martha	M
N	Nordpol	N
O	Otto	O
P	Paula	pay
Q	Quelle	coo
R	Richard	air
S	Samuel	S
T	Theodor	te
U	Ulrich	uh
V	Viktor	fowe
W	Wilhelm	vee
X	Xanthippe	eeks
Y	Ypsilon	ip-seelon
Z	Zeppelin	tsett

0	null
1	einz
2	svy
3	dry
4	fear
5	funf
6	zex
7	zeeben
8	acht
9	noin

Italian

A	Ancona	a (as in bat)
B	Bologna	B
C	Como	chee
D	Domodossola	D
E	Empoli	e (as in bet)
F	Firenze	effay
G	Genova	gee
H	Hotel	acka
I	Imola	ee
J	I lunga	ee-lunga
K	Kursaal	kappa
L	Livorno	ellay
M	Milano	emmay
N	Napoli	ennay
O	Otranto	o (as in dot)
P	Padova	P
Q	Quarto	coo
R	Roma	erray
S	Savona	essay
T	Torino	T
U	Udine	oo
V	Venezia	voo
W	Washington	doppio-voo
X	Ics	eeks
Y	York	ip-seelon
Z	Zara	zeta

0	zair-oh
1	unno
2	doo-ay
3	tray
4	quatro
5	ching-kwe
6	say
7	settay
8	otto
9	novay

Spanish

A	Antonio	a (as in bat)
B	Barcelona	bay (vay largo in Lat. Am.)
C	Carmen	say
D	Dolores	day
E	Enrique	ay
F	Francia	effay
G	Gerona	hay (h as in loch)
H	Historia	achay
I	Inés	ee
J	José	hota (h as in loch)
K	Kilo	cah
L	Lorenzo	ellay
M	Madrid	emmay
N	Navarra	ennay
O	Oviedo	o (as in dot)
P	París	pay
Q	Querido	coo
R	Ramón	erray
S	Sábado	essay
T	Tarragona	tay
U	Ulises	oo
V	Valencia	oovay (vay corta in Lat. Am.)
W	Washington	oovay-dovlay (dovlay-vay in Lat. Am.)
X	Xiquena	ekis
Y	Yegua	ee-gree-ay-ga
Z	Zaragoza	seta

0	zair-oh
1	unno
2	dos
3	tres
4	quatro
5	sinko
6	sayce
7	see-ate-ay
8	otcho
9	noo-way-vay

Appendix 8
Greek & Russian Alphabets

Greek

Capital	Lower-case	Principal nearest equivalent English letter or sound
Α	α	a
Β	β	v
Γ	γ	g
Δ	δ	d
Ε	ε	e
Ζ	ζ	z
Η	η	ee
Θ	θ	th
Ι	ι	i
Κ	κ	k
Λ	λ	l
Μ	μ	m
Ν	ν	n
Ξ	ξ	x
Ο	ο	o
Π	π	p
Ρ	ρ	r
Σ	σ	s
Τ	τ	t
Υ	υ	ee
Φ	φ	f
Χ	χ	ch
Ψ	ψ	ps
Ω	ω	o

Russian

Capital	Lower-case	Principal nearest equivalent English letter or sound
А	а	a
Б	б	b
В	в	v
Г	г	g
Д	д	d
Е	е	e
Ё	ё	o
Ж	ж	zh
З	з	z
И	и	ee
Й	й	j
К	к	k
Л	л	l
М	м	m
Н	н	n
О	о	o
П	п	p
Р	р	r
С	с	s
Т	т	t
У	у	oo
Ф	ф	f
Х	х	ch
Ц	ц	ts
Ч	ч	ch
Ш	ш	sh
Щ	щ	shch
Ъ	ъ	˝ ('hard sign')
Ы	ы	y
Ь	ь	´ ('soft sign')
Э	э	eh
Ю	ю	yu
Я	я	ya

Notes